JOURNAL FOR THE STUDY OF THE OLD TESTAMENT SUPPLEMENT SERIES

42

Editors
David J A Clines
Philip R Davies

Department of Biblical Studies
The University of Sheffield
Sheffield S10 2TN
England

Professor William McKane
in the quadrangle of St. Mary's College, St. Andrews

A
WORD
IN
SEASON

Essays in Honour
of

William McKane

Edited by
James D. Martin
and
Philip R. Davies

Journal for the Study of the Old Testament
Supplement Series 42

Copyright © 1986 JSOT Press

Published by
JSOT Press
Department of Biblical Studies
The University of Sheffield
Sheffield S10 2TN
England

Printed in Great Britain
by Redwood Burn Ltd.,
Trowbridge, Wiltshire.

British Library Cataloguing in Publication Data

A word in season : essays in honour of William
   McKane.—(Journal for the study of the Old
   Testament. Supplement series, ISSN 0309-0787; 42)
   1. Bible. O.T.—Criticism, interpretation, etc.
   I. Martin, James D.   II. Davies, Philip R.
   III. McKane, William   IV. Series
   221.6   BS1171.2

   ISBN 1-85075-016-5
   ISBN 1-85075-047-5 Pbk

CONTENTS

PART B   Post-Biblical Studies

PREFACE

This collection of essays in honour of Professor William McKane on the occasion of his sixty-fifth birthday is not along the usual lines where an international body of highly celebrated scholars are invited to write in honour of a dedicatee with whom they have a more or, sometimes, less close connection. This is essentially a 'family' volume, since all of the contributors have had, at some stage in their careers, a close connection with Willie McKane. Some were taught their first Hebrew by him in his Glasgow days, while some have pursued their doctoral research either directly under his supervision or with his less direct guidance and inspiration. Others have been colleagues in the past or are such in the present. Some of the contributors fall into more than one of these categories, and for some their association and friendship with Willie goes back for almost thirty years. Those of us who form this 'extended family' felt that we wanted to honour a man who, in many respects, has been our 'father' in Old Testament scholarship, whose example we have tried to follow in however inadequate a way.

Willie McKane is a dedicated scholar whose literary productions are recorded elsewhere in this volume, but he is not one whose life is centred solely and exclusively on his scholarly activities. Monday morning coffee in St. Mary's usually centres on a discussion of the weekend's soccer or rugby or, depending on the season, cricket. Willie's interests have concentrated on two main areas of Old Testament study which are already encapsulated in the title of one of his earlier books, *Prophets and Wise Men* (1965). From here he has enriched the study of Old Testament wisdom literature by his commentary on Proverbs (1970) and of Old Testament prophecy both by his article on 'Prophecy and Tradition' in *Tradition and Interpretation*, the SOTS volume of 1979 edited by G.W. Anderson and by his volume on *Jeremiah 1–25* in the new I.C.C. series. Some of the contributors have written on topics within the general spheres of prophecy and wisdom. Others have ranged further afield, for not all families follow directly in their father's footsteps. We hope, however, that what we offer will be accepted by our dedicatee as tokens of our regard for his scholarship and our thanks for his friendship over the years.

James D. Martin

Philip R. Davies

Abbreviations

AV	Authorized Version
BA	*Biblical Archeologist*
BDB	Brown, Driver and Briggs, *Hebrew and English Lexicon*
BHS	*Biblia Hebraica Stuttgartensia*
BJRL	*Bulletin of the John Rylands University Library of Manchester*
BKAT	Biblischer Kommentar, Altes Testament
BO	*Bibliotheca Orientalis*
BSOAS	*Bulletin of the School of Oriental and African Studies*
BWANT	Beiträge zur Wissenschaft vom Alten und Neuen Testament
BZAW	Beihefte zur Zeitschrift für die alttestamentliche Wissenschaft
CBC	Cambridge Bible Commentary
CBQ	*Catholic Biblical Quarterly*
CBQMS	Catholic Biblical Quarterly Monograph Series
GNB	Good News Bible
HAT	Handbuch zum Alten Testament
HSM	Harvard Semitic Monographs
ICC	International Critical Commentary
IEJ	Israel Exploration Journal
IDBSup	*Interpreter's Dictionary of the Bible, Supplementary Volume*
JAOS	*Journal of the American Oriental Society*
JB	Jerusalem Bible
JCS	*Journal of Cuneiform Studies*
JSOT	*Journal for the Study of the Old Testament*
JSS	*Journal of Semitic Studies*
JTS	*Journal of Theological Studies*
KAT	Kommentar zum Alten Testament
K–B	Koehler—Baumgartner, *Lexicon in Veteris Testamenti Libros*

KHAT	Kurzer Hand-Commentar zum Alten Testament
NCBC	New Century Bible Commentary
NEB	New English Bible
OTL	Old Testament Library
OTS	*Oudtestamentische Studiën*
OTWSA	*Oud-Testamentiese Werkgemeenskap in Suid-Afrika*
RQ	*Revue de Qumran*
RScR	*Recherches de Science Religieuse*
SBLMS	Society of Biblical Literature Monograph Series
SEÅ	*Svensk Exegetisk Årsbok*
SVT	Supplements to *Vetus Testamentum*
TBC	Torch Bible Commentaries
TDOT	*Theological Dictionary of the Old Testament*
TGUOS	*Transactions of the Glasgow University Oriental Society*
UF	*Ugarit-Forschungen*
VT	*Vetus Testamentum*
WMANT	Wissenschaftliche Monographien zum Alten und Neuen Testament
WUNT	Wissenschaftliche Untersuchungen zum Neuen Testament

LIST OF CONTRIBUTORS

Ernest W. Nicholson is Oriel Professor of the Interpretation of Holy Scripture at the University of Oxford

Philip R. Davies is Senior Lecturer in Old Testament at the University of Sheffield

John F.A. Sawyer is Professor of Old Testament Language and Literature at the University of Newcastle-upon-Tyne

Robert B. Salters is Lecturer in Hebrew and Old Testament at the University of St. Andrews

Peter W. Coxon is Lecturer in Hebrew and Old Testament at the University of St. Andrews

William Johnston is Professor of Hebrew at the University of Aberdeen

James D. Martin is Senior Lecturer in Hebrew and Old Testament at the University of St. Andrews

James C. Vanderkam is Associate Professor in the Department of Religion and Philosophy at North Carolina State University, Raleigh

Bryan Paradise is Curate of Christ Church, Harrogate

Derek R.G. Beattie is Lecturer in Semitic Studies at the Queen's University of Belfast

James G. Fraser is Lecturer in the Department of Near Eastern Studies at the University of Melbourne, Australia

PART A

BIBLICAL STUDIES

ISRAELITE RELIGION IN THE PRE-EXILIC PERIOD
A DEBATE RENEWED

Ernest W. Nicholson

Oriel College, Oxford

A Retrospect

Old Testament research in recent years has entered a period of fresh discussion of a range of fundamental issues, including, for example, Israelite origins, the background of the patriarchal traditions, the dating of the oldest Pentateuchal literary strata, how the Pentateuch as such came into existence. But among them none is more prominent than the nature and development of Israelite religion in the pre-exilic period. The emerging debate, in some instances indeed upheaval, on these and other issues follows a period of relative stability, as we may now see the situation in the middle decades of this century to have been. With regard specifically to the subject with which we are concerned here, the current period is in ways reminiscent of the generation of discussion and controversy which followed the publication of Wellhausen's *Prolegomena* a little more than a century ago.[1]

Wellhausen drew a sharp dichotomy between Israelite religion before the advent of the eighth-century prophets and that which developed in the wake of their preaching.[2] In the centuries before these prophets, religion rested upon the conviction of an indestructible bond between Yahweh and his people: it was a 'natural relationship', as that of a son to father, and was not conditioned upon observance of the terms of a 'pact' or 'treaty' (ברית). Law was conceived of as part of Yahweh's 'help', guidance, to Israel. In the preaching of the prophets of the eighth century, however, the commandments were newly conceived of as demands, on the fulfilment of which his continued relation to Israel entirely depended. To these 'ethical monotheists'[3] Yahweh was 'the God of righteousness in the first place, and the God of Israel in the second place, and even then only in so far as Israel came up to the righteous demands which in His grace He had revealed to him'.[4] Thus 'the natural bond between the two was severed, and the relationship was henceforth viewed as conditional . . .

The ethical element destroyed the national character of the old religion'.[5] Over against what it had been, what now emerged represented a 'denaturalization' of religion. The old relationship was soon replaced by one characterized as a legally binding ברית which was introduced by the Deuteronomic authors in the period following the time of these prophets.

Others rejected the dichotomy which Wellhausen thus drew, and argued for much greater continuity between the earlier and later stages in the history of Israelite religion. It is a misconception, they contended, to depict the relationship between Yahweh and Israel as ever having rested upon a 'natural bond'; rather, from the outset it was a religion of 'election', historically manifested in the deliverance of the people from bondage in Egypt and subsequently formalized at Sinai by the making of a covenant which laid down the ethical commandments henceforth binding upon Israel as the people of Yahweh. In fact a high ethical element characterized Israelite religion from the outset, and among the scholars of this period who held this view there were not lacking those who further argued against Wellhausen that the so-called 'ethical decalogue' (in an original, shorter form) was the moral content of the covenant at Sinai.[6] The prophets of the eighth century were not innovators in the manner believed by Wellhausen. Rather, 'their constant purpose was simply to uphold and renew the old faith which in their time had been forgotten or left aside'.[7]

This polarization of opinion characterized the generation of discussion of this issue which followed the publication of Wellhausen's *Prolegomena*. But in the period which followed the First World War it was the second of the two views briefly depicted above which, on the basis of new methods and insights and under the influence of other developments at this time, gained the support of the great majority of scholars, establishing itself first in Germany and eventually, especially in the years following the Second World War, in Britain and the United States. By contrast, the sort of development of Israelite religion argued by Wellhausen increasingly lost support, and from the 1940s onwards may be said to have everywhere gone into almost total eclipse.

The foundations of the consensus on the early period of Israelite religion as the decisively formative stage of its distinctiveness were quickly laid in the years immediately following the First World War, with no small debt to the 'history-of-religions movement'. Even though as a movement this was now going into decline, it had given a decided and lasting impulse to tracing traditions, concepts and institutions to their remotest origins, in keeping with one of its fundamental axioms: 'There is no subject-matter in the world which does not have a pre-history, no concept which does not have a point of origin.'[8] It also pioneered the methods—*Gattungsgeschichte* and *Traditionsgeschichte*—which enabled scholars to penetrate to the earlier periods of the history of Israel and of its religion in a way that went far beyond what Wellhausen had considered possible, and it had already made significant gains by means of them.[9]

In the post-war years the earliest periods of the history of Israel and of its religion were decisively opened up by such scholars as Alt and Noth, by the former in a series of brilliant essays such as 'Die Landnahme der Israeliten in Palästina' (1925), 'Der Gott der Väter' (1929), 'Die Ursprünge des Israelitischen Rechts' (1934), and by Noth in his famous monograph *Das System der zwölf Stämme Israels* (1930). The importance of this latter work in particular cannot be overemphasized. The theory which it so compellingly presented of the nature and structure of Israelite society as a sacral confederation of tribes in the pre-monarchical period became the most widely accepted view on this issue for a generation to come, and became virtually the 'given' for further research into the origin and history of central Old Testament traditions, beliefs and institutions. The vital contribution which Noth's 'amphictyony' hypothesis made to the widespread acceptance of the view that the early period of Israelite religion was the formative and normative stage of its distinctiveness is so well known as to require no illustration here; it is no exaggeration to claim that as long as this theory remained regnant, that view remained secure.

But the trend towards a consensus on this view had in fact already set in among German scholars in the years immediately preceding Noth's monograph. Perhaps the most striking indication of this is the way in which the 1920s brought to an end a controversy which had been rife throughout the preceding period concerning the origin and place of the notion of a covenant between Yahweh and Israel in the development of Israelite religion.[10] A decisive contribution towards the resolution of this controversy came from an unexpected source— the sociologist M. Weber in his *Das Antike Judentum* which was first published as a series of articles in 1917-19 and then in 1921 as the third volume of his *Gesammelte Aufsätze zur Religionssoziologie*.[11]

Like earlier scholars who had rejected Wellhausen's view on this, Weber too emphasized the covenant as an ancient and distinctive feature of Israelite religion.[12] But what was decisive about his work was that it shifted attention to the *function* of the covenant as a religious institution which constituted the unity of the tribes of early Israel and was normative in their social organization under their common God Yahweh with whom they entered the covenant. Weber's work had an immediate influence upon Old Testament scholarship in Germany. Wellhausen's view that the covenant was a late *theologoumenon* now rapidly faded in the face of this new understanding of it as constitutive of Israelite religion and society from the earliest period. A similar understanding of its origin and role was argued by Noth in his monograph referred to above, and later in his study of the laws of the Pentateuch.[13] 'Election' and 'covenant' as the foundation pillars of Israelite religion and of its distinctiveness among the religions of its environment were the subjects of works which were to be of lasting influence from, for example, Weiser,[14] Galling,[15] and most notably Eichrodt who employed the covenant and its theology in a large-scale programmatic manner for his monumental *Theologie des Alten Testaments*, the first volume of which appeared in 1933.[16]

The space here allowed does not permit a detailed charting of how this fresh presentation of the distinctiveness of early Israelite religion was further consolidated and commanded an increasing consensus, first in Germany and subsequently in both Britain and the United States. It was the presupposition of, and in turn further enhanced by, important works from such internationally influential scholars as von Rad and Zimmerli in the inter-war and post-war period. Concurrent wider trends in theology not only provided a congenial context in which it could thrive, but also gave additional impetus to its widespread acceptance. The increasingly grim situation in Germany in the inter-war years, and notoriously the deepening anti-semitism with its shrill call for the abandonment of the Old Testament, gave sombre urgency to the rediscovery of the abiding and distinctive features of Old Testament faith, whilst national-socialism's glorification of German *Volkstum* made equally urgent renewed interest in, and emphasis upon, the coming into existence of 'the people of God' to which not only the New Testament but also the Old Testament with its central traditions of 'election' and 'covenant' bears witness.[17] Neo-orthodoxy, which had emerged in the shadow of the First World

War and a fundamental aspect of which was a sharp rejection of 'natural theology' and 'religion', with a corresponding emphasis upon the in-breaking of God *von oben nach unten* ('from above to below'), also gave new relevance to the history of Israel as the arena of God's self-manifestation, and thus to the distinctiveness of Israelite faith among the 'religions' of its environment. This accounts in part for the preoccupation with *Heilsgeschichte*, to the downgrading of the Old Testament's wisdom tradition and literature which bear witness to Israel's closer dependence upon its cultural environment, and also for the peculiar handling of 'creation-theology' which was regarded— one thinks here especially of the work of von Rad[18]—as originally an alien element, only secondarily appropriated by Israel but transformed from its roots in 'natural theology' by being integrated into Israel's primal and central confession of faith in Yahweh's actions in history.[19]

The emphasis placed upon the distinctiveness of early Israelite religion by the 'biblical theology movement' in the United States from the 1940s onwards, with which the writings of such influential British scholars as H.H. Rowley had some affinities, needs no detailed presentation here, since it has been well described by Brevard Childs.[20] By this time the influence of recent German scholarship, especially works by Alt, Noth and Eichrodt, had extended there, though the American 'movement' had, as Childs has shown, its own peculiar matrix and causes. Led by G.E. Wright and other leading American scholars, this 'movement' depicted Israel's faith as having been from the outset a radical departure from the religious thought-world of its ancient Near Eastern environment. W.F. Albright's well-known *From the Stone Age to Christianity*, already published in 1940, gave an initial impulse, whilst further influential support came from a collection of essays by specialists in Egyptian and Mesopotamian religions under the title *The Intellectual Adventure of Ancient Man* which was published in 1946.[21] The contrast between 'mythopoeic' thought and biblical 'revelation through history' was persistently emphasized; Wright wrote of the 'Israelite mutation' when seen against the religions of its time.[22] As against these religions, Israel's religion was grounded in a faith in the 'God who acts' (the title of one of Wright's most influential books).[23] Albright and Wright and, in England, Rowley chose to employ such terms as 'incipient' or 'practical' monotheism as the only adequate description for Israel's understanding of God from the time of Moses. There was a particular emphasis upon 'Hebrew mentality' as contrasted with Greek thought-patterns, and manifesting itself even in the Hebrew language.[24] Archaeological discoveries were called upon as empirical evidence for the peculiar and mutational nature of Israelite religion from its earliest stages.

To sum up: during the middle decades of this century it was very widely agreed among scholars both in Europe and the United States that the early period of the history of Israelite religion was crucially formative of its distinctiveness. With much variation in detail, a majority of leading scholars associated the emergence of a highly distinctive Yahwism with the pre-monarchical period and, with greater or lesser emphasis, the pre-settlement period, a Yahwism characterized by, for example, a strict exclusivism (which some ventured to describe in some such way as 'practical' or 'incipient' monotheism) expressed in terms of a solemn covenant between God and Israel, and although incorporating features of Canaanite religion, nevertheless in its nature and ethos radically discontinuous with the religious thought-world of its environment. Israelite religion, it was agreed, was marked off from the outset in the most fundamental respects as virtually a stranger among the religions of its ancient Near Eastern neighbours, and was endowed with such distinctive characteristics that it was able to survive them, notwithstanding the many threats which confronted it over the centuries, not least among which was the danger during long periods of its history, especially during the monarchy, of a decline and fall into a degenerate syncretism with indigenous Canaanite religion.

By contrast, the sort of development of Israelite religion which had been argued by Wellhausen and many others who associated themselves with his view in the preceding period became almost universally abandoned. By contrast also, a school of thought which emerged in the 1930s under the leadership of S.H. Hooke and which argued that Israelite religion is to be understood as having been much more integrated into, and in significant ways a reflection of, a 'myth and ritual pattern' common to the major religions of the ancient Near East remained a minority position.[25]

Renewed Controversy

In recent years, however, this consensus has collapsed in the face of a critical reappraisal of, and fresh controversy concerning, the main findings of research upon which it was fundamentally dependent. Thus, for example, Noth's 'amphictyony' theory, which contributed so significantly to it, has been widely abandoned,[26] and new and controversial theories of Israelite origins and of the nature of early Israelite society are being argued.[27] Controversy has also once again arisen concerning the origin of the notion of the covenant between Yahweh and Israel which has been so important for the understanding of early Israelite religion as radically innovative. That it was in reality a *theologoumenon* introduced at a late stage in the pre-exilic period, just as Wellhausen maintained, has been freshly and vigorously argued, in more detail indeed than ever before.[28] Further, that the exclusive worship of Yahweh, which is an integral and prominent feature of the covenant-theology, was the *sine qua non* of early Israelite religion which the consensus-view regarded it as having been[29] has likewise come in for increasing challenge in recent years,[30] and the well-attested worship of a plurality of gods in Israel during the monarchical period is seen, not as a falling away from an earlier, pristine faith in, and allegiance to, one God alone but as evidence that Israelite religion as it emerged and developed in Palestine was for centuries of its history polytheistic. In addition, an ample demonstration of the belief in divine actions in history among ancient Near Eastern religions generally has undermined the well-known emphasis upon 'the mighty acts of Yahweh in history' as qualitatively differentiating Israelite religion from the religious thought-world of its environment.[31] This in turn has reinforced the increasing criticism of the emphasis upon *Heilsgeschichte* as a too narrow definition of the character of Israelite religion, and as having been at the expense of other influential traditions and beliefs in its make-up—for example creation-theology. A further trend is a new willingness to assess more positively what Israelite religion had in common with the religions of its environment which hitherto have been too often employed merely as a foil for highlighting the polarities between them.[32] To all this has to be added the renewed controversy in recent years concerning the dating of the oldest literary strata of the Pentateuch (JE). Against the hitherto widely favoured dating of these to the earlier period of the monarchy—in the case of J to the Solomonic period—some are now arguing for a period of composition in the very latest stages of the pre-exilic period or even the exilic period.[33] This in turn has added to controversy concerning how far back into Israelite history one can reliably trace the history of traditions, beliefs and institutions reflected in these strata, since the 'base line' from which one begins can vary by centuries according to the date one accepts for the composition of the literary strata as such.[34]

The result of all this is a renewed division of opinion in recent years concerning the nature and development of Israelite religion in the pre-exilic period reminiscent of that which characterized the pre-First World War generation of discussion briefly sketched above.

On the one hand, currently finding increasing support is the view that Israelite religion throughout centuries of its history was a much more typical ancient Near Eastern religion, and that the ways in which it ultimately departed from the religious thought-world of its environment to become truly idiosyncratic are to be attributed to a late period in its history. The recent scholarly literature in which this view, or aspects of it, has been argued is extensive, and a survey and assessment of it is well beyond the scope of this essay.[35] In offering a brief indication of it, I have concentrated largely upon the work of H.H. Schmid as the most constructive and programmatic in which this view has been argued.[36]

On the other hand, the radically mutational nature of early Israelite religion remains favoured by many. Of special interest, however, is the fresh expression it has found in connection with a new and controversial understanding of the origins of Israel and of the nature of pre-monarchical Israelite society. The most notable protagonist of this is N.K. Gottwald, a brief summary and assessment of whose work is given below.[37]

Before turning to this, a further observation concerning this new phase of research and discussion may here be added: it takes place against the background of, and has been partly stimulated by, a changed and more diversified theological climate generally. Two trends have been of significance.

First, Neo-orthodoxy has gone into decline; there has been an 'anthropological turn' and something of a revival of 'liberal theology'. Such topics as 'religion and culture', 'faith and reason', 'religion and society', 'natural theology', 'phenomenology'—the 'orphans' of the period of dialectic theology—are once again firmly on the theological agenda. In this new climate it is no coincidence that in Old Testament study there is now, for example, a renewed interest in the wisdom tradition, for so long regarded virtually as 'the erring child of the house' in assessing the roots and peculiar character of Israelite religion, and in creation-theology, for so long overshadowed and deprived of any real significance by the focus upon 'revelation through history' and the 'theology of redemption'. Further, since both wisdom and creation-theology were prominent features of the religious thought-world of Israel's environment, this renewed interest in the Old Testament's handling of them has brought with it renewed interest in their significance and role in ancient Near Eastern religions which in turn has given added impetus to the renewed interest in what Israelite religion owed to these religions. In short, the creative interaction between Israel and its cultural and religious environment, the investigation of which was an axiom of the 'history-of-religions movement' in the days of 'liberal theology'[38] and then faded under the impact of Neo-orthodoxy, is once again a focus of interest and new research.

Second, however, there is the relatively recent emergence of 'liberation theology' which has also been attracting increasing attention—and contention—and for which the Old Testament, with its 'foundation story' of the deliverance of slaves from oppression and their subsequent constitution in freedom in a land given to them by God, has been a primary source. Allowing for some over-simplification, it can be said that whilst the current theological trend referred to in the foregoing paragraph has influenced the emergence of the first of the two opposing views mentioned above, 'liberation theology' is a dominant influence upon Gottwald's restatement of the understanding of early Israelite religion as radically mutational. Here, as we shall see, the emphasis is upon such features as election, covenant, the exclusive worship of Yahweh ('mono-Yahwism')—suitably re-interpreted in terms of 'liberation', 'egalitarianism', and the like—as essentials of the religion ('ideology') of premonarchic Israel as a mutational society.

Opposing Opinions: Two Examples

1. The 'liberated' tribes of early Israel and their religion

G.E. Mendenhall first proposed this view,[39] and although Gottwald, with whose work I am mainly here concerned, has both extensively developed and in significant ways gone beyond it, it is first necessary to note briefly Mendenhall's thesis.

This is that Israel originated, not in the invasion of Canaan by semi-nomadic clans from outside, but by a process of what he terms 'withdrawal' on a massive scale on the part of large groups among the indigenous population of Canaan in the Late Bronze Age, a 'withdrawal' politically and subjectively from further obligation to the city-states to which they had hitherto belonged and under whose rule they had been oppressed and exploited. What happened was a 'peasants' revolt against the network of interlocking Canaanite city states'.[40] According to Mendenhall, the Amarna letters with their record of political upheaval in Canaan and the biblical account of the 'invasion' of Canaan represent one and the same process. Though the groups which had been in Egypt in bondage under the Pharaoh were a statistically negligible element of Israel, they in fact were those who upon their entry into Canaan provided the religiously based dynamic for the revolution. After their escape from Egypt they had formed a community in the desert under their God and liberator Yahweh with whom they entered a covenant which formalized and determined the responsibility and freedom of each member of the group. Their arrival in Canaan 'polarized the existing population all over the land'.[41] Their loyalty to a single Overlord, Yahweh, their adherence to a simple body of norms (the stipulations of the decalogue), and their solidarity as a group which had experienced liberation were 'attractive to all persons suffering under the burden of subjection to a monopoly of power which they had no part in creating, and from which they received virtually nothing but tax-collectors'.[42] Consequently, 'entire groups having a clan or "tribal" organization joined the newly-formed community, identified themselves with the oppressed in Egypt, received deliverance from bondage, and the original historic events with which all groups identified themselves took precedence over and eventually excluded the detailed historical traditions of particular groups who had joined later'.[43] Thus the new community, Israel, was the result of a revolution against both the political *status quo* of the time and the religion upon which this was founded and from which it derived legitimation. What now came into existence was 'the kingdom of Yahweh' in which Yahweh alone was king, and the existing power structures centring upon the monopoly control of the state were rejected. The basis of the new religion was 'the rejection of control of human beings by force, and the proclamation that only God was in control—through the voluntary subjection of all members of the community to those policies of the sovereign stipulated in the Decalogue-Covenant. This was the constitution of the "Kingdom of God"; that it existed at all is a historical miracle'.[44]

Gottwald shares and defends Mendenhall's 'revolt model' of Israelite origins: 'Early Israel was a slowly converging and constellating cluster of rebellious and dissenting Canaanite peoples distinguished by an anti-statist form of social organization with decentralized leadership.'[45] Historically, according to Gottwald, Israel originated in the period of the declining power of imperialist Egypt and of the city-states of Canaan from c. 1350 BC onwards, and he identifies two stages in its emergence: 'Elohistic Israel'—the name Isra*el* itself is a pointer to this first stage—followed by 'Yahwistic Israel'. The descendants of the Amarna Age *'apiru*, he argues, 'gained strength in the Palestinian highlands, at first as separate bands, increasingly as models for peasants to emulate, then as cultic-sociopolitical-military associations of previously separate groups (Elohistic Israel), and finally as a greatly expanded association of former *'apiru*, Shosu, peasants, and transhumant pastoralists from Canaan and Egypt under the name Israel, but with a new religious identity of Yahwism'.[46] He ascribes the patriarchs to 'Elohistic Israel', arguing that in Genesis they are already pictured as leaders of semi-autonomous 'socioeconomic' groups who lived in treaty relations with Canaanite cities at Mamre-Hebron, Jerusalem, and Gerar in the south of Palestine (cf. Gen. 14.26).[47] The union of groups to which they belonged 'probably falling within the period 1350–1250 BC, expressed the growing consciousness of the antifeudal movement as a powerful social movement in its own right, able to co-operate in the search for new forms of liberated social organization and a cult [El, the God of Israel] appropriate to such aims'.[48]

'Yahwistic Israel', he then argues, came about through an organizational leap forward by virtue of an increase in the number, socio-economic types, and previous historical experiences of the groups entering the community. The groups from Egypt 'became a powerful catalyst in energizing and guiding the broad coalition of underclass Canaanites. Their experience became exemplary for all Israel, fundamentally shaping . . . the entire format of the Israelite traditions'.[49] It was they who introduced the cult of Yahweh. There were negative and positive reasons why the Canaanite 'underclass' association turned to 'a totally, or largely, strange deity': 'Negatively, there was disappointment and frustration with El as a deity for validating an antifeudal social order, inasmuch as El had come to be so largely appropriated as the high father god of the very feudal city-states that Israel was challenging head-on. Positively, there was the overwhelming, demonstrated, military and cultic-ideological appeal of the Levites in convincing the coalition that Yahweh, who had defeated Egypt on its own ground, could defend an enlarged anti-imperial and antifeudal order in Canaan.'[50]

Whilst adopting and elaborating Mendenhall's theory of Israelite origins, however, Gottwald castigates him for not having properly completed what he had begun by failing to understand Israelite religion in a thoroughgoing sociological manner as a 'function' of early Israel as an 'egalitarian', 'anti-feudal' and 'anti-imperialist' society, and also for having failed to perceive that Israelite religion was just as much a projection of the power interests of its tribal 'egalitarian society' as the religions of its environment were projections of the 'stratified, feudal societies' to which they belonged and which they legitimated.[51] Gottwald writes:

> The weakness of the biblical-theology paradigms of Israel's 'uniqueness' was that they were formulations of religious idealism which failed to root the religious organization and ideology of early Israel in its distinctive social-constitutional framework. The intent of biblical theology to characterize the distinctiveness of early Israel is better served by depicting the religion of Yahweh as the symbolic bonding dimension of a synthetic egalitarian, inter-tribal counter-society, originating within and breaking off from hierarchic, stratified Canaanite society.[52]

Accordingly, he continues:

> All of the primary aspects of the religion of Israel, including its most idiosyncratic elements, hitherto viewed autonomously in the theological tradition, can be viewed more intelligibly in a socially organic manner that 'demythologizes' them into functions and expressions of socio-economic and communal-cultural existence instead of into states of existential or mystical consciousness.[53]

Yahwism is thus portrayed as 'the function of communal egalitarianism'. For example, with regard to Yahwistic exclusivism:

> Yahweh is unlike the other gods of the ancient Near East as Israel's egalitarian intertribal order is unlike the other ancient Near Eastern social systems. Yahweh forbids other gods in Israel as Israel forbids other systems of communal organization within its intertribal order. The social-organizational exclusionary principle

in Israel finds its counterpart in a symbolic-ideological exclusionary principle in the imagery of deity.[54]

Yahweh's uniqueness lay in the fact that 'he' was the symbol of a single-minded pursuit of an egalitarian tribal social system, a symbol drawn out of a common pool of ancient Near Eastern belief in individuated high gods, but appropriately refined and altered to fit the distance that lay between ancient Near Eastern society and Israelite society.[55]

In short, 'Yahweh was so different from the other gods because "he" was the god of such a different people.'[56]

The notion of 'election' is similarly re-interpreted:

'The Chosen People' is the distinctive self-consciousness of a society of equals created in the intertribal order and demarcated from a primarily centralized and stratified surrounding world.[57]

Likewise, the 'covenant charter' was a 'function' of this egalitarian society:

The cosmic religiopolitical charters of social life elsewhere in the ancient Near East mirrored and legitimated submission to the stratified world of class inequality, to the dependence of the many on the few for physical sustenance and for human identity. The covenant charter of early Israel mirrored and legitimated commitment in struggle toward the intentional 'destratification' of the human world, to the elevation of all Israelites to the status of free producers—both of their physical lives and their religiocultural identities . . . The covenant charter thus attests the enormous power of a social movement embracing the interests and identities of an entire populace that no longer waits to be given its due and its meaning from an elite.[58]

With regard to the religion or, as he prefers, 'ideology'[59] of early Israel, therefore, Gottwald has adopted a number of the main findings of the 'biblical theology movement' and translated them into the sociologial terminology appropriate to his Marxist 'historical cultural-material method of approach'.[60] At the same time, his understanding of early Israelite society constitutes a restatement of some of the 'biblical theology movement's' findings with regard to early Israelite religion: it was a mutational religion born of a mutational society. But how convincing is this suggestion?

A general observation may first be made before turning briefly to a number of more specific objections. At the beginning of his book Gottwald writes of the difficulties of reconstructing the early history of Israel on the basis of the largely later literary sources which the Old Testament affords. Yet time and again in reading the book one's credulity is strained at the amount of information—in places elaborate and detailed—which he is nonetheless apparently able to call upon. In reality, the answer to this is not that the sources after all yield more information than one would suspect; on many issues on which Gottwald writes freely, they remain mute. Rather, the explanation appears to lie in the confidence Gottwald has in his sociological method. This appears to be indicated by his statement as follows:

> ... while reiterating that sociology cannot supply literary and historical solutions when literary and historical data are absent, it is possible to say that what must remain uncertain in specifically literary or historical terms can take on another kind of *certitude* [italics mine] in social terms. We need not wait for the future resolution of historical questions for the social significance of the religion of ancient Israel to be demonstrated.[61]

This appears simply to claim that the theory is self-vindicating when empirical evidence for it is absent or not always present. Gottwald emphasizes that 'all the theory in the world is only as good as the empirical observations on which it is based'.[62] Yet time and time again his own very elaborate theory falls victim to this sound principle. All too often the theory is imposed upon the texts, and alleged 'empirical observations' turn out to be creations of the theory rather than what the texts, on any plausible reading of them, offer in support of the theory. Thus, for example, the 'Song of Deborah' (Judges 5) is interpreted as relating to a war between 'egalitarian' Israel and 'hierarchic', state-monopolist Canaanites whom the anti-feudal Israelites had been economically despoiling, looting them and viewing it as 'the rightful reappropriation of wealth that had been extracted by kings, aristocrats, landowners, and merchants from the raw labor of the lower classes'[63]—all this being argued on the basis of an unusual reading of three words in verse 7 and a redivision of the Masoretic Text (with no support for any of this in the ancient versions) and a surely highly tendentious reading of verse 8b.[64] Or again, an idiomatic usage of the verb ישב is argued, so that in strategic texts the ישבי הארץ ('the inhabitants of the land') become 'rulers' or 'kings of the land' whence the move is made to 'those who rule *abusively* or *oppressively*'—just as the theory demands.[65] But even if in such texts as Judges 1 relating to the 'conquest' the expression were to be understood in some instances as connoting specifically 'rulers' or 'kings of the land', the issue does not at all appear to be the way they rule or the nature of the society in which they rule but that the *land* over which they rule is being claimed by Israel to whom it has been promised by Yahweh. That an 'egalitarian', anti-feudal, anti-imperialist Israel was in the events described in such texts seeking to overthrow 'abusively' and 'oppressively' ruling kings and leaders is what the theory demands but not at all what the texts themselves indicate or are concerned with. Or again, the overall peaceful tone of the patriarchal narratives in Genesis 12ff. is ignored, and attention is focused upon Genesis 14 and 26. But in neither of these passages can the patriarchs seriously be viewed as 'underclass' Canaanites in search, with others, 'for new forms of liberated social organization'. This again is what the theory (of 'Elohistic Israel') demands rather than what these narratives portray. In Genesis 14 Abram is an ally of Canaanite kings who appear indeed to be subordinate to him and his group (something which Gottwald acknowledges but, since it is not congenial to his theory, explains as the result of 'anachronizing Israelite tradition, which makes of Abraham an epic figure who foreshadows David's empire'),[66] whilst in Genesis 26, where Isaac is described as being more powerful than Abimelech (verse 16), Abimelech is portrayed in morally upright terms (cf. verses 9-11) when, on Gottwald's hypothesis, we expect him to be one who rules 'abusively' and 'oppressively'. Neither feudalism nor anti-feudalism as such has any part in what is described in these narratives, and the claim that the patriarchs and their communities are to be understood as 'underclass' Canaanites is in the face of the evidence they provide.[67] A further key text is Exodus 15 in which, according to Gottwald, the Pharaoh is 'perceived as *the* historico-political Enemy, the epitome of those oppressive rulers which the imperial-feudal systems of Near Eastern statist society necessarily produce and which Israel and her God just as necessarily must oppose and defeat'.[68] But this passage has nothing to say about economic and social conditions in either Egypt or Palestine,[69] here too the theory is being read grandly into the text.

What 'certitude in social terms' can there be when so much has to be read into texts such as these which are quite devoid of interest in

the ideological issues Gottwald seeks to advance and some of which
in fact militate against his theory?

A further example of this latter may be given. According to
Gottwald the Edomites, Ammonites, and Moabites came into existence
by the same process of 'retribalization' as Israel; their origins 'fall
apparently within the same broad category of anti-imperial and anti-
feudal sociopolitical formation'.[70] But why then did these peoples
evidently so soon adopt kingship and a 'statist' form of society which,
ex hypothesi, they so recently had been glad to have rid themselves of,
and not only adopted it but maintained it for centuries? Gottwald's
explanation of this is what he himself describes as 'highly conjectur-
al'.[71] Just as difficult for his theory is why Israel, the alleged epitome
of revolutionary, 'anti-statist' societies of this time, also adopted
kingship and a 'statist' form of social organization, and why, when
after the bitter experiences of Solomon's reign the northern tribes
rebelled against this king's oppressive policies, they did not resort to
their erstwhile form of de-centralized society but established their
own state and dynasty, and this by divine designation, we are told (1
Kgs 11.29ff.). If it is the case that there was initial opposition to the
institution of monarchy, it appears to have quickly dissipated.
Neither Ahijah nor any of the prophets who succeeded him, including
even Elijah, and who became involved in the overthrow of dynasties
in northern Israel, evidently sought the abolition of kingship as such
and a revival of a de-centralized tribal form of society.

Gottwald's stance *vis à vis* the 'biblical theology movement'
requires a further comment. Among his criticisms of these earlier
scholars is that they virtually denied any 'commonality in religious
patterning between Israel and its neighbors'.[72] This is a criticism
which may be fully accepted. He also correctly points out, following
Albrektson, that the notion of divine actions in history was by no
means a feature peculiar to Israelite religion among the religions of
antiquity. He himself offers a brief depiction of the general structure
of belief in the ancient Near East in which Israel fully participated,[73]
followed by a description of the ways in which Israelite religion
nonetheless 'stands out as a highly idiosyncratic version of the
common theological pattern'.[74]

Yet it does not seem that Gottwald himself makes much of the
'commonality' between Israelite religion and the religions of its
environment. For all his strictures upon earlier scholars, he differs
but marginally from them in respect of what they understood to be

the primary and characterizing features of early Israelite religion as radically innovative. In his book the emphasis remains on such features as election, covenant,[75] the exclusive worship of one God— none of which belonged to the 'commonality' referred to. Similarly, creation-theology, which in some respects at least does belong to his 'commonality' but which was given short shrift in the writings of these scholars, is just as much out of the picture in Gottwald's long and detailed work. (In his brief treatment of 'Common High-God Paradigms' in the ancient Near East he does not explicitly deal with the theme of creation, and it is nowhere mentioned, as far as I can see, among the topics listed in his extensive index.) It seems that for Gottwald, just as much as in the case of these earlier scholars, the emphasis remains upon Yahweh's 'actions in history', understood in the specific sense of 'liberation' and the emergence of 'egalitarian' Israelite society. In short, the only substantial difference between Gottwald and the representatives of the 'biblical theology movement' is that they failed, in his opinion, to make proper use of the distinctive features of early Israelite religion which they believed to have uncovered, that is, failed to interpret them correctly in terms of the social reality which he believes they symbolized.

We have seen, however, that in recent years a number of the widely agreed conclusions of earlier scholars concerning the radically innovative nature of early Israelite religion have been freshly challenged. This has been accompanied by a new consideration of precisely the 'commonality' between Israelite religion and the religious thought-world of its time, an adequate investigation of which Gottwald no less than the scholars he has criticized on this count has failed to carry through. In particular, there has been a reappraisal of 'creation' not merely as a common theme of ancient Near Eastern religions, including Israelite religion, but of creation-theology as the 'broad horizon' of Israelite faith and belief; that is, there has been a shift to the theme of the 'divine ordering of the world' as the framework and religious 'given' which Israel shared with its neighbours and within which the distinctive features of Israelite religion had to be and were worked out. On such a view, one begins not with the 'particularist' themes such as election and covenant, but with the 'universalist' theme of creation-faith and thence moves on to the peculiar development of Israelite religion; the movement is, we might say, from 'God and the world' to 'God and his people'. Israelite religion is then understood as having been initially and indeed for centuries of its history a much more typically ancient Near Eastern religion, and those features which ultimately differentiated it sharply from the religious thought-world of its environment are viewed, not as the product of one founding period at the beginning, or at least not largely so, but as the outcome of a protracted history of inner-Israelite thinking and controversy about God, man and the world which reached its decisive stages only with the beginnings of the 'classical' prophets of the eighth century BC.

2. 'Creation-theology' in the religions of the ancient Near East and in Israel

Schmid writes of a common ancient Near Eastern perception of a comprehensive divine ordering of the world (*Weltordnungsdenken*), and employs the term 'creation-theology' in a broad sense to designate this. The evidence he adduces may be briefly summarized as follows.[76]

The creation myths described how the world was created by the gods against the forces of chaos in the *Urzeit*. In reality, however, these myths reflected society's experience of the confrontation in the here and now between the 'right order' of the human world and all that threatened it. That is, creation was not merely an event of the remote past, but much more vitally concerned the present: the cosmic order was not merely given; it had to be sustained. It was society's guarantee against the ever present forces of destruction, in cosmic terms, of the forces of chaos which might manifest themselves in, for example, disruptions of the fertility of nature, attacks by enemies (seen as allies of these cosmic forces of chaos), and the like.

A perception of *Weltordnung* informed all activities of society's life, the total well-being of which depended upon upholding it. In the cultic sphere the annual New Year festival centred upon a realization in the present, a cultic 'actualization', of the triumph of the creator gods over chaos in creation and so sought to 'renew' the 'right order' of the world, including the fertility of nature, for the year to come. Or when at any time calamity struck—that is, the cosmic order was under assault—the cult and its rituals (lament, sacrifice, magic, etc.) played an important role in restoring the 'right order'. In the political sphere enemies were seen as earthly representatives of the cosmic forces of chaos, so that defence against them was itself part of the endeavour to maintain the sacred order of the world. This sacred order was also reflected in society's laws, understood as having been decreed by the gods at the foundation of the state; in this way the just ordering of society was brought into close relationship with the creation of the world itself.[77] Hence a breach of these laws was *ipso facto* a breach of the order of creation, and could be understood as having dire consequences in the sphere of nature or in the sphere of politics, since law, politics, and nature were but different aspects of the one all-embracing cosmic order. The concept of the divine order of the world likewise informed the ideology of kingship in the ancient Near East. The king—whether as incarnation or 'son'—was the divinely appointed vice-gerent of the creator deities and as such was seen as the earthly guardian and guarantor of the sacred order of creation, responsible through his actions and functions for the social and political well-being of the state, including the fertility of the land, in accordance with the divinely willed order of the world. The ordering of social life is further evidenced in the wisdom literature of the ancient Near East: to live wisely was to be in harmony with the cosmic order of which wisdom was fundamentally constitutive[78] (hence the use, for example, in Egyptian wisdom and legal texts of the word *Maat* which is also employed to designate the 'primal order' or the 'right order' of the created cosmos itself).[79]

The sense of the all-pervading order of the world accounts for another familiar feature of ancient Near Eastern thought, namely, the belief in a direct relationship between a misdeed and what must befall as a result of it: a violation of the divinely established 'right order' issues in dire consequences for its perpetrator; unless otherwise purged or expiated, the offence rebounds on the malefactor, whether as a necessary result of the inherent nature of things, or as punishment visited directly by the gods, as sustainers of the divinely willed order of the world, upon the offender.

Schmid writes of all this as evidence of an endeavour to comprehend the manifold experiences of reality as an ordered unity.[80] But it is clear that by this he means something rather more than some sort of abstract theology. By *Weltordnung* he means the organization and conduct of society as grounded in, and therefore validated by, the divine ordering of the world. That is, his considerations point to the 'social reality' of religion. I shall return to this below.

For evidence that Israel shared with its neighbours the view of a comprehensive world order grounded in and informed by a creation-theology, in the broad sense of this term, Schmid points, for example, to the probability that in Israel too there was an annual New Year festival which centred upon Yahweh's triumph over chaos in creation, and thus proclaimed his divine kingship as creator and sustainer of the world. He draws attention also to the motif of the battle against chaos (*Chaoskampf*), which belonged to the typology of Canaanite and Mesopotamian religions, as having also been known in Israel, and to the way in which this motif appears not only in cosmological contexts but also in political contexts, thus indicating that in Israel too enemies were regarded as none other than a manifestation of chaos which must be driven back.[81] In Israel too, at least in the case of the Davidic dynasty, there emerged an ideology of kingship which bears close resemblance to that of the surrounding nations: the king is Yahweh's 'son' on whose behalf Yahweh defeats the enemies (Pss. 2; 89; 110); he exercises the role of Yahweh's vice-gerent as the guardian and maintainer of Yahweh's righteousness among the people, and associated with the role of the king in this respect is the very fertility of the land (e.g. Ps. 72). Likewise in Israel wisdom was believed to be grounded in, and to reflect, the divinely created 'right order' of things; wisdom and righteousness were closely related to one another.[82] In the ethical sphere there is evidence that Israel, no less than its neighbours, believed in the 'deed-and-its-effect' syndrome, and Schmid understands the basic structure of this to underly the prophetic indictment of Israel. They 'follow the general knowledge of the time and criticize the people in terms of what is "order" in the sphere of interpersonal relationships. And this is the same order that is found in the context of creation faith as well as in the sphere of law and of wisdom.'[83] Yahweh watches over this 'order' so that Israel's violation of it which the prophets relentlessly expose must and will be met with Yahweh's judgment. Creation-thought also informs the prophetic announcement of the inbreaking of salvation after divine judgment. Thus, for example, Second Isaiah begins with the announcement that Israel has double paid for its sins (Is. 40.1ff.): 'once the marred order is restored through punishment (here the exile), the world returns again to its order, it again becomes whole and healthy ... Whenever portrayals of this blissful (*heil*) future rework motifs dealing with primeval time, the connection with creation faith is obvious. However, in an indirect way this connection can be seen in numerous other passages: in those cases, among other, where salvation (*Heil*) is described with the concept of $ṣ^edāqā$ (righteousness). [Is. 45.8, 23f.; 46.12f.; 51.6, 8; 54.14, 17.] In these instances "righteousness" is not understood narrowly as a legal matter, but as universal world order, as comprehensive salvation.'[84] Schmid proceeds to argue that the concept of a single, harmonious order of the world can be discerned as the controlling background of such diverse materials as the narratives of the primaeval history in Genesis 1–11, the patriarchal narratives in Genesis 12ff., including the divine promises to the ancestors, the Exodus traditions, and the development of eschatological faith. Thus he concludes that 'the controlling background of OT thought and faith is the view of a comprehensive world order and, hence, a creation faith in the broad sense of the word—a creation faith that Israel in many respects shared with her environment'.[85]

In this fundamental way Israel participated fully in the religious thought-world of its environment. But there are in addition other strong indications that for much of its history Israelite religion may be described as a 'Canaanization' of Yahwism.[86] There is well-known evidence, for example, that Yahweh was identified with El, the highest god of the Canaanite pantheon, a number of whose epithets and descriptions have been associated with Yahweh. In this way Yahweh would have assumed the role of El as creator, sustainer and guardian of the divinely willed order of the world. Further, there is some evidence that, in typical Canaanite fashion, a number of subordinate deities were worshipped alongside the national God Yahweh (e.g. Shalim, Shaḥar, Shamash, Resheph, Astarte), and there is abundant testimony that Baal, the most active god of the Canaanite pantheon, was widely worshipped in Israel, in some circles probably identified with Yahweh.[87] It seems also very likely that the cult of the Canaanite goddess and Baal's consort Anath among the fifth-century Jews at Elephantine was inherited by them from much earlier Israelite times. To all this may now be added the evidence from Palestinian inscriptions from c. 800 BC of the worship of Asherah as Yahweh's consort, just as she (Athirat) was the consort of El in Canaanite religion.[88]

Clearly, however, whilst a number of features originally adopted from Canaanite religion remained permanent features of Israelite religion, the faith of Israel as we encounter it in the Old Testament has decisively rejected others. How is this to be accounted for? How did the religion of Israel acquire its umistakeable distinctiveness among the religions of its environment?

Schmid writes of a long history of inner-Israelite controversy. Whilst the adoption by Yahwism of certain features of Canaanite religion evidently caused no controversy (e.g. the identification of Yahweh with aspects of El), others did—notably the worship of Baal who more and more became the rival of Yahweh. The books of Kings provide ample evidence of a continuous dispute on how God, people and the world are to be understood.[89] But it was not until the preaching of the prophets of the eighth century that this controversy reached its decisive stage and took on a new dimension. Briefly stated—if I understand Schmid correctly—what the preaching of these prophets represented was a radically reoriented perception of the divine *Weltordnung*.[90] The presupposition of Israel's inherited 'world-view' was that Yahweh's ordering of the world had for its goal the well-being (שלום) of Israel; any threats to this could be warded off by the usual means (lament, sacrifice, etc.). But these prophets announced Yahweh's rejection of Israel, the end of Israel. No longer the שלום of Israel but Yahweh's will for righteousness stands at the centre—if need be at the cost of Israel; that is, the preaching of these prophets represented a shift from a 'state-ideological' concept of the divine ordering of the world to a radically theocentric one. It represented a sharp polarization between God and the world, an emphasis on the radical transcendence of Yahweh with a corresponding relativizing of Israel in the face of Yahweh's will for righteousness.

The significance which Schmid thus attaches to the preaching of these prophets is clearly reminiscent of Wellhausen's assessment of them to which I referred at the outset of this essay, and he fully acknowledges this.[91] In this respect his views represent something of a revolt against the so-called 'revolt against Wellhausen' which characterized the period of research outlined earlier. I shall return to this below. At this point I offer two observations about Schmid's work, the first concerning his emphasis upon *Weltordnung* in Israelite religion, and the second concerning his bold claim, which represents such a reversal of von Rad's well-known treatment of creation-faith in the Old Testament, that 'creation, namely, the belief that God has created and is sustaining the order of the world in all its complexities' is 'plainly the fundamental theme' of the Old Testament.[92]

Schmid's emphasis upon *Weltordnung* in Israelite religion and in the religions of its environment, as well as his claim concerning the preaching of the eighth-century prophets, is implicitly fully in line with certain aspects of the modern study of the sociology of religion, and may be further elucidated briefly as follows.[93]

First, the concept of *Weltordnung* as used by Schmid is in line with the sociological analysis of religion as part of what has been termed a society's 'world-building' activity, that is, its endeavour to impose meaning upon its manifold experiences of the world. As a microcosm is related to a macrocosm, the humanly perceived 'right order' of the world, including both nature and society, was perceived as a reflection of the cosmic order created and willed by the gods/God. Second— and this too is exemplified in Schmid's work—religion in this way legitimated the social order, its structures and institutions, that is, it represented a 'mystification' of the humanly perceived world *sub specie aeternitatis*. There is every reason for believing that this was no less the case in Israel than in other ancient Near Eastern societies; Israel believed its wellbeing to be permanently guaranteed by Yahweh, precisely as part of the 'order' established by him.

Third, however, sociologists such as P. Berger stress also the historical role of religion as an agent of de-legitimation or 'demystification', and this too is a way of understanding what Schmid has in mind in claiming that the preaching of the eighth-century prophets effected a shift from a 'state-ideological' understanding of the divine ordering of the world to a radically theocentric one: their emphasis on the transcendence of Yahweh and their corresponding relativizing of Israel represented a 'demystification' of Israel *sub specie aeternitatis* by declaring Israel in the face of God's righteousness to be devoid of inherent sanctity or divinely willed permanence.

But what of Schmid's claim that creation, 'the belief that God has created and is sustaining the order of the world in all its complexities', is 'plainly the fundamental theme' of the Old Testament? It is hazardous to put the matter like this, for it too easily gives the impression that simply this is what the Old Testament is 'about'.[94] Further, it might be objected that there is after all comparatively little in the Old Testament that is overtly and systematically stated about Yahweh's ordering of the world in the sense which Schmid has in mind. It is surely the case that 'God and his people' is the theme which is in the foreground rather than 'God and the world'. Further, what creation, that is 'orderly and harmonious world', is, or should be, is, as he points out, a general human perception, common not only to the religions of the ancient Near East, including Israel, but one also arrived at in a different way by the Enlightenment centuries later.[95] Clearly, simply this belief would be inadequate as a description of what the Old Testament is 'about'.

But, if I understand him correctly, it is not Schmid's intention that a background and largely unarticulated concept of *Weltordnung* should overshadow what the writers of the Old Testament consciously described and asserted. By describing creation, the notion of 'orderly and harmonious world', as the fundamental theme of the Old Testament I understand him to mean that it is so in the sense that what is explicitly described and asserted there is ultimately concerned with, and witnesses to, the concept of 'orderly and harmonious world', and that it is the task of exegesis to demonstrate how this is so. In short, I take it that Schmid employs the description 'fundamental theme' as another way of saying that creation-faith is the 'broad horizon' of Old Testament faith.

Nevertheless, his statement that this fundamental theme is 'the belief that God has created and is sustaining the order of the world in all its complexities' has to be qualified in an important way, but one which I think Schmid would approve. It is that this is only so in the sense that this sustaining involves God's activity to *transform* the world from what it is perceived to be into what he as creator purposes it to be, 'orderly and harmonious world'. Is not this more precisely the 'horizon' of Old Testament faith, that God who has created the world 'supports the world order and seeks to bring it into realization'?[96] In this 'horizon' the task of Old Testament exegesis would then be to show how God seeks to bring creation, 'orderly and harmonious world', into realization concretely through his people— through his election of them, the vocation to which this summons them in the covenant (which constituted his 'order' for them), his judgment of them, his renewal of them after judgment, and his promises to them for the future and their role as 'a light to the nations'. Beyond this, the question is also placed on the agenda of the contribution the Old Testament's testimony to what constitutes 'orderly and harmonious world' can make to the task of theology in a modern world which is no less occupied with the major theme of 'orderly and harmonious world'.

A final observation brings us back to where we began this essay, that is, to Wellhausen whose assessment of the contribution of the great prophets has in its essentials been re-argued by Schmid. As already indicated, this is something which Schmid fully acknowledges. But it is clear also that in arguing this view he has been able to draw upon a great deal that has happened in research since Wellhausen's time, especially our greatly increased knowledge of the religions of

Israel's environment compared with what was available to Wellhausen. As also indicated above, it represents a reversal in this matter of the so-called 'revolt against Wellhausen', and it is with this 'revolt' that my concluding observation is concerned.

Central to it was the accusation that Wellhausen had imposed an *a priori* 'evolutionary' pattern, whether derived from Hegel or from the natural sciences, upon the history of Israelite religion seen as having emerged from primitive beginnings through various stages of development to the monotheism of much later times.[97] But there is reason for believing that the 'revolt' against his views, the full flowering of which is represented by the consensus-view outlined in the opening section above, was in part influenced by assumptions and presuppositions of no less a theoretical and *a priori* nature than those which allegedly governed Wellhausen's work.

This was surely particularly so in the case of the 'history-of-religions' movement. Under the influence of a revived Romanticism,[98] this movement stressed the notion of the individuality, (*Eigenart* or *Eigentümlichkeit*) of peoples, an individual character or 'national spirit' (*Volksgeist*) which distinguishes each from the others, giving each its own peculiar stamp. Each is individually endowed with its own peculiar capabilities, gifts and tendencies which in multifarious ways affect its comprehension of reality and hence also its development which cannot therefore be understood along the lines of any mechanistic or abstract theory of growth; each strives to realize its own *Eigenart*, and necessarily so.

To understand the unique value and status of, for example, Israel's religion, which is the historian's goal, is to fathom its *Eigenart* in its growth and becoming from its origins. Hence Gressmann, in his work referred to earlier, stressed the importance of looking not only 'backwards' (*rückwärts*) but also 'sideways' (*seitwärts*) at the surrounding cultures: the aim of both exercises, which belong together in research, is to determine the *Eigenart* of Israel. He re-emphasized this in a programmatic essay on the future tasks for Old Testament research published in 1924—just when the foundations of the consensus-view described above were being laid—stressing that 'each people has its own individual soul, with its specific capabilities and gifts, its own personal character, which distinguishes it from all others'.[99]

The specifically Idealist terminology in which such an approach was expressed largely disappeared in the generation which followed, but the evidence suggests that the notions themselves remained in some measure influential upon scholars of this period who, as we have seen, placed a similar emphasis upon Israel's *Eigenart* and laboured to demonstrate how much this had been formed already at the beginnings of Israel's history. Thus, for example, a prominent representative of this period, G.E. Wright, could write of that 'something' in early Israel which 'predisposed and predetermined the course of Biblical history'.[100]

But clearly this is no less an *a priori* approach than the alleged 'evolutionary' approach of Wellhausen which it is intended to rebuff and replace. *Of course* the faith of Israel as it found expression in the Old Testament drew upon features already there at the beginnings; *of course* there was continuity between the later and the earlier periods. But there was no inherent necessity which compelled Israelite religion to develop in the particular way it did. Indeed, the testimony of the Old Testament is surely that it might have been otherwise, for it points to an Israel which had evidently a propensity for doing many things which the Old Testament condemns, for example the worship of many gods rather than exclusive allegiance to one God. The very fact that there was prolonged controversy on this issue—to mention a prominent example—is itself an indication that the development of Israelite religion into what it in fact became was not the only possibility that lay open to it at the beginning. Far from predetermining the future development of Israelite religion in one inexorable direction, or already setting down all that was essential for what has found expression in the Old Testament, it seems much more likely that early Israelite religion was polyvalent; that is, a number of different, in part sharply conflicting, directions of development lay open to it. Thus, to take again the example referred to above, it seems likely that whilst for some circles from the earliest period the worhip of Yahweh was intolerant of the worship of other deities as well, for others it was not; the resulting controversy between the adherents of each of these outlooks was by no means settled all at once.[101]

Schmid is surely correct to eschew all schemes of 'pure beginnings' or of 'evolution from lower to ever higher forms', and to stress this polyvalent nature of early Israelite religion.[102] Only after a long controversy, the vigour of which can still be seen in the pages of the Old Testament, concerning the nature of Yahweh and his claims upon Israel did the faith of the Old Testament come to be. Those, evidently a minority, who in the course of this controversy broke through to an understanding of the world as created and ordered by Yahweh as God alone, Israel's God from the land of Egypt, were vindicated by the eventualities of history which were seen to point to Yahweh as God alone, in whom alone, therefore, Israel was summoned to place its trust.[103]

It is a very great pleasure to contribute this essay to a volume in honour of Professor William KcKane to whom I owe a lasting debt for a multitude of kindnesses to me and most of all for his wise and stimulating guidance when I was a student in Glasgow many years ago.

NOTES

1. First published as *Geschichte Israels I*, Berlin, 1878, and in subsequent editions as *Prolegomena zur Geschichte Israels*; ET: *Prolegomena to the History of Israel*, Edinburgh 1885. (References below are to the latter.) Wellhausen's article 'Israel' was first published in the ninth edition of *Encyclopaedia Britannica*, vol. XIII, 1881, and was republished as an Appendix to the English translation of the *Prolegomena*. Again, references below are to it as contained in the latter.

2. On Wellhausen's assessment of the prophets see Professor McKane's perceptive article 'Prophet and Institution', *ZAW* 94 (1982), 251-66.

3. Wellhausen frequently employs this term, which he appears to have derived from A. Kuenen.

4. *Prolegomena*, 417.

5. 'Israel', 473f.

6. For a survey of opinions on this at that time see, for example, E. Osswald, *Das Bild des Mose*, Berlin, 1962.

7. R. Kittel, *A History of the Hebrews*, I, London and Edinburgh, 1895, 243ff. (ET from *Geschichte der Hebräer*, I, Gotha, 1888).

8. 'Es gibt keinen Stoff in der Welt, der nicht seine Vorgeschichte, keinen Begriff, der nicht seinen Anknüpfungspunkt hätte', H. Gressmann, *Albert Eichhorn und die Religionsgeschichtliche Schule*, Göttingen, 1914, 35.

9. For a survey see D.A. Knight, *Rediscovering the Traditions of Israel* (SBL Dissertation Series, 9), Missoula, Montana, 1975.

10. I have described this at greater length in a forthcoming book *God and His People: Covenant and Theology in the Old Testament*.

11. An English translation of *Das Antike Judentum* under the title *Ancient Judaism* was published in 1952.

12. For a fuller treatment I again refer to my forthcoming book on covenant (see note 10).

13. *Die Gesetze im Pentateuch*, Halle, 1940, reprinted in his *Gesammelte Studien*, Theologische Bücherei, Munich, 1960, 9-141; ET: 'The Laws in the Pentateuch: Their Assumptions and Meaning', in *The Laws in The Pentateuch and Other Essays*, Edinburgh and London, 1966, 1-107.

14. A. Weiser, *Die Bedeutung des Alten Testaments für den Religionsunterricht*, Giessen, 1925, and *Glaube und Geschichte im Alten Testament* (BWANT, 4:4), Stuttgart, 1931. Both of these are reprinted in his *Glaube und Geschichte im Alten Testament und andere ausgewählte Schriften*, Göttingen, 1961.

15. K. Galling, *Die Erwählungstraditionen Israels*, BZAW 48, Giessen, 1928.

16. W. Eichrodt, *Theologie des Alten Testaments*, vol. I, Leipzig, 1933; vol. II, 1935; vol. III, 1939.

17. See the comment of O. Keel, *Monotheismus im Alten Testament und seiner Umwelt*, ed. O. Keel (Biblische Beiträge, 14), Fribourg, 1980, 23.

18. See especially his 'Das theologische Problem des alttestamentlichen Schöpfungsglaubens', in BZAW, 66, Berlin 1936, 138-47, reprinted in his *Gesammelte Studien*, Theologische Bücherei, Munich, 1958, 136-47; ET: 'The Theological Problem of the Old Testament Doctrine of Creation', in *The Problem of the Hexateuch and other Essays*, Edinburgh and London, 1968, 131-43.

19. See the comments of H.H. Schmid, *Altorientalische Welt in der alttestamentlichen Theologie*, Zürich, 1974, 9f., 145ff. The first chapter in this book is now available in English translation as 'Creation, Righteousness and Salvation: "Creation Theology" as the Broad Horizon of Biblical Theology', in B.W. Anderson (ed.), *Creation in the Old Testament* (Issues in Religion and Theology, 6), Philadelphia and London, 1984, 102-17.

20. B.S. Childs, *Biblical Theology in Crisis*, Philadelphia, 1970.

21. Eds. H. Frankfort and others, Chicago, 1946.

22. See especially his *The Old Testament Against Its Environment* (SBT, 2), London, 1950.

23. G.E. Wright, *God Who Acts, Biblical Theology as Recital* (SBT, 8), London, 1952.

24. A description of this and its collapse in the face of criticisms from J. Barr and others is provided in Childs, *Biblical Theology in Crisis*, esp. chapter 4.

25. A survey of the period up to 1951 is given by G.W. Anderson, 'Hebrew Religion', in *The Old Testament and Modern Study*, ed. H.H. Rowley, Oxford, 1951, 283-310.

26. For a discussion see, for example, A.D.H. Mayes, *Israel in the Period of the Judges* (SBT 2/29), London, 1974.

27. See, most notably, G.E. Mendenhall, 'The Hebrew Conquest of Palestine', *BA* 25 (1962), 66-87, and *The Tenth Generation*, Baltimore, 1973;

C.H.J. de Geus, *The Tribes of Israel*, Assen and Amsterdam, 1976; N.K. Gottwald, *The Tribes of Yahweh: A Sociology of the Religion of Liberated Israel, 1250-1050 B.C.E.*, Maryknoll and London, 1979.

28. L. Perlitt, *Bundestheologie im Alten Testament* (WMANT, 36), Neukirchen, 1969.

29. Von Rad's statement 'Ein Jahwekultus ohne das erste Gebot ist wirklich nicht vorstellbar' ('Yahwism without the first commandment is positively inconceivable') is representative of this view. (*Theologie des Alten Testaments*, I, 6th ed., Munich, 1969, 39; *Old Testament Theology*, I, Edinburgh and London, 1962, 26.)

30. See, for example, G.W. Ahlström, *Aspects of Syncretism in Israelite Religion* (Horae Soederblomianae, 5), Lund, 1963; Morton Smith, *Palestinian Parties and Politics That Shaped The Old Testament*, New York and London, 1971; B. Lang (ed.), *Der Einzige Gott: Die Geburt des biblischen Monotheismus*, Munich, 1981, and *Monotheism and the Prophetic Minority: An Essay in Biblical History and Sociology* (The Social World of Biblical Antiquity Series, 1), Sheffield, 1983; F. Stolz, 'Monotheismus in Israel', in O. Keel, *Monotheismus*, 144-84.

31. B. Albrektson, *History and the Gods* (Coniectanea Biblica, Old Testament Series, 1), Lund, 1967.

32. This can already be seen in F.M. Cross's important work *Canaanite Myth and Hebrew Epic*, Cambridge Mass., 1973. For a comment on Cross's contribution see B.S. Childs, *Biblical Theology in Crisis*, 75f.

33. For example, J. Van Seters, *Abraham in History and Tradition*, New Haven and London, 1975; H.H. Schmid, *Der sogenannte Jahwist*, Zürich, 1976; H. Vorländer, *Die Entstehungszeit des jehowistischen Geschichtswerkes* (Europäische Hochschulschriften), Frankfurt, Bern and Las Vegas, 1978; M. Rose, *Deuteronomist und Jahwist* (Abhandlungen zur Theologie des Alten und Neuen Testaments), Zürich, 1981.

34. See, for example, J. Van Seters, *Abraham in History and Tradition*, esp. Part II.

35. Extensive bibliographies are provided in the works of Lang and Stolz (n. 30 above).

36. H.H. Schmid, *Altorientalische Welt*. See also his *Wesen und Geschichte der Weisheit* (BZAW, 101), Berlin, 1966, and *Gerechtigkeit als Weltordnung* (Beiträge zur Historischen Theologie, 40), Tübingen, 1968.

37. N.K. Gottwald, *The Tribes of Yahweh*.

38. Cf. H. Gressmann, *Albert Eichhorn*, 38, 39ff.

39. See note 27.

40. 'The Hebrew Conquest', 73.

41. *Ibid.*, 74.

42. *Ibid.*, 74.

43. *Ibid.*, 74.

44. *The Tenth Generation*, xiii.

45. N.K. Gottwald, 'Domain Assumptions and Societal Models in the Study of Pre-monarchic Israel' (SVT, 28), 1975, 93.

46. *The Tribes of Yahweh*, 496f.

47. *Ibid.*, 493.

48. *Ibid.*, 495.

49. *Ibid.*, 496.

50. *Ibid.*, 496.

51. This pronounced difference between Gottwald's view and Mendenhall's is very evident in the latter's response to *The Tribes of Yahweh* in 'Ancient Israel's Hyphenated History', *Palestine in Transition: The Emergence of Ancient Israel*, eds. D.N. Freedman and D.F. Graf (The Social World of Biblical Antiquity Series, 2), Sheffield, 1983, 91-103.

52. *The Tribes of Yahweh*, 692.

53. *Ibid.*, 692.

54. *Ibid.*, 693.

55. *Ibid.*, 693.

56. *Ibid.*, 693.

57. *Ibid.*, 692.

58. *Ibid.*, 701.

59. *Ibid.*, 65f.

60. *Ibid.*, 631ff.

61. *Ibid.*, 17.

62. *Ibid.*, 13.

63. *Ibid.*, 506.

64. *Ibid.*, 503-507. חדלו 'they ceased' in its two occurrences in 7a is understood as 'grew fat', and עד, which in the MT belongs to 7b and means 'until', is linked to 7a and understood as 'booty'. But rather than describing bounty that came to Israel as a result of Deborah's achievements, the verse surely has the function of describing the misery, the plight, of Israel which Deborah arose to meet and from which Israel was then delivered under her leadership. Understood in this traditional way, the overall structure of the poem is similar to that of other narratives of threat and deliverance in the book of Judges. (See the comment of J.A. Soggin, *Judges*, London, 1981, 86.) 8b, 'Not a lance, not a shield was to be seen among the forty thousand of Israel', underlines the plight of Israel in the face of its enemy; to see what is here stated as portraying 'the hierarchic pitted against the egalitarian' (Gottwald, 507) is merely tendentious.

65. *The Tribes of Yahweh*, 515ff.

66. *Ibid.*, 493.

67. Cf. the more sober assessment in this respect by C.H.J. de Geus, *The Tribes of Israel*, 180f.

68. *The Tribes of Yahweh*, 509.

69. See the comments of J. Barr, 'The Bible as a Political Document',

BJRL 62, 1980, reprinted in his *The Scope and Authority of the Bible* (Explorations in Theology, 7), London 1980, 107f.

70.   *The Tribes of Yahweh*, 429.

71.   *Ibid.*, 433.

72.   *Ibid.*, 671.

73.   *Ibid.*, 676-91.

74.   *Ibid.*, 679.

75.   It is remarkable that in his copiously documented work Gottwald apparently makes no reference to Perlitt's notable study of the origin of this concept which was published in 1969.

76.   H.H. Schmid, *Altorientalische Welt*, 10ff.; 'Creation, Righteousness and Salvation', in B.W. Anderson, *Creation*, 103ff.

77.   *Altorientalische Welt*, 11f.; 'Creation, Righteousness, and Salvation', 104f.

78.   Detailed treatment of this is given in Schmid's *Wesen und Geschichte der Weisheit*, and *Gerechtigkeit als Weltordnung*.

79.   *Altorientalische Welt*, 12f.; 'Creation, Righteousness and Salvation', 105.

80.   *Altorientalische Welt*, 33.

81.   Cf. F. Stolz, *Strukturen und Figuren im Kult von Jerusalem* (BZAW, 118), Berlin, 1970, 12-101.

82.   See especially Schmid's *Gerechtigkeit als Weltordnung*, 96ff.

83.   'Creation, Righteousness and Salvation', 106. (*Altorientalische Welt*, 15.)

84.   Creation, Righteousness and Salvation', 107. (*Altorientalische Welt*, 16.)

85.   'Creation, Righteousness and Salvation', 110f. (*Altorientalische Welt*, 21.)

86.   *Altorientalische Welt*, esp. ch. 2.

87.   See H.W. Wolff, *Hosea* (Biblischer Kommentar, XIV/1), Neukirchen-Vluyn, 1965, 60; ET: *Hosea*, Philadelphia, 1974, 49f.

88.   For a recent discussion see J.A. Emerton, 'New Light on Israelite Religion: The Implications of the Inscriptions from Kuntillet 'Ajrud', *ZAW* 94 (1982), 2-20. (Schmid himself was not able to draw upon this evidence, which followed the publication of his main works.)

89.   *Altorientalische Welt*, 49. See also F. Stolz, 'Monotheismus in Israel', 174-79.

90.   *Altorientalische Welt*, 49-51.

91.   *Altorientalische Welt*, 54 note 78, and 60 note 94.

92.   'Creation, Righteousness and Salvation', 111. (*Altorientalische Welt*, 25.)

93.   I have in mind P. Berger's *The Social Reality of Religion*, London, 1969, upon which the following remarks are based.

94. See the comment on this in J. Barton, 'Ethics in Isaiah of Jerusalem', *JTS* n.s. 32 (1981), 16f.

95. 'Creation, Righteousness and Salvation', 111. (*Altorientalische Welt*, 25.)

96. 'Creation, Righteousness and Salvation', 110. (*Altorientalische Welt*, 20.)

97. But see the incisive criticism of such an assessment of Wellhausen by L. Perlitt, *Vatke und Wellhausen* (BZAW, 94), Berlin, 1965.

98. See R.A. Oden, 'Hermeneutics and Historiography: Germany and America', in *Society of Biblical Literature, Seminar Papers*, Chico, 1980, 135-57.

99. 'Jedes Volk hat seine individuelle Seele, mit ihren spezifischen Fähigkeiten und Gaben, seine persönliche Note, die es von allen anderen unterscheidet.' H. Gressmann, 'Die Aufgaben der alttestamentlichen Forschung', *ZAW* 42 (1924), 10.

100. G.E. Wright, *The Old Testament Against its Environment*, 14f., 28f. (Note especially Wright's telling reference to Rudolph Otto's markedly Romantic statement on p. 14.)

101. See Schmid, *Altorientalische Welt*, 156f.; cf. H.-P. Müller's discussion 'Gott und die Götter in den Anfängen der biblischen Religion', in O. Keel, *Monotheismus*, 99-142.

102. *Altorientalische Welt*, 155ff.

103. *Altorientalische Welt*, 157.

SONS OF CAIN

Philip R. Davies

University of Sheffield

The Story of the Curse

Since before the beginnings of biblical criticism, the contents of Genesis 1–11 have rarely been out of theological or literary discussion, whether informed or ignorant. These chapters have been the focus of debates on documentary sources, on the nature of 'myth' and, in more recent times, their own theology and literary structure have been investigated time and again.[1] However, this present minor addition to the volume of secondary literature is not directly concerned with chapters 1–11 as a unit, but with a particular story contained within them, distinguishable by *literary* criteria and, as I hope to show, by a coherent ideology and purpose.[2] The story in question begins at Genesis 2.4b and ends at 9.29; it begins with the creation of mankind and ends with the restoration of life on earth after the Flood.

Its structure may be defined in terms of both chiasm and recapitulation.

Chiasm

The chiastic structure itself is in fact capable of two formulations, the first of which is as follows:

A	4.2	Cain as a worker of the ground (עבד אדמה)
B	4.5	Cain's offering refused
C	4.11	Cain cursed from the ground (ארור מן־האדמה)
B′	8.20	Noah's offering accepted
C′	8.21	Curse (קלל) on the ground 'because of man' not to recur
A′	9.20	Noah a man of the ground (איש־האדמה)

The appeal of this construction is enhanced by the fact that the elements in the above table occur in two tight clusters (that is, of course, when 9.1-19 is extracted from the narrative as being part of a different, 'P', narrative, later intertwined with our narrative; see below on the importance of this source-critical procedure). It does, of course, on my notation, exhibit an eccentric ABC/B'C'A' pattern, although by amalgamating the sacrifice and the response to it, the pattern could be redefined as AB/B'A' (a sacrifice and its reception are not elements easily inverted). But also to be noted is the lack of symmetry in A/A': Cain is a 'tiller' (עבד) of the ground, Noah a 'man' (איש) of the ground. The statement about the curse after Noah's sacrifice is also expressed differently: the curse referred to is aimed at the ground for mankind's sake, not at mankind directly: Cain himself is cursed 'from the ground'.

The second formulation of the chiasm is this:

A	2.5	Man (אדם) as a 'worker of the ground' (לעבד האדמה: cf. 3.23)
B	3.17	Curse on the ground 'because of man' (בעבורך . . . ארורה)
C	4.4	Rejection of human offering
C'	8.20	Acceptance of human offering
B'	8.21	Curse (קלל) on the ground 'because of man' (בעבור אדם) not to recur
A'	9.20	Noah a man of the ground (איש־האדמה)

This construction produces an ABC/C'B'A' pattern and sustains a closer verbal correspondence than the previous construction between the two references to the curse (B/B'); בעבור אדם. However, in neither case do we find perfect symmetry; indeed, ארר in 3.17 and 4.11 is replaced by קלל in 8.21, and עבד האדמה in 2.5 and 4.2 by איש האדמה in 9.20.

From a formal structural point of view, it seems better to take the curse referred to in 8.21 as that pronounced to Adam, because it is the first curse in our story and the verbal connection between 3.17 and 8.21 is closer. Furthermore, the curse on Cain is to deny him a livelihood from the ground, while Adam will have to labour for its produce. The curse referred to in 5.29 refers to 'toil' (עצבון), and the provision of a regular seasonal cycle in 8.22 also implies alleviation of agricultural labours. Indeed, both of these two texts reveal that the curse on Cain is not seen, from the perspective of the entire story, as hereditary.

Hence, the second formulation is preferable in our view, although a more complicated account embracing the sacrifice and curse of Cain might be feasible. The chiasm as I formulate it discloses the classic sequence of problem/complication/resolution, with the curse as the problem, and the Cain and Flood episodes as the major complications, initiated by mankind and by God respectively. It remains to be seen how the rest of the material in the story serves this plot, and what exactly is the manner of resolution of the problem, the curse.

To begin with, it would be both naive and careless to conclude that the chiastic structure leaves the narrative at the point where it began, with the curse undone and humanity living happily ever after. The text does not state that the curse is revoked, only that there will be no further curse; mankind does not return to Eden, or any Eden, and the effects of the curse—thorns and thistles, death—persevere.[3] Indeed, verbal discrepancies between the two poles of the chiasm have already been observed—the different word for 'curse' and the replacement of 'worker of the ground' by 'man of the ground'. The structural, verbal and contextual aspects of 8.21-22 certainly impart the definitive resolution of *something*, and, as I have suggested, that something seems to be the curse on the ground pronounced in Eden. But it is not simply a matter of undoing what has been done. The problem of the curse is resolved, but the curse itself is not revoked. What occurs is a *volte face* in which the original, negative curse is 'resolved' by a positive 'counter-curse'—effectively a blessing; the blessing of the seasonal cycle. Superficially, God's resolution after the end of the Flood appears to be simply an undertaking not to bring another Flood. But if the 'curse' to which this statement refers is not the Flood itself, a different interpretation of the divine undertaking becomes necessary, and we see instead an effective resolution of the original curse on the ground. The divine statement presupposes that the effects of the original curse will continue; but they will be offset by divine help in promoting agriculture through regular ordering of the seasons. In the same way, the pristine condition of mankind will not be restored; God acknowledges, perhaps even condones the wickedness which bars the way back to the original Edenic relationship. God will not undo his curse, nor can mankind's condition be undone.

The curse, then, is not repealed: what transpires is that God now operates in some way *against* it and in favour of mankind.[4] Accordingly, the story does not leave things where they began, but marks a

new beginning on a different level—more precisely, on different
terms, which accommodate both the original curse and the wicked
nature of mankind.[5]

Recapitulation

Another line of approach to the curse story reveals a *recapitulation*
which reinforces our conclusion that the story ends with a new
beginning in a different key. As has been already observed, the
statement (9.20) that Noah was a 'man of the ground' does not
correspond exactly with the description of Adam as a 'worker of the
ground'. In repeating, but not exactly, the description of Adam, the
phrase both rounds off one construction and commences another.
However, it cannot be severed from the verses which follow it, for
which it provides the necessary pretext, and obviously forms an
intrinsic part. We are therefore invited to consider the episode of
9.20-27 as belonging to the curse story; more precisely, to compare
the adventure of Noah with that of his predecessor Adam. In so
doing, we discern in 9.20-27 a *recapitulation* of Genesis 2–3, but one
in which contrasts are emphasized. Adam is a 'worker', Noah a
'man', of the ground. Noah plants his own fruit, the vine. (I shall not
speculate here on the possibility of the vine as a provider of
'knowledge': *in vino veritas* is not a Hebrew proverb.) Noah's waking
up parallels the 'opening of the eyes' of Adam and Eve, and the
subsequent realization in both cases is that of a state of nakedness.
On awaking, Noah 'knows' (how?) what has transpired (compare 3.7,
and cf. also 4.1; it may well be that some sexual connotation is
involved in the case of Noah also[6]). The result of the escapade is a
curse, pronounced this time not by a god but by a human. And there
may also be seen a certain parallelism between the expulsion from
the garden to the world outside and the projection from a place still
beyond history, where the family of Noah live, to the historical world
of the reader, the land of Palestine, and the fortunes of its various
inhabitant races, the descendants of Shem, Ham and Japheth. The
curious little episode of Genesis 9.20-27 has long teased scholars; it
seems to me that whatever its ultimate origin (if it had any pre-
existence, which is not certain), it now functions as a *parody* on the
story of Eden. And what does the parallelism between this Noah
story and the Eden story imply for the literary shape of the curse
story? It emphasizes, of course, that the curse story has an open
ending: formally, its plot may be terminated with the amelioration of

the curse, but this by itself constitutes a new beginning, and by means of this epilogue (this is how I would prefer to consider 9.20-27) the future possibilities of the new divine-human relationship are suggested.

Hence, the epilogue in 9.20-27 also affords us deeper access to the ideological formation of the curse-story in that it indicates the significance of that story for what may transpire *subsequently*. In that regard, it suggests what the story 'adds up to'. In the new order of things inaugurated by the countering of the divine curse, we see mankind left to its own devices. It is not created to work in God's garden; its fruit is not provided for it; but neither is any forbidden, nor is it subject to a curse. Rather, it now finds its own way, doing its own planting, eating its own fruit, doing its own cursing. Its fate, in other words, is now in its own hands, more or less. With the creation of the seasonal cycle it is, moreover, time-conditioned in a way which its existence in Eden appears not to have been. It is, nevertheless, a creature the 'imagination of whose mind (לב) is evil from its youth'. The behaviour of Noah and one of his sons testifies to this evil imagination; the story also, it may seem, gently mocks the behaviour of the new humanity through its parody of Eden. The fruit of the vine is a most appropriate symbol for the fruit of the new world, where life is not paradisal, but requiring human labour for its provision, yet with the divine gift of pleasurable relief. Wine does not make life perfect, but it does enable one to face the imperfections with, at the very least, equanimity. This last observation may strike one as fanciful over-exegesis: but who can confidently claim to have exhausted the ingenuity of a good story-teller?

If the preceding analyses—which are by no means very penetrating, but only sufficient for the purpose—seem cogent, then we have achieved the definition of a story whose boundaries are precisely delineated and some of whose themes have begun already to emerge.[7] At this juncture, we are obliged to address the problem of the source-critical division between 'P' and 'J'.[8] The story we are dealing with is written in a style which is entirely different from the 'P' material, and purely on such literary criteria—which are well enough known to require no rehearsal—we are justified in removing from our narrative the whole of chapter 5 (except for v. 29; see below), and 9.1-17. One is not at all obliged—despite occasional assumptions or assertions to the contrary in contemporary scholarship—to insist on 'final form' in pursuing a literary analysis. Indeed, where the object of analysis is the product of an author who is identified by a certain style of writing, it is perverse to ignore inconsistencies of style. Source-criticism, at present so much berated by 'literary critics', is not in itself an historical but a literary technique. That it may be, and in the main has been, utilized most often in the service of historical reconstruction is beside the point. Hence source-critical considerations comprise an important element in the next section of this essay.

Mankind is Descended from Cain

The biblical text in its present form contains two lines of descent from Adam. The first is given, though not in a genealogical table, in 4.1-2, 17-25: the second, a formal genealogy, occupies chapter 5. They may be conveniently referred to as respectively the 'Cainite' and 'Sethite' genealogies.[9]

Genesis 4 (Cainite)	*Genesis 5 (Sethite)*
Adam	Adam
	Seth
	Enosh
Cain	Kenan
Enoch	Mahalalel
Irad	Jared
Mehujael	Enoch
Methushael	Methuselah
Lamech	Lamech
(Noah)	Noah

A comparison of the two lists shows that all of the names in the Cainite list can be identified with names in the Sethite list, minor differences in spelling being allowed for. Adam, Lamech and Enoch are identical in both lists; Methushael, Irad and Cain are, respectively, variants of Methuselah, Jared and Kenan. Mehujael and Mahalalel may perhaps also be equivalents. The additional entries in the Sethite list are Seth and Enosh. The order is also a little different, but the last three are in a common sequence.

From a comparison of the lists two points become obvious, although they have seldom been followed up in scholarly research. The first is that the two additional names in the Sethite list are those which are also introduced into the Cainite list at 4.26. The second is that although Lamech is the last name given in the Cainite list, he does not complete that list. We have to supply Noah after Lamech, on the basis of 5.29 (see below).

The Cainite genealogy is commonly identified as 'J' and the Sethite as 'P'. Both 'J' and 'P' stories follow with an account of the flood, in which the hero is Noah. The integration of the two versions of the Flood story has produced a single Noah. But up to the beginning of the Flood there are actually two Noahs. 'J''s Noah must be the son of 'J''s Lamech, the Lamech of chapter 4, not 'P''s Lamech, the Lamech of chapter 5. So, according to the 'J' story, *Noah is descended from Cain*. The task of turning two Noahs into one has been achieved in the biblical text—not with the greatest elegance, but well enough to deceive most readers—by interrupting the Cainite genealogy just before Lamech has any sons, and by inserting instead 4.25-26a, which is an obvious redactional linkage by means of which two genealogies which are clearly *alternative* (given the parallel names) are presented as *parallel*. By proleptically introducing Seth and Enosh at 4.26, the blender of the 'J' and 'P' versions fits the Sethite genealogy into the Cainite. Whether or not by accident, this redactor also matches up *all* the individual names—and hence also the total number—of the two genealogies. The redactor seems to have been even-handed in his treatment of the two versions, for in v. 25 he both follows 'P' in using אלהים and 'J' in the formula וידע אדם עוד את־אשתו ותלד בן (modelled on 4.1). The use of יהשה in v. 26b marks the resumption of the Cain genealogy, probably as an introduction to the mention of Noah who would become the hero of the Flood.

But 'J''s Noah is not entirely from the biblical text. There is one possible hint of his presence and one certain reference. The hint is in 4.26, where the use of יהוה may betray 'J', in which case the very unexpected improvement in human behaviour, in calling upon Yahweh rather than elaborating on the delights of multiple vengeance, may originally have been associated with 'J''s Noah, son of the vengeful Lamech, rather than the non-'J' Enosh, as in the biblical text. The certain reference to the 'J' Noah occurs in 5.29. Here, in the middle of a genealogy characterized by the use of אלהים and by the use of a recurring pattern unrelieved by variation or expansion, we find (a) a deviation from the pattern, (b) the sole occurrence in the entire chapter of יהוה, and (c) a reference to a curse which has been described earlier in the 'J' story, but not the 'P'. This verse, therefore, appears to be a fragment of the Cainite genealogy, and its preservation shows us that the Cainite genealogy did indeed once reach as far as Noah. The producer of the biblical text, however, having disposed of the surplus Cainite Noah, can use this little piece of the 'J' story here, 'Yahweh' and all, because only one Noah is now left to be referred to, and, since the one Noah will subsequently procure relief from toil and from the cursed ground, v. 29 serves as a helpful bond to secure the composite Noah story of the present biblical text.

Our interest, nevertheless, is not in the biblical form of the story in which two Noahs are combined, but in one of the components of the biblical account, the story of the curse, the 'J' narrative (or, to be pedantic, part of it, since no argument is being made here for the scope of 'J' beyond chapters 2–9). The results of the preceding source-critical analysis serve for us two ends. First, they confirm that the curse story contained no Sethite line of descent, but *only a Cainite one—from which Noah descended—and hence all mankind.* Second, they reveal how in the story Noah is identified by his father Lamech as being the occasion for the alleviation of the curse on the ground. The description of the curse in 5.29 also seems to confirm our choice of formation for the chiastic structure, for it points to the curse spoken to Adam in 3.17 rather than that pronounced on Cain in 4.11. The three references to the Adamic curse share the words ארר and אדמה, and although מן־האדמה occurs in both 4.11 (Cain) and 5.29, עצבון is common to 3.17 and 5.29. In the light of 5.29, then, we ought strictly to reformulate the chiastic pattern to include a reference to the curse theme at the centre of the story as well as at the extremes; indeed, its position marks the structural centre of the story, since it lies immediately between the Cain and Flood episodes, which are the two major complications of the plot, brought about respectively by human and divine violence.[10]

Thus, the thrust of the arguments in this section is that there is in the curse story only one line of human descent, which runs from Adam through Cain to Noah. Noah, and, indeed, all mankind in that epoch, are represented as living under a divine curse on the ground and also as being descendants of a murderer and outcast.

The 'Wickedness of Man'

The countering of the curse after the Flood is preceded in 8.21 by the words 'for the imagination of man's mind is evil from his youth'. It seems, then, that the curse is closely related to the evil in mankind.

Since the curse is spoken to Adam, it seems to follow that the act which occasions the curse is the act which constitutes the origin of mankind's evil: Adam is the first 'sinner', by whom 'sin entered the world'. However, the same phrase as in 8.21 is also used in 6.5, following the story of Cain and the episode in 6.1-4. This is the first mention of human wickedness in the story and suggests, on the contrary, that the wickedness has just come about. It may be that God counters his curse despite human wickedness; it does not necessarily follow that wickedness was the reason for the curse in the first place. Rather, it seems that the wickedness was the reason for the *Flood*. Hence, we may not have to look to Adam for the origin of human wickedness—at least, not the immediate origin.

Nevertheless, the almost unanimous view of scholarship both ancient and modern is that human wickedness originated with Adam's and Eve's original disobedience. Yet it is in fact difficult to establish, rather than merely to presuppose, that Gen. 2–3 narrates Eve's and Adam's behaviour in terms of wickedness, or indeed that the Eden episode is presented in such terms. Rather, the acts of Adam and Eve are described in terms of an acquisition, contrary to divine intentions, of a divine quality of knowledge, which is better seen as a precondition of the development of human 'wickedness'. The outcome of the events in chapters 3–4 is a relationship different from that once prevailing between creator and creature. What happens *before* the curse requires careful definition, and not merely on its own terms, but within the terms of the whole curse story.

To read the chapters 3–4 in terms of sin-punishment, which is the most usual interpretation among biblical critics, is to misconceive entirely the level at which the narrative operates. It is not concerned essentially with the moral dimension of the human act, seen as disobedience or 'sin', but with the *motive* and *consequence* of that act. The motive is presented straightforwardly and at some length. The original constitution of mankind is from the 'dust of the ground' and his diet 'of every tree of the garden'—save one, which is forbidden without any reason being given. The choice presented to the woman by the snake is not a temptation to disobey in itself: that is, neither does the snake intend to cause, nor the humans to perpetrate, disobedience as such and for its own sake. The snake offers a truthful statement of the nature of the tree, namely that its fruit will confer some kind of divine status and knowledge. After inspecting the tree and its fruit, the woman chooses to believe the snake, and eats because she wants what the fruit offers. The result is that, as it were, a mutation of the species occurs whereby its 'eyes are opened', and it is 'godlike'. The motive of the woman's act (the man's motive is not given) is ambition for the effects of the fruit. The consequences are as desired, except for God's intervention. God's response may indeed be termed a punishment, but the importance of the response is not as an act of punishment for its own sake. It lies first in its consequences for the creatures, and secondly in its consequences for the divine-human relationship. A series of regressions is imposed: the most cunning snake becomes the lowly eater of dust, the woman who persuaded the man becomes subservient, and the man who took the fruit will in future find no fruit without toil. Moreover, he will return to the dust from which he was created. But the significant point of this divine riposte is that *what has occurred can only be countered, not undone*; mankind may suffer toil, but has the open eyes and knows good and evil like God; his expulsion from the garden lest he acquire individual immortality (and thus, presumably, achieve total divinity) cannot undo his 'knowledge' which enables him to procreate and thus to populate the entire earth. Gen. 3–4 furnishes an anthropology which defines mankind as a species caught somewhere between its own ambition and its creator's restraint, fashioned from אדמה but estranged from it, poised between the realms of earth and heaven, deprived of immortality but endowed with wisdom, and the knowledge of how to breed. Humanity is neither what its creator originally conceived nor what the creature itself aspired to. The divine curse, rather than a permanent punishment on mankind, is presented (with hindsight, perhaps) as prompting the evolution of humanity, for it brings about the beginnings of a social order comprising woman, man and ground (and snake?). Work and sex, the new lot of humans, are the basic human activities, after all. This is a sophisticated and indeed a moving analysis of the human condition, and one which inevitably, in its theistic context, leads to the problem of the relationship between mankind and God.

In an actantial model of the narrative programme on the lines proposed by Greimas, God would have to be marked as both opponent and helper,[11] and not only in that his curse aids human development. He creates, he provides (food, woman), then again provides (clothing). He also forbids, then curses, and expels. The last two of these negative acts have positive results from the point of view of human evolution, and even the forbidding of the fruit is open to speculation on this score; the man, the tree, the fruit, the snake, the woman, are all created by God, and in several cases this is explicitly stated. The provision of the tree right in the middle of the garden and the ban on its fruit appear rather like a catalyst to create the chain reaction. But this line of deduction takes us beyond the immediate argument, which must concern itself now with the theme of human-divine relationships.

I have tried to show that the Eden story does not introduce the theme of wickedness, but rather the main themes of the curse story—human development and the divine-human relationship. To each successive development in humankind God responds in consistent fashion: he restricts, but his actions promote rather than retard the process of development. At each stage (fruit-eating, homicide, eugenics or whatever) God reacts restrictively, yet beneficial results emerge; from Cain's line come cities, ironmaking, music; from the 'sons of God' and human women come 'mighty men', 'men of renown'. Even at the Flood, where God apparently seeks not to correct or counter but to annihilate, the outcome is good; the curse is countered, the seasonal cycle is ordered. In the Flood episode God's reaction is the last resort; yet he immediately ensures the survival of humanity, and at the end showers benefits upon it—so the pattern is repeated. But at the end of our story, of course, these themes are concluded: the processes of human development and divine reaction terminate, and a new and permanent relationship is established.

Human wickedness, then, is not the central theme of the curse story, but an element in it. To resume the thread of our argument, we now have to consider where human wickedness arises. For, obviously, wickedness does arise, even though a mere two verses assert this by way of explanation for the Flood (6.5-6). There are two other points in the story at which 'wickedness' (its nature yet to be defined)[12] might originate: the murder of Abel by Cain and the descent of the 'sons of God'. Either, or both, of these, are more plausibly seen—and more explicitly depicted—as being the origin of that wickedness which brings the Flood. It is in these two episodes, taken together, that we find the story's explanation of the origin of human wickedness. Framed by the Eden episode and the Flood episode, which narrate respectively the imposition of the curse and its resolution, Genesis 4 + 6.1-4 form the nucleus of the story. Their theme is apparently the increase of the human race and—more importantly—the development of human nature along two intrinsically related lines: violence and civilization. The Eden episode, I have argued, has not explained the origins of either, but only disclosed the *precondition* for them, namely, divine 'knowledge of good and evil', and expulsion into a world needing to be mastered.

Cain and the Descent of the 'Sons of God'

Our discussion begins with 6.1-4. These verses are, as usually conceded, something of a puzzle. In the first place, they hardly constitute a complete account, striking many scholars as a relic of something once more substantial. In the second place, their function in context is uncertain. How do their contents relate to the following Flood episode? Are they a mere interlude, having no immediate connection, or do they provide the immediate occasion for the Flood? The suggestions to be developed here attempt to address both of these questions together and explain the problems in terms of the composition of the whole story.

Whether or not 6.1-4 formally constitutes a fragment of a once larger narrative, it surely implies familiarity by the reader with a more complete story. It is difficult to escape the conclusion that the meaning of these verses depends on a knowledge of matters not given in the text. The critic can hardly conclude that the contents have been created in their present form *de novo* by the author for a specific function, because no plausible function offers itself. However, it is equally impossible to postulate an accidental truncation of a passage originally intended to be more extensive.

There exists a fuller account of a descent of divine beings to the earth in 1 Enoch 6–11.[13] The Enoch text combines two versions of what is essentially the same story—one featuring as villain Semihaza, one 'Asael/Azazel—whose basic elements are as follows:

1. Some of the 'sons of heaven' descended and married mortal women (6.6)
2. They taught various arts and sciences, including astrology, medicine, botany, cosmetics, sword-, knife- and armour-making (7.1; 8.1-3)
3. They begat giants who brought oppression and bloodshed upon the earth (7.2)
4. The earth cried out to God (9.2)
5. The sons of heaven were commanded to be bound for seventy generations (10.4.12)

The 1 Enoch passage has been evaluated differently by various scholars. For Milik, it represents an essentially older version of the story than that in Genesis 6.[14] Barker agrees with this assessment.[15] Most other scholars, however, regard it as a late haggadic development of the biblical story. In a detailed analysis of the 1 Enoch passage, P.D. Hanson[16] has concluded that a basic story concerning a group of angels led by Semihaza has been amplified by the inclusion of sections in which Azazel is the villain. Hanson suggests that the Azazel story was developed organically out of the Semihazah story in order to relate that story to the scapegoat ritual of Leviticus 16. But this is improbable. While the Ethiopic has Azazel, the Qumran Aramaic has 'Asael, which also seems to be underlying the Greek. Yet Azazel is certainly known as the villain of the myth according to the (Hebrew) Qumran fragments 4Q180-181.[17] The exact name of the villain in the 1 Enoch version is not important; we have ancient evidence of three alternative names, one of which is Azazel. It is the existence of the myth itself which is the issue, and not the name of the ringleader of the 'angels'.

But, other objections aside,[18], there is a major obstacle against Hanson's thesis—and at the same time to all those who take for granted that the 1 Enoch story is a haggadic expansion of the biblical story and look for its *point d'appui* in the Hellenistic epoch.[19] It is that the biblical texts in question—Leviticus 16 as well as Genesis 6.1-4—remain unaccounted for. Gen. 6.1-4 implies a more complete myth about the descent of heavenly beings, and Leviticus 16 implies knowledge of an Azazel. To suppose that a complete myth, or myths, were first truncated in the Old Testament and then later expanded again from the truncated form in 1 Enoch is not only unnecessarily elaborate but a considerable challenge to credulity.

An explanation of Leviticus 16 is not part of the purpose of this essay, but insofar as it impinges on the story alluded to in Gen. 6.1-4 it will be offered. The ceremony of the scapegoat culminates in the sending of a goat into the wilderness 'to/for Azazel' (לאזזל). There is no consensus among commentators on the passage (many of whom do not bother to consider 1 Enoch) as to who or what Azazel was, but they generally assume that those who described and performed the ritual did know. What, then, are they likely to have known? The answer offered by 1 Enoch 6–11 is straightforward: the purpose of sending the goat into the wilderness is that in the wilderness is Azazel! According to the Enoch story he is buried under a rock

awaiting judgment. The reason for sending the sins to Azazel is that
Azazel is responsible for bringing them into the world. The ritual
accomplishes the removal of sins from Israel and their transfer to the
divine being who brought them and upon whom the punishment of
God has been decreed. The ultimate destruction of Azazel will
therefore secure the ultimate destruction of the accumulated sins of
Israel.

There is a species of scholarship which eschews simple answers,
and especially simple and logical answers to curious rituals; hence
the explanation offered by 1 Enoch of the scapegoat ritual will not
win widespread consent. Another crucial question is, of course, the
dating of the 1 Enoch story. So long as it is dated no earlier than the
most ancient manuscripts in which it appeared (3rd century BCE at
the earliest?), its dependence upon the biblical material must be
accepted, as is the case with the majority of scholars. However, there
is a growing consensus that the traditional material in this story is
very ancient. In this respect, a number of scholars are in agreement.[20]
Between the dating of Leviticus 16 and the date of the earliest Enoch
manuscript (from Qumran) not a great timespan exists. The question
of the priority of the 1 Enoch story and Leviticus 16 requires no
strong *a priori* bias in favour of the biblical passage.

The argument thus moves to another stage: it appears that the
author of Gen. 6.1-4 knew the Azazel story (with or without the
name 'Azazel', but more probably with). In the first place, as already
suggested, 6.1-4 appears to presuppose a more complete account of a
descent of heavenly beings. If it was not the Azazel story, it was
presumably another one rather similar. Second, and more controver-
sially but also more important, *the major elements of the Azazel story
which are lacking from 6.1-4 are found in chapter 4.* These elements
are as follows:

Genesis		1 Enoch
4.11	blood shed upon the earth	9.1
4.11	the earth cries out	9.2
	(blood cries out)	9.10
4.12f.	villain cast into desert	10.4f.
(4.15, 24	sevenfold, seventy-sevenfold	
	seventy generations	10.12)
4.22	instruments of bronze and iron	
	swords, knives, shields, breast-	
	plates	8.1
4.23-4	widespread violence	9.1ff.

These parallels do not carry equal weight; nor should they, even cumulatively, be taken too far; their extent suggests only a limited, yet deliberate, degree of correspondence between the Cain story and that of the descent of the 'sons of heaven'. It is not being suggested that the Cain story is entirely explicable on the basis of these parallels. The numerous traditional elements which have been supposed in Genesis 4—Kenite genealogy, stockbreeder-agriculturalist rivalry, aetiology of nomadic folk, song of revenge—provide almost all of the *raw material* of the whole narrative. But the *plot* which has determined the manner of assembly of these diverse fragments, I suggest, is disclosed by the parallels with the ancient Hebrew myth. That is to say, the Cain story tells of the introduction into the world of human aggression in the form of violence towards other men, together with violence towards materials—in the form of technology. Cain is the first wicked man; he is also the first technocrat.[21] His descendants—the entire human race—become progressively more violent and more 'civilized', in the sense that they discover arts and sciences—first the building of cities, a prerequisite of civilization (4.17), then music (4.21), and metalwork (4.22).

The realization that Cain is a transformation of Azazel, as it were, answers the two problems about 6.1-4. This account has been included because it represented the (generally prevalent?) Hebrew myth about the origin of violence and of civilization; it is truncated because its substance has no place in the narrative: these things have come into the world not by divine rebellion but by human initiative. What remains of the story is emasculated into an aetiology of the race of giants, and at the same time now functions as a kind of 'last straw' finally provoking God to bring the Deluge.

Incidentally, the literary technique and the ideological direction of the Cain episode imitate those of the Eden episode. Both are constructed from traditional themes and motifs—the snake, the tree of immortality (etc.) on the one hand, the herdsman/agriculturalist and the marked nomad (etc.) on the other. Moreover, for each story as a whole there is no extant parallel; each is, as far as we can know, an original creation. The two episodes, indeed, have to be regarded as part of a single account, because they are incomplete individually. *Together*— and only together—chapters 2–4 tackle the great paradox of humanity: its createdness and its creativity, its material finitude and its intellectual infinitude, its estrangement from the worlds both of nature and of divinity. They account for the development of humanity as a

conscious, (im)moral, aggressive and ambitious creature, not, as did
the extant Hebrew myth, as the outcome of a divine incursion into
the human world by 'sons of God', but by an act of human initiative
not entirely unprompted by God. The great mystery of humankind,
that is, its capacity for evil, its restless ravaging of its environment, its
godlike imagination and creativity, are not laid at the door of a
heavenly revolt, which betrays a divided heaven, but at the door of
the creature itself; as 1 Enoch 98.4 puts it, sin did not come from
heaven but 'man of himself created it'—yet with some degree of
connivance, wilful or otherwise, from the one God. The thrust of
Gen. 2–4, then, is a significant revision of what may have been the
prevalent explanation of the origin of mankind's nature, which is at
the same time anthropologically more profound and theologically
more congruent with monotheism.

But neither God nor mankind can exist indifferent to one another,
and the focus of the curse story is on the God-mankind relationship.
Is there any means of reconciling the humanity in the story with the
God in the story? If not, the story itself is religiously futile; it will
provide no paradigm for a human religious life. Within the narrative
confines, the alternative to reconciliation appears to be uncreation.
The Flood story thus appears as a false ending; but the pretence is
sustained for no more than a verse, for the choice of Noah immediately
contradicts and undermines the intention behind the Flood, and thus
keeps the reader in hope of a more positive resolution, without any
clear idea of what that will be. Thus the Flood actually turns out, as
already suggested, to be the second major complication.

The Flood

Between the beginning of the Flood episode and its end occurs the
great divine conversion. At the outset, humanity's wickedness is
taken as an excuse for its destruction; at the end, as an excuse for its
preservation.[22] What has intervened to effect this *volte-face*? The
immediate cause of the change of heart appears to be the sacrifice of
Noah. But the very fact that Noah was already preserved from the
Flood compels us to look back to the beginning of the episode itself,
where we encounter the second great paradox of the story: in the
first, God so ordered things that mankind should be caused to eat
what God had forbidden; here, in the second, God decides to 'blot
out' mankind (6.7), yet immediately afterwards Noah pleases him so

that (7.1, the next 'J' verse) he is told how to survive. Were it not for the intervention of the block of 'P' material in 6.9-22 the incomprehensibility of God's behaviour would be even more apparent: he decides to destroy mankind, then decides to save one family, thereby negating the effect of the destruction. 'P', recognizing the paradox, insists that Noah is righteous—and the availability of the Sethite line of descent permits this; but for 'J' Noah is a direct descendant of Cain, and is not singled out as righteous. The writer of the curse story is not above resorting to the mystery of divine motivation when needed; in narrative form he can convey the paradox that God wills the frustration of his own plans, whether these be to deprive mankind of the fruit of a tree of divine knowledge, or to destroy the entire race.

However, the dramatic *dénouement* of the curse story, from its crisis in the intended obliteration of creation to the acceptance of humanity as it is, is not settled at a stroke by some piece of inscrutable divine psychology. The dramatic change of mind by God which resolves the story requires a substantial narrative vehicle, and this the description of the Flood provides. But is this description merely a vehicle, or does it carry part of the freight as well? I woud suggest that the character of the Flood itself is significant. It assists in the resolution of the divine-human relationship by prompting a human initiative of submission, and this it does because it is acknowledged not so much as a divine act of 'uncreation' (this is how 'P' displays it) but rather as one of supreme violent bloodshed. The Flood is a display of divine superiority in both violence and creativity (i.e. in its harnessing of the elements of the cosmos). Man may be like God to a degree, but only a small degree. One might say that as mankind sought to be like God, so God now behaves like mankind.

At all events, this demonstration of divine aggression (and perhaps the realization that only a God can deliver from divine violence) ultimately elicits from Noah a sacrifice. One will search in vain among the commentaries for any intelligent answer to the question 'what kind of sacrifice', for the question itself is unintelligent. The nature of the sacrifice is irrelevant; its accomplishment, on the other hand, counts for all. It is a gesture of submission, of acknowledgment, perhaps containing elements of fear and appeasement. It constitutes that gesture which elicits divine indulgence. The gesture is certainly not indicative of repentance, and neither signals nor effects any change in the nature of God or mankind. The outcome of the exchange which follows the Flood is an accommodation to the realities: for God, mankind's nature is what it is, and will ever be so; for mankind, God's power lies beyond the horizons of human ambition, and mankind will have to deal with God as one whom it cannot become, as it once desired.

Reflection: the Gospel of the Curse

The resolution of the curse signals the establishment of a *modus vivendi*. Neither the nature of mankind nor the nature of God are fully defined, but only the context of their relationship. Whether our story forms part of a larger epic—as many scholars hold—is another issue entirely, and not to be pursued at this moment. This particular story has reached its conclusion: its plot has been accomplished, its aims achieved. But despite its modest extent, our story has accomplished an enormous task in two areas: it has transformed the mythology of Israel in a radically monotheistic but also humanistic direction, and it has provided a 'gospel'.

The gospel? The gospel is, in the first place, that it is of the essence of human nature to be wicked, or at least to have a 'bad imagination of the mind': this badness is the inevitable consequence of mankind's acquisition of divine knowledge which released it from the status of pure creature and made it a creator, both of its environment and, to an extent, of itself. Each human being carries the responsibility for its own acts. In the second place, the gospel preaches no prospect of any other kind of human existence. That existence is one which God appears not to like, although there is more than a hint that he willed it at some level of his subconscious. It is a relationship which God finally endorses by superimposing on his curse what amounts to a blessing, renouncing the threat of superior violence against mankind, but guaranteeing the beneficent use of divine power to provide for his well-being through the regular ordering of the seasons. As I observed earlier, the antics of Noah and his sons, which I have chosen to regard as an epilogue to the curse story, highlight the shortcomings of human nature after the Flood, but only by way of reinforcing the extent of divine indulgence. Mankind's nature, in its wickedness, is accepted by, if not agreeable to, God. For mankind's part, the limits of human power have been defined in that however far it may progress in its violence and its mastery of nature, only God can create a world and destroy it, and without divine power and divine favour, the ambitions of mankind are rather futile. Hence, we may add to the achievements of our story a rationale of the sacrificial cult. Sacrifice is not here a gesture reducible to appeasement, bribery, repentance or atonement, but the acceptance of the unchallengeable status of a deity over against a human. It is mankind's respect to God; God's respect to mankind is to accept its 'bad' nature.

This Old Testament gospel is not the gospel of St. Paul; many would deny—if they even accept my reading of the story—that this 'gospel' is a gospel at all. Some may find in it a creed of humanism, for the 'God' of the story is a fictional character who can without great difficulty be exegeted as a symbol of all that constitutes the contingencies of human life—disease, death, accident—contingencies which have so often been deified and in our society sometimes continue to be in the form of superstition. Other readers may find here the seeds of a 'covenant theology' in which the legal status of the agreement between God and mankind presupposes a measure of equality and freedom on both sides. It is possible to find here in the depiction of a God who accepts humans as they are and requires only acceptance in return some (imperfect?) anticipation of the Christian gospel. Yet again, it may appear to enshrine the spirit of Judaism rather than of Christianity (and Judaism has a gospel no less than Christianity).

All these possibilities exist. But Jews, Christians or agnostics, we are all sons of Cain. I hope Professor McKane, from whom, among other things, I learnt to engage seriously with the moral as well as the academic challenge of biblical exegesis, will forgive the title of the paper. He has inspired more of this paper than its title.

NOTES

1. For a most convenient summary of the history of research, see C. Westermann, *Genesis 1–11* (Erträge der Forschung, 7), Darmstadt, 1972; cf. also his *Genesis 1- 11* (BK), Neukirchen, 1966-74 (ET London, 1984) *ad loc.*, for a fuller bibliography. For a (somewhat dense and complicated) discussion of the literary and ideological structure of the material, see W.M. Clark, 'The Flood and the Structure of the pre-Patriarchal History', *ZAW* 83 (1971), 184-211. See also D.J.A. Clines, 'Theme in Genesis 1–11', *CBQ* 38 (1976), 483-507.

2. The definition of Genesis 1–11 (or, for that matter, the Yahwistic material within it) as a literary unity has yet to be demonstrated on literary grounds. The main criteria for its isolation as a distinct literary entity have been (a) its *content* ('myth' over against 'saga' or 'prehistory' over against

'history'), (b) its *thematic coherence*—displaying a clear ideational structure such as sin-punishment-grace or breaking bounds-limitation or creation-recreation (on these see Clines, *art. cit.*), or (c) its supposed structural function within the Yahwistic composition (cf. especially the theory of von Rad in his 'The Problem of the Hexateuch', in *The Problem of the Hexateuch and Other Essays* [ET], Edinburgh, 1966, 1-78 [especially 63-67]). The last two items seem to presuppose chapters 1–11 not as an independent literary composition but as a preface or prologue to a larger work.

3. As Clines, for example ('Theme', 497), has pointed out.

4. I am reminded of a similar device in the book of Esther, where, since the 'law of the Medes and the Persians' cannot actually be revoked, Artaxerxes is obliged to circumvent it. Just as the king in Esther is compelled by his own decree, so perhaps God here is compelled by his curse and can revoke it only in the sense of acting against its intent. See D.J.A. Clines, *The Esther Scroll* (JSOTS, 30), Sheffield, 1984, 16ff.

5. Accordingly, I find myself (with W.M. Clark) not too distant from the interpretation of R. Rendtorff, who translates 8.21 'I will no longer regard the earth as cursed, or treat it as such'. But I cannot accept his translation, since I do not see the divine curse as actually being revoked or ignored. See R. Rendtorff, 'Genesis 8.21 und die Urgeschichte des Yahwisten', *KD* 7 (1961), 69-78.

6. This suspicion is an ancient one. See the discussion and proposal by F.W. Bassett, 'Noah's nakedness and the curse of Canaan', *VT* 21 (1971), 232-37.

7. Ought the story of Babel in Genesis 11.1-9 to be considered as a constitutive part of the same story, as it is usually taken to be? This suggestion would restore all the 'J' material of Genesis 1–11 to a literary unity. But I find no adequate grounds for its inclusion, since the episode has no structural links with the curse story either on the literary or the ideological level. The only possible *literary* connection between 11.1-9 and 2–9 seems to be in the use of שם in 11.4, which might be related to the name of Noah's favourite son. Yet it is difficult to discern any clear function for this other than idle wordplay; the device (if it be such) plays no obvious *structural* role, and it is difficult to conclude that the coincidence is deliberate. Also there are contra-indications. While the episodes of the curse story each build upon the preceding one to form a continuous account, the Babel story makes no reference to Noah's family; in its opening words and phrases, כל הארץ, בנסעם and מקדם, such an absence is conspicuous.

There is likewise no *thematic* link between the Babel story and the curse story. Although the sin-punishment pattern, seen still by many scholars as the plot of Genesis 1–11 (whether in its 'J' passages or in its present form) is discernible in the Babel story, both the 'sin' and the 'punishment' are of less moment than any of the preceding instances adduced. It seems to me that a much more cogent case can be made for understanding the Babel story as a prelude to the Abraham cycle (following ancient Jewish exegesis, which often looks to the Babel story to explain Abraham's departure from Ur), or perhaps a link between the curse story and the patriarchal stories.

8. I use the conventional sigla in inverted commas not because I question the validity of the source-critical analysis, but because I do not recognize by them the literary entities to which they are taken to refer. The well-known criticisms of R. Rendtorff (*Das Überlieferungsgeschichtliche Problem des Pentateuchs* [BZAW, 147], Berlin, 1977) and H.H. Schmid (*Der Sogenannte Jahwist*, Zurich, 1977) are more than enough, in my opinion, to justify this reserve.

9. A convenient recent review, with bibliographical data, of the problem of the two genealogies may be found in J.C. VanderKam, *Enoch and the Growth of an Apocalyptic Tradition* (CBQMS, 16), Washington, 1984, 23-28.

10. The phrase 'then men began to call upon the name of Yahweh'—if, as suggested, it was originally assigned to the time of Noah—perhaps reinforces the central position of the birth of Noah which is marked by Lamech's reminiscence of the curse. Just as the solution of that curse is anticipated in Lamech's remark, so the coming together of mankind and God in Noah's sacrifice is perhaps anticipated by this curious phrase. One could speculate further that the remark about 'calling on the name of Yahweh' concludes the first, man-made complication (the Cainite development) just as the divine relief from the curse concludes the second, God-made complication, the Flood. But such a suggestion may lie, I suspect, on the border between literary appreciation and sheer fancy.

11. An interesting collection of structuralist interpretations of Gen. 2–3 may be found in *Semeia* 18 (1980). However, the particular actantial analysis implied here is not suggested.

12. It is possible that a distinction between 'wickedness' and the 'evil imagination of the human mind' ought to be drawn within the terms of this story, but as far as I have been able to see, it would not affect the general arguments of this paper.

13. For English translations, see R.H. Charles (ed.), *Apocrypha and Pseudepigrapha of the Old Testament*, Oxford, 1913, II, 191-95; J.H. Charlesworth (ed.), *The Old Testament Pseudepigrapha*, New York, 1983, I, 15-19. The version of the story in Jubilees 5 (see Charles, II, 20f.) appears to be based, unlike the Enoch version, entirely on Genesis 6.1-4.

14. 'Problèmes de la littérature hénochique à la lumière des fragments araméens de Qumran', *HTR* 64 (1971), 349; cf. his *The Books of Enoch*, Oxford, 1976 (with M. Black).

15. M. Barker, 'Some Reflections Upon the Enoch Myth', *JSOT* 15 (1980), 7-29. The recent commentary by M. Black (with the collaboration of J.C. VanderKam), *The Book of Enoch or I Enoch*, Leiden, 1985, *ad loc.*, also agrees with Milik's contention.

16. 'Rebellion in Heaven, Azazel, and Euhemeristic Heroes in Enoch 6–11, *JBL* 96 (1977), 195-233.

17. See Milik, *Books of Enoch*, 248-52.

18. Hanson's source-criticism is in any case rather more precise than the nature of the textual material permits, and his account of the structure of the Semihazah and Azazel elements is exceedingly elaborate, relying on themes derived (with admittedly great erudition) from Hurrian, Ugaritic and Greek mythology. Furthermore, his suggestion that a single account should be converted into a double account as a deliberate act of editorial expansion is improbable; it is surely more likely that the combination in our 1 Enoch text is the result of an editorial combination of sources already available.

19. Such as G.W.E. Nickelsburg, 'Apocalyptic and Myth in 1 Enoch 6–11', *JBL* 96 (1977), 383-405, and J.J. Collins, *The Apocalyptic Imagination*, New York, 1984, 38ff. Cf. also M. Delcor, 'Le mythe de la chute des anges et de l'origine des géants comme explication du mal dans le monde dans l'apocalyptique juive: Histoire des traditions', *RHR* 190 (1976), 3-53.

20. Hanson, *art. cit.*; M. Stone, 'The Book of Enoch and Judaism', *CBQ* 40 (1978), 479-492. The latest investigation of Enoch traditions, VanderKam's *Enoch and the Growth of an Apocalyptic Tradition* (see n. 9 above) also documents the evidence for their antiquity.

21. The ascription to Cain of responsibility for the inauguration of wickedness is both ancient and widespread. Cf. Wisdom 2.24; 'it was through the devil's envy that Death entered into the cosmic order' has been taken by many interpreters to refer to Cain (cf. D. Winston, *The Wisdom of Solomon* [AB], 121 for discussion). The interpretation gains some support from Wisdom 10.1-3, which contrasts Adam with Cain, the 'wicked man . . . on whose account the earth was flooded'. Winston (*ibid.*) also cites Theophilus *Ad Autolycum* 2.29 who attributes death to the devil's envy, occasioned by the production of offspring by Adam and Eve and by Abel's pleasing God, and worked out *through the murder of Abel by Cain*, a notion also found in Irenaeus, *Adversus Haereses* 1.30.9, where death as well as envy are the results of Cain's murder. Cf. further Pirqe deRabbi Eliezer 22 ('From Cain arose and were descended all the generations of the wicked, who rebel').

22. As noted by D.L. Petersen, 'The Yahwist on the Flood', *VT* 26 (1976), 438-46. But his conclusion that the Yahwist treats the Flood episode ironically is somewhat *faute de mieux*, although irony is by no means absent from the account, and features quite prominently in the following episode of the sons of Noah (as argued above).

'BLESSED BE MY PEOPLE EGYPT' (ISAIAH 19.25)
The Context and Meaning of a Remarkable Passage

John F.A. Saywer

University of Newcastle-upon-Tyne

Modern commentators on Isaiah 19.16-25, from Lowth (1778) and Duhm (1892) to Wildberger (1978) and Clements (1980),[1] are agreed on two things. First, it represents some kind of high point in the Old Testament. In G.A. Smith's words it is the 'most universal and "missionary" of all Isaiah's prophecies'.[2] In this unique passage, Egypt and Assyria, elsewhere symbols of oppression and brutal tyranny, are united in harmony with Israel and blessed by the Lord of hosts. According to Wildberger, we are in these verses not far from Paul's 'to the Jew first and also to the Greek' (Rom. 1.16).[3] Second, the passage is somehow related to events in Hellenistic Egypt.[4] According to Josephus, v. 19 was cited by the expatriate priest Onias in a letter to Ptolemy VI Philometor (181–145 BC), requesting permission to build a temple at Leontopolis in Egypt: 'For this indeed is what the prophet Isaiah foretold, "There shall be an alter in Egypt to the Lord God", and many other such things did he prophesy concerning this place' (*Ant.* 13.68). There is plenty of evidence in the ancient versions and commentaries that Is. 19.16-25 was interpreted and re-interpreted in the light of Jewish attitudes towards that temple.[5] The fifth city in v. 18, for example, is variously named 'the city of destruction' and 'the city of righteousness' (cf. 1.26), the former presumably by opponents (including the Masoretes; cf. AV), the latter by supporters (including some of the Greek translators).

The first of these two points of agreement, concerning the theological significance of the passage, clearly transcends the immediate historical circumstances which gave rise to the second. But since all our Hebrew manuscripts, together with the ancient versions and commentaries, have been influenced by those historical circumstances, a commentary must take them into account, if only to clear a path through later interpretations to what the author originally meant.

There is a third context to be considered, however, in addition to that of the original author and the Hellenistic context. The present literary context of the passage, among the 'oracles against the foreign nations' (chs. 13–23), invites us to imagine the prophecy on the lips of the eighth century prophet Isaiah,[6] and to ask whether the author of Is. 19.16-25 chose his words with that context in mind. To catch the individual nuances and associations of the language, we must therefore try to think ourselves back into these three periods, and then let the text speak for itself.

The Original Context

Few would nowadays argue that any part of this passage goes back to the eighth century BC. The arguments of Erlandsson and the late Professor Mauchline, that the year 701 BC was the 'requisite occasion' for the original proclamation,[7] are peremptorily dismissed by Clements, for example.[8] In fact, as we shall see, valuable insights are to be gained by such an approach, but they concern the author's intention to give his message Isaianic force, not the actual date of composition. Mauchline is right to stress that the 'advanced theological outlook' of the passage does not in itself preclude an eighth century date, but when we take into account the language, which is without a doubt far removed from eighth century Isaianic usage,[9] it becomes unrealistic as well as unnecessary to argue for an eighth century date.

The Egyptian connections, which go back, as we have seen, at least as far as the Septuagint and Josephus, have prompted others to argue for a Hellenistic date. Cheyne (1895) suggests the reign of Ptolemy I Soter (d. 283), with a possible allusion to his throne-name in v. 20 ('saviour'), or his son Ptolemy II Philadelphus (283-246), to whose reign tradition attributes the first Greek translation of the Hebrew Bible.[10] Duhm (1892) and Marti (1900) recognize the hand of an Egyptian Jew living around 160 BC.[11] More recently Kaiser (1973) concludes that the reign of Ptolemy III Euergetes (246-221) is the earliest possible date. He sees in vv. 16-17 a possible allusion to the Ptolemaic occupation of Judah in 301 BC, and in the mention of Egypt and Assyria in vv. 23-25 references to Ptolemaic–Seleucid relations culminating eventually in the Peace of Apamea in 118 BC.[12]

Such an approach correctly picks up significant allusions to Hellenistic history which are present in the manuscripts and ancient versions. But these surely belong to the history of interpretation rather than the debate about the actual date of composition. The discovery of the second century BC Isaiah Scroll at Qumran, which of course contains our passage in its present context, without a trace of its having been a late interpolation, virtually rules out so late a date.[13] As in the case of the other extreme, 701 BC, this view must be rejected as highly improbable.

More convincing are the arguments of those who point to parallels with the exilic literature.[14] The concern for God's people in Babylon (e.g. Jer. 29), Egypt (e.g. Jer. 44) and other developing diaspora communities is one obvious example. The generous world-wide perspective ('Weitherzigkeit') associated with Deutero-Isaiah may be cited as another.[15] From a slightly later period the Book of Jonah contains even closer parallels.[16] There the Assyrian citizens of Nineveh are, by implication, 'the work of God's hands' (cf. Jonah 4.10-11), just as they are in Is. 19.25. In both, the Assyrians are transformed from a symbol of brutality and ruthlessness, into the object of divine compassion. Is. 56; 66.18-21, Zech. 2.12-17 (EVV 2.8-13) and Mal. 1.11 are more examples from about the same era. Like the so-called 'Isaiah apocalypse' (chs. 24–27), 19.16-25 appears to build on earlier intimations of universalism, many of them Isaianic, and press them forward towards Job, 'the wise man from the east' who discovers Yahweh, Daniel, who turns Nebuchadnezzar and Darius to God, and even Col. 3.11 'where there is neither Greek nor Jew, circumcision nor uncircumcision, barbarian, Scythian, bond nor free'. We shall probably not be far out if we date the passage to the fifth century BC,[17] and envisage our author placing this message on the lips of an eighth century prophet, in exactly the same way as the author of the Book of Jonah has done. Let us now consider the meaning of the passage in that context.

In an interesting study published in 1951[18] and largely neglected by recent commentators, André Feuillet correctly moves away from attempts to identify actual historical and geographical references in the passage, and concentrates instead on literary affinities. He recognizes, for example, in v. 18 an allusion to the five cities defeated by Joshua in the spectacular finale to the story of the Israelite conquest of Canaan (Josh. 10.1-27).[19] One of these was Jerusalem, and this provides a clue to the identity of the fifth city, 'the city of righteousness', restored on the basis of LXX and a familiar epithet for the 'new Jerusalem' (cf. 1.26).[20] The passage is then an impressive prophecy about the conquest and conversion of Egypt, built upon traditional accounts of the victories of Joshua and the conversion of Canaan. Others have noted allusions to the Exodus traditions, especially in vv. 19-22.[21] Like the authors of Chronicles and Jonah, not to mention 'Deutero-Isaiah', the ending of Amos (9.11-15) and countless other such passages, many of them introduced like the present one by the formula 'on that day . . .', our author is clearly building on traditions preserved elsewhere in the Hebrew Bible. It should not be difficult to grasp what he is saying without seeking to identify any actual historical events alluded to.

We shall begin with the 'promised land' motif that runs through the passage from beginning to end. The subject of the first part is described as 'the land of Judah', a striking *hapax legomenon*. Then there are the five cities, Canaan and the land of Egypt in v. 18, the 'boundary' in v. 19, the highway leading from Egypt to Assyria in v. 23, and finally the richly allusive term 'Israel my heritage' in v. 26 with which the prophecy ends. Feuillet is certainly right to look for allusions to the conquest traditions here, particularly when we are thinking in terms of a writer living some time after the end of the Babylonian exile. At that time the promise 'to Abraham and his seed for ever' was an enigma and the Jews were seeking to come to terms with diaspora conditions. Jeremiah had advised some of them to 'build houses and live in them; plant gardens and eat their produce . . .' (29.5). Isaiah 19 contains a similar message for Jews in Egypt:

> Do not be afraid; this time the Egyptians will be afraid of you. Build cities and live in them. Take the language of the promised land with you ('the language of Canaan'). Build a new Jerusalem. Start again: like Abraham when he came to Canaan, build an altar to the Lord (Gen. 12.6-7); set up a pillar there as Jacob did (Gen. 28.18). When things go wrong and you cry for help, God will send you a saviour as he did in the days of the Judges (e.g. Judg. 3.9, 15; 6.14-15).

Such a paraphrase highlights the author's purpose. Jeremiah sent his message to the Babylonian exiles in the form of a letter; Isaiah 19.16-22 contains a very similar message, in a different form. Like the author of the Book of Jonah, our author has placed his 'letter to the exiles' on the lips of an eighth century prophet. Just as Onias, some three centuries later, cited Isaiah's authority for his actions, so here the anonymous author of Is. 19.16-25 claims the same authority for his message to the exiles in Egypt: Egypt will be a land of promise too, with its own *Heilsgeschichte*, its own Jerusalem.

The closest parallel comes at the end of the passage: 'Blessed be my people Egypt, and Assyria the work of my hands' (v. 25). Jeremiah's letter to the exiles specifically urges them to pray for the host community in Babylon: 'Seek the welfare of the city where I have sent you into exile, and pray to the Lord on its behalf, for in its welfare you will find your welfare' (29.7). Does not the blessing of Egypt in Is. 19, at the end of a description of Israel settling there, correspond exactly to the Jeremiah passage? An entirely new situation obtains: Jews in Egypt and Mesopotamia praying for the peace and welfare of their new homelands. That Isaiah should have preached thus in eighth century BC Jerusalem would be almost unbelievable (we shall return to that context later); but in the light of Jeremiah's letter, and the attitude towards the Assyrians advocated in the Book of Jonah, it is somewhat less surprising to find a fifth century BC statement of these views.

There has been some discussion about the significance of placing Israel 'third with Egypt and Assyria' (v. 24). It could be that it means third in order of precedence behind Egypt and Assyria, rather like Jonah (Jonah 4) or the elder brother in the Parable of the Prodigal Son (Luke 15.25-32): as a rebuke to an exclusivist people or a summons to adopt a more generous attitude towards other nations. But in view of the emotive 'promised land' theme, and in particular the concluding ישראל נחלתי 'Israel my heritage', surely the point is less carping. Is not Israel the object of the verb 'blessed' at the beginning of v. 25, a new Israel, living in harmony with her neighbours? A kind of triad will be completed, three great nations, basking in the peace and prosperity of God's blessing.[22] There will be one language (the language of Canaan [v. 28], the promised land); all the people will worship one God (vv. 22-23); they will travel freely to and from Egypt and Mesopotamia (v. 23); and all the families of the earth, not just Israel, will be blessed (Gen. 12.3; cf. Ps. 47.10).[23]

There are many allusions and associations in this rich passage. It is hoped that this attempt to see into the original author's mind has elucidated some of them. We move on now to the question of what the text meant in the Hellenistic period.

The Hellenistic Context

Our evidence for later interpretations comes, first, from the Masoretic text itself, which contains one or two readings that do not go back to the original author. עיר ההרס 'the city of destruction' in v. 18 is one, and מושיע ורב 'a saviour and a great one' in v. 20 is probably another, as we shall see. Then there are the versions, in particular the Greek translations which were written in all probability either in Egypt or with Greek-speaking Egyptian Jews in mind. The Targum Jonathan is also an important witness to how the text was understood in official Jewish circles, while the Isaiah Scrolls from Qumran give us a glimpse into sectarian interpretation at about the beginning of the Christian era. Finally early commentaries, such as the midrashic literature, together with the mediaeval commentaries of Rashi, Kimḥi and the rest give us further information on how people reacted to this remarkable passage.

As we saw, there is good reason to suppose that the original text of v. 18 referred to a city in Egypt called 'the city of righteousness' (= 'a new Jerusalem'), and that the Masoretic עיר ההרס 'city of destruction' reflects Pharisaic attitudes to the temple of Onias at Leontopolis, possibly after its destruction in 73 AD.[14] Other ancient authorities express similar suspicious or polemical attitudes towards the rival temple. The Mishnah classifies worship at the Temple of Onias as illicit (*m. Menaḥ.* 13.10). The Tosephta condemns it as a crime punishable by excommunication (*t. Menaḥ.* 13.12-13). The Targum on Isaiah 19.18 has 'the city of Beth Shemesh (= Heliopolis) which is destined for destruction'. Given this unsympathetic or hostile attitude on the part of Palestinian Judaism towards the situation in Egypt, we might expect to find other examples of a decline from the original author's universalistic intentions.[25] Thus Rashi (1040–1105 AD) explains that the great blessing in vv. 24–25 comes to Israel third in *chronological* order: 'The name of Israel will be raised on high and they will be as much to be reckoned with as one of these kingdoms in blessing and greatness'. The trend goes still farther in an eighteenth-century commentary which suggests that שלישיה may mean 'government, authority' (from שליש 'officer' as in Exod. 14.7), not 'third' at all: '. . . Israel will be a ruling power over Egypt and Assyria'.[26]

Another example of how the Masoretic text appears to reflect the beliefs and attitudes of Pharisaic Judaism, rather than those of the original author, occurs in v. 20. The Hebrew text has ישלח להם מושיע ורב 'he will send them a saviour and a great one' for an original ישלח להם מושיע ורב 'he will send them a saviour and will defend them . . .'[27] Rashi and Kimḥi understand this as 'a saviour and a prince', thinking of Israel's guardian angel Michael, 'one of the chief princes' (cf. Dan. 10.13). It must be remembered that the Masoretic text comes to us from a context in which Jewish eschatology was well developed, whatever the intention of the original author may have been.[28]

The Greek versions were written for a rather different readership. As long ago as 1948 the late Professor Seeligmann accumulated ample evidence to show that the Septuagint version of Isaiah 'regarded the diaspora of Egypt . . . as the rightful recipient of the prophetically promised salvation.'[29] In 11.16 and 28.5, for example, where 'the remnant' is mentioned, the translator adds ἐν Αἰγύπτῳ 'in Egypt'. Here in v. 25 he need only add the preposition ἐν 'in' to change 'my people Egypt' into 'my people in Egypt'.[30] In 6.12 and 14.2, the notion of an expanding, flourishing 'remnant', not mentioned in the Masoretic text, is introduced by the Greek translator, in the latter example, closely related to the term γιώρας 'proselyte'.[31] The Greek version, in other words, was written for Greek-speaking Jews in Egypt, and has to be read, first and foremost, in that context, not only as a witness to what the Hebrew originally meant.

In the first place, not one of the Greek versions aims a whisper of criticism at the Temple of Onias at Leontopolis. Some contain the odd hybrid name πόλις ασεδεκ, which looks like a cryptic representation of a Hebrew original עיר הצדק 'city of righteousness'[32] while others add the word ἡλίου 'of the sun', to make the reference to Heliopolis (the nome where Leontopolis was situated) explicit.[33] Now only readers with a knowledge of Hebrew could have understood what ασεδεκ meant, and it may be that there is another cryptogram of the same type, this time requiring a knowledge of Arabic. Codex Sinaiticus has πόλις ασεδ ἡλίου and it is tempting to imagine that here is a reference to Leontopolis itself (as well as Heliopolis), since asad is the normal Arabic word for 'lion'. The connection between this verse and the Temple at Leontopolis was well-established from the time of Josephus at the latest, and if one translator can incorporate a Hebrew word into his Greek, then it is not impossible that another, probably from a later age, might play the same game with Arabic. Others merely reject the word ασεδ as a scribal error, or suggest that it is a transcription of the Hebrew עיר חסד 'loyal city', an expression not attested elsewhere.[34] However we take it, the phrase refers to Leontopolis, where some Jews believed Onias had built a New Jerusalem 'as the prophet Isaiah had foretold'.

In v. 20 LXX has σημεῖον εἰς τον αἰῶνα 'a sign for ever' (reading לְעַד for וּלְעַד). This too expresses Jewish hopes for the Temple at Leontopolis which must go back before its destruction in 73 AD, and were certainly not shared by Jews living outside Egypt.[35]

It would be natural to expect the Greek versions to spell out for us in some way who the 'Saviour' in v. 20 was.[36] For example, according to one tradition Ptolemy I Soter (= 'Saviour') was noted for his 'kindness and love of mankind' and settled large numbers of Jews in Egypt, among them a distinguished high priest called Hezekiah. Yet none of the Greek versions translates the noun מושיע by σωτήρ, and this could be deliberate, since according to another tradition, recorded in Josephus (*Ant.* 13.74-9), this Ptolemy was a hard taskmaster, and his acts in Palestine proved the contrary to what was indicated by his title.[37] Perhaps the term κρίνων 'passing judgment', for Hebrew ורב, gives us a clue. Ptolemy VI Philometor, according to Josephus (*Ant.* 13.74-9), decided in favour of the Jews on two separate occasions, once in connection with the founding of Onias's Temple, and once to settle a dispute with the Samaritans. It was during his reign too that Egypt and Syria were united in a marriage alliance, and movement between the two countries was facilitated. Could this be the background of v. 23? On the other hand, there is an umistakeable anti-Egyptian slant at the end of the verse: 'The Egyptians will *serve* the Assyrians' (for Hebrew ' . . . will *worship with* the Assyrians') and 'my people in Egypt' (for 'my people Egypt').

The Isaiah Scroll from Qumran (IQIsᵃ) has 'city of the sun' in v. 18, which, like the LXX readings, would encourage Onias and his followers.[38] In fact Leontopolis and Qumran may originally have been 'two branches of a common Zakodite movement which rejected the Jerusalem Temple and its priests'.[39] Jeshua ben Sira and his grandson, who translated his work into Greek for the Jews in Egypt, were probably also part of the same Zadokite movement.[40] Codex Sinaiticus actually describes ben Sira as 'a priest from Salem' (Sir. 50.27), like Melchizedek (Gen. 14.18; Ps. 110.4; Heb. 7; 11QMelch).[41]

Further investigation will no doubt reveal more examples of how this text has been activated by events in the Hellenistic world. Both as literature in their own right, and as witnesses to the meaning of the original Hebrew, these texts still have much to tell us, provided we keep the issues discussed in the present section distinct from those exclusively concerned with the original meaning of the text discussed

in the previous section. It remains now to look briefly at a third level
of interpretation, equally distinct, and for which a quite different
context must be reconstructed.

The Literary Context

As we saw, arguments to prove that Is. 19.16-25 was actually
composed in the eighth century BC are unconvincing. Yet the fiction
that it was is important too, since clearly the author wishes us to
imagine Isaiah addressing these words to his contemporaries. Our
final task is therefore to treat the text as part of the whole 'vision of
Isaiah the son of Amoz, which he saw concerning Judah and
Jerusalem in the days of Uzziah, Jotham, Ahaz and Hezekiah, kings
of Judah' (Is. 1.1). To ignore this level of intepretation would be to do
violence to our text by divorcing it from the literary framework to
which it now belongs. One might add that, since it was the whole
Bible that was canonized, not its separate parts, Biblical commentators
have a special responsibility to expound the book as a whole, in
addition to the archaeological exercises by which its separate strata
are exposed.[42]

That the author of the books of Malachi or Jonah should have
written in such marvellously universalistic terms is one thing; but
that an eighth century prophet should have spoken thus would be
nothing short of a miracle. Yet this is what our author wishes us to
imagine. We are to look away from the diaspora situation of his own
day and focus on the memorable events that shook Jerusalem and
Judah towards the end of the eighth century BC. Isaiah had witnessed
the devastating series of Assyrian campaigns, advancing to the gates
of Jerusalem itself, (8.7-8; 10.28-32; 36.1) and the pathetic failure of
Egypt to withstand them (20.3-6; 37.9). He also saw the miraculous
deliverance of Jerusalem from the armies of Sennacherib (chs. 36–
37). What would 19.16-25 mean against that background?[43]

First, the reference in v. 17 to 'what the Lord of hosts has proposed
against Egypt' points back to v. 12 explicitly and establishes that
vv. 16-25 are intended as a continuation of the 'oracle concerning
Egypt' which begins in v. 1.[44] Just as the oracle against Moab in ch.
15 is immediately followed by a prophecy of mercy to 'the outcasts of
Moab' (16.1-5), so now the oracle against Egypt turns from confusion
and destruction (vv. 1-15) to salvation (v. 20), healing (v. 22) and
blessing (vv. 24f.). But there is more to it than that. Salvation comes

from Judah. It is to Zion that Moabites (16.1) and Ethiopians (18.7) bring gifts when their punishment is over; it is in Zion that the outcasts of Moab are to find refuge from the destroyer (16.4). It is in the new Jerusalem, 'city of righteousness' (v. 18), that the Egyptians are going to worship the Lord of hosts. This is another 'In that day . . . ' passage, which, like the ending of Amos (9.11-15), adds hope to judgment and so transforms the whole prophecy from one of doom to one of new life and rebuilding after destruction.[45] But it also transforms it from being one of the oracles of doom against the foreign nations (chs. 13–23), which in themselves had little to say to the beleaguered citizens of Jerusalem, into a prophecy 'concerning Judah and Jerusalem' (1.1; 2.1). Visions of a new Jerusalem appear in almost every chapter, from the beautiful 'faithful city' poem in ch. 1 and the famous 'swords into ploughshares' prophecy in ch. 2, to the 'new heaven and a new earth' prophecy in ch. 65 (vv. 17-25; cf. 66.18-24). The 'oracles concerning the foreign nations', like the present one, are no exception.

In such a context the problem of what v. 17 refers to becomes clear: 'the land of Judah will become a terror to the Egyptians'. Surely this must be, as Mauchline pointed out, the miraculous triumph of Judah over Sennacherib in 701 BC.[46] The fact that Isaiah did not actually utter these words at that time, or that the defeat of the Assyrian army never happened,[47] is of no importance if we are concerned to discover what the author of the passage is saying. He invites us to imagine the legendary Isaiah commenting on that legendary victory. The spectacular events described in chs. 36–37 begin with Sennacherib's attack on 'all the fortified cities of Judah' (36.1) and end with the miraculous slaying of 185,000 Assyrians and the ignominious retreat and subsequent assassination of their king Sennacherib (37.36-38). The role of the Egyptians is mentioned twice in the prose account (36.6-9; 37.9), and it is clear from passages like 20.3-6 and 31.3 that they were at the mercy of Assyria at that time. How much more had they to fear from 'the land of Judah', who had defeated Assyria and had good reason to turn their supernatural powers on Egypt next.

This brings us to the question of why, out of all the available words for 'fear, terror, panic', the author chose the enigmatic word חגא in v. 17. There are perhaps two clues to the special nuance of the word, which occurs only here. In the first place, the form of the word, which makes it look like Aramaic rather than Hebrew, is suggestive.

Are we intended to recognize in it the frightening overtones of something foreign to the Egyptians, quite new to their experience and all the more terrifying for that? All but one of the Aramaisms of this type cited by the grammarians refer to something frightening (Is. 19.17; Ezek. 19.2; Dan. 11.46; Lam. 3.12) or destructive (Jer. 50.11) or unpalatable (Num. 11.20; Ruth 1.20) or evil (Qoh. 10.5).[48] It is also significant that Modern Hebrew חגא denotes a foreign or non-Jewish festival.[49] This obvious association of חגא with חג 'festival' may provide a second clue to the author's intention in choosing this rare word for 'fear'. In the whole book of Isaiah, only one חג 'feast' is described, and that description is an unforgettably grotesque and spine-chilling one:

> You shall have a song as in the night when a holy feast is kept; and gladness of heart, as when one sets out to the sound of the flute to go to the mountain of the Lord, to the Rock of Israel. And the Lord will cause his majestic voice to be heard and the descending blow of his arm to be seen, in furious anger and a flame of devouring fire, with a cloudburst and tempest and hailstones. The Assyrians will be terror-stricken at the voice of the Lord, when he smites with his rod. And every stroke of the staff of punishment which the Lord lays upon them will be to the sound of timbrels and lyres; battling with brandished arm he will fight with them...' (Is. 30.29-32).

This description, worthy of Hieronymous Bosch, brings together jubilant celebrations at a feast in Judah with the terror of Judah's enemies. Does the word חגא do the same? Is this a sinister pun in which the author is deliberately alluding to that Isaianic 'terror-feast'? Or perhaps in this Egyptian context, there is an allusion to the night of the Passover at which not only the Egyptians, but also Philistia, Edom, Moab and Canaan were seized with terror (Exod. 15.13-18).[50]

For the ancient historian, no doubt events in second century BC Hellenistic Egypt will be of particular interest; literary and religious developments in fifth century BC Judaism are important too. But for those claiming this passage as a 'high point in Old Testament theology', then surely its literary framework in the Book of Isaiah as it stands must take pride of place. One final example will illustrate this. For the original author of the passage, as we saw, Egypt and Assyria were symbols or literary allusions, while for the eighth century prophet, they meant far more. Egypt was a vain hope in whom some of his foolish contemporaries were placing their faith:

Woe to those who go down to Egypt for help and rely on
horses . . . The Egyptians are men and not God, and their horses
are flesh and not spirit.
When the Lord stretches out his hand, the helper will stumble, and
he who is helped will fall, and they will all perish together (31.1-3).

The Assyrians were his people's worst enemy, responsible for oppression and wholesale destruction. It is to such people, then, that he apparently directs this prophecy of forgiveness and hope. In the same way the Book of Jonah, divorced from its eighth century BC context (2 Kgs 14.23-17.7), preaches forgiveness to the gentiles, symbolized by the citizens of Nineveh, long since dead and buried. But the author deliberately chose Jonah as his hero, not Noah or Moses or Haggai or Ezra, in order to preach forgiveness to his country's bitterest enemies. The distinction is worth making; it is there in the text for all to see; and it raises a high point in Old Testament theology even higher. Adapting Wildberger's comment quoted at the beginning of this paper, we are in these verses, theologically and morally, not far from the words of Jesus on the cross: 'Father, forgive them; for they know not what they do' (Luke 23.24).

With the greatest pleasure I offer this as my contribution to a Festschrift for one whose devotion to the subtlest nuances of the Hebrew text has been a model to me and to many others, since we were colleagues in Glasgow, in the days of Mauchline and Mullo Weir, twenty years ago.

NOTES

1. R. Lowth, *Isaiah: A New Translation with a Preliminary Dissertation and notes, critical, philological and explanatory*, London, 1778 (15th ed., 1887), 240-41; B. Duhm, *Das Buch Jesaja*[4] (HAT), Göttingen, 1922, 122-23; H. Wildberger, *Jesaja 13-27* (BK), Neukirchen-Vluyn, 1974-78, 746; R.E. Clements, *Isaiah 1–39* (NCBC), Grand Rapids & London, 1980, 170. See also A.J. Heschel, *The Prophets*, New York, 1962, 185-86.

2. G.A. Smith, *The Book of Isaiah*, London, 1889, 275; cf. T.K. Cheyne, *Introduction to the Book of Isaiah*, London, 1895, 99: 'we can hardly imagine a more "swanlike end" for a dying prophet'.

3. Wildberger, *op. cit.*, 746; cf. Duhm, *op.cit.*, 122. O. Kaiser, *Isaiah 13– 39* (OTL), (transl. R.A. Wilson) London, 1974, 111.

4. See especially V. Tcherikover, *Hellenistic Civilization and the Jews*, Philadelphia, 1959, 272-87; M. Delcor, 'Le Temple d'Onias en Egypte', *RB* 75 (1968), 188-205; P.M. Fraser, *Ptolemaic Alexandria*, Oxford, 1972, Vol. I,

83f., 281-86; R. Hayward, 'The Jewish Temple at Leontopolis: A Reconsideration', *Essays in Honour of Yigael Yadin*, *JJS* 33 (1982), 429-43.

5. Cf. G. Vermes, 'Bible and Midrash: Early Old Testament Exegesis', *Cambridge History of the Bible*, Vol. I, Cambridge, 1970, 223f.

6. Cheyne, *op. cit.*, 106. Many commentators on the passage, like Onias and Lowth, of course, assume that Isaiah was the author and interpret the passage accordingly. See below.

7. J. Mauchline, *Isaiah 1–39* (TBC), London, 1962, 162.

8. Clements, *op. cit.*, 170.

9. G.B. Gray, *Isaiah 1–27* (ICC), Edinburgh, 1912, 332f.; cf. K. Marti, *Das Buch Jesaja* (KHAT), Tübingen, 1900, 156; Cheyne, *op. cit.*, 100.

10. *Loc. cit.*

11. *Loc. cit.*

12. *Op. cit.*, 110.

13. Cf. Wildberger, *op. cit.*, 738.

14. E.g. Wildberger, *op. cit.*, 745f.

15. E.g. Duhm, *op. cit.*, 127f; Kaiser, *op. cit.*, 110; E. Jacob, *Theology of the Old Testament* (ET), London, 1958, 217-23.

16. Jacob, *op. cit.*, 222, n. 2.

17. As Jacob, Wildberger, Clements and many others do.

18. A. Feuillet, 'Un sommet religieux de l'Ancien Testament. L'oracle d'Is. 19.19-25 sur la conversion de l'Egypte', *RScR* 39 (1951), 65-87.

19. *Op. cit.*, 69ff.

20. Cf. Gray, *op. cit.*, 335; Feuillet, *op. cit.*, 72; Kaiser, *op. cit.* 107; I.Z. Seeligmann, *The Septuagint Version of Isaiah*, Leiden, 1948, 68; Hayward, *op. cit.*, 439-40.

21. E.g. Kaiser, *op. cit.*, 105; Wildberger, *op. cit.*, 742f.

22. I.W. Slotki (*Isaiah*, London, 1949, 93) speaks of a 'triple alliance' and a 'league of nations'.

23. Cf. Slotki, *loc. cit.*; Wildberger, *op. cit.*, 745; Jacob, *op. cit.*, 222; Kaiser, *op. cit.*, 110-2.

24. Vermes, *op. cit.*, 223f.; Delcor, *op. cit.*, 201-3; Hayward, *op. cit.*, 438-443.

25. Cf. Duhm, *op. cit.*, 123; Gray, *op. cit.*, 341.

26. *Metzudat David* ('Tower of David') by D. Altschuler, Berlin, 1770 (printed along with the commentaries of Kimḥi and Rashi in Rabbinic Bibles).

27. Cf. BHS, Kissane, Kaiser, Wildberger. 1QIsaᵃ has 'and will come down (sc. from heaven)', which agrees with the eschatological interpretation of Rashi, Kimḥi and probably MT. Cf. Wildberger, *op. cit.*, 72. But see n. 38 for a different interpretation of the Qumran evidence. The Greek Codex Marchalianus (6th cent. AD) identifies the 'saviour' in this verse as Jesus: ὅπερ ἑρμηνεύεται Ἰησους.

28. Cf. J.F.A. Sawyer, 'Hebrew terms for the resurrection of the dead', *VT* 23 (1973), 218-34, esp. 228ff.

29. Seeligmann, *op.cit.*, 117.

30. *Ibid.*, 116f.

31. *Ibid.*, 117.

32. See above, n. 20.

33. Cf. *Septuaginta, Isaias*, ed. J. Ziegler, Göttingen, 1939, 191. 1QIsa[a] has עיר החרם 'City of the Sun'. Heliopolis is called בית השמש in Jer. 43.13. Tcherikover, *op.cit.*, 277f.; Fraser, *op.cit.*, I, 83; II, 162-63.

34. For a full discussion of the problem, see especially Gray, *op.cit.*, 335-37; Seeligmann, *op.cit.*, 68.

35. Vermes, *op.cit.*, 223f.; Delcor, *op.cit.*, 202f.

36. Cf. Cheyne, *op.cit.*, 105f.; Hayward, *op.cit.*, 440f.

37. Cf. Tcherikover, *op.cit.*, 56.

38. Hayward (*op.cit.*, 441) suggests that the 1QIsa[a] reading in v. 20 'and will descend' (see above, n. 27) refers to 'going down to Egypt', and that the 'saviour' is thus Onias, founder of the Temple. He cites E. Kutzscher, *The Language and Linguistic Background of the Isaiah Scroll (1QIsa[a])*, Leiden, 1974, 245.

39. Hayward, *op.cit.*, 443.

40. J.F.A. Sawyer, 'Was Jeshua ben Sira a Zadokite priest?', *Proc. of VIII World Cong. of Jew. St.*, I, Jerusalem, 1982, 65-71.

41. *Ibid.*, 65. For the connection between Melchizedek, Jerusalem and the Zadokite priesthood, see H.H. Rowley, 'Melchizedek and Zadok', *Bertholet Festschrift*, 1950, 461-72.

42. Cf. B.S. Childs, *Introduction to the Old Testament as Scripture*, London, 1979, e.g. 60; J. Goldingay, *Approaches to Old Testament Interpretation*, London, 1981, 132-37; J.F.A. Sawyer, 'A change of emphasis in the study of the Prophets', *Israel's Prophetic Tradition*, eds. R. Coggins *et al.*, Cambridge, 1982, 240-46.

43. The most useful materials for this section are of course the commentaries of the Church Fathers, Jewish commentators like Rashi and Kimḥi, and more recently Lowth, G.A. Smith, Mauchline and others who take seriously the text as it stands, however far removed from a reconstructed original.

44. Cf. Duhm, *op.cit.*, 119; Gray, *op.cit.*, 332.

45. Clements, 'Patterns in the Prophetic Canon', *Canon and Authority*, eds. G.W. Coats and B.O. Long, Philadelphia 1977, 42-55, esp. 44; Sawyer, *op.cit.*, 242f.

46. Mauchline, *op.cit.*, 161f. Although Mauchline may not have known it, this was Rashi's view too.

47. See especially R.E. Clements, *Isaiah and the Deliverance of Jerusalem* (JSOTS, 13), Sheffield, 1980.

48. *GK* 80h; *B-L* 511x. The one exception is the puzzling שׁנא 'sleep' in Ps. 127.2. M. Wagner (*Die lexikalischen und grammatikalischen Aramäismen im alttestamentlichen Hebräisch* [BZAW, 96], Berlin 1966, 128) merely records these as textual variants.

49. A. Even Shoshan, *Millon Hadash*, Jerusalem, 1977, II, p. 366, quotes examples of wordplays on חגא/חג from Ben-Zion (1870-1932) and Bialik (1873-1934) among others. The Vulgate has *festivitatem*. The Targum Jonathan, incidentally, has חגא at Is. 30.29. Aramaic for a 'pagan festival' is חגתא see J. Levy, *Wörterbuch über die Talmudim und Midrashim*, Darmstadt, 1963, II, 13.

50. Kaiser, *op.cit.*, 106.

LAMENTATIONS 1.3:
LIGHT FROM THE HISTORY OF EXEGESIS

R.B. Salters

University of St. Andrews

2 Kgs 25.8-12 describes how in 587 BC the Babylonian army swept into Jerusalem and burned down the Temple of Yahweh, the royal palace and many other houses. The passage goes on to record the tearing down of the city walls and the taking captive to Babylon of many of the inhabitants, leaving only the poorest. There is no doubt that these events are, for the book of Lamentations, in the past, though perhaps only in the recent past, and one would be in good company if one were to make the assumption that the author, at all points, is looking back at Jerusalem razed to the ground.

While the view that Jeremiah is the author has been generally abandoned, the majority of scholars would argue that the book of Lamentations has one author, though this too has been challenged. As regards the dating of the five poems, Hillers[1] argues that there is insufficient evidence for their precise chronological ordering, though Rudolph[2] makes out a case for treating chapter 1 as having been written shortly after the first capture of Jerusalem in 597 BC, and not, as with chapter 2, after 587 BC; consequently, although great misfortune is spoken of in this chapter, a few passages may bear the interpretation that the Temple still stands, though desecrated, and that the festivals go on, though poorly attended (cf. vv. 4, 10). Though perhaps not of vital importance for the exegesis of every single passage in the chapter, there are some where the dating could be of significance, and this should be kept in mind as we proceed.

Verse 3 is one verse where the foregoing concerns may be relevant.

גלתה יהודה מעני ומרב עברה
היא ישבה בגוים לא מצאה מנוח
כל רדפיה השיגוה בין המצרים

The translation and the exegesis of this verse have long presented problems to the scholar. These problems have not been resolved, though in the various translations of the Bible difficulties are seldom noted or acknowledged.

One of the problems is the lack of confidence with which one may tackle the Hebrew text of these laments; such is the nature of the literary style that the context does not always provide a reliable guide, and one may be left to interpret a verse in the same way as one has to interpret one of the Wisdom sentences in Proverbs, that is, almost in isolation. Three translations juxtaposed reveal where the problems lie:

AV: Judah is gone into captivity because of affliction and because of great servitude: she dwelleth among the heathen, she findeth no rest: all her persecutors overtook her between the straits.

JB: Judah is exiled after her downfall and harsh enslavement. She dwells among the nations now, but finds no relief there. Her pursuers all overtake her in places where there is no way out.

NEB: Judah went into the misery of exile and endless servitude. Settled among the nations, she found no resting place; all her persecutors fell upon her in her sore straits.

The chief difficulty in this verse lies in the meaning of the first line, though the problems are all inter-related. Is it a present condition that is being described or a past event? What is that condition or event? Is there more than one condition? What is the syntax in the first line? Who are the nations? What lies behind the hunting terminology in the last line?

The subject of the first line is Judah. The poet personifies the state as he does the city in vv. 1f., though it is the people of Judah which he has in mind and not the land. This is clear from the rest of the verse.

As far as the consonantal text is concerned the difficulties are minimal. The LXX ἀπὸ ταπεινώσεως αὐτῆς καὶ ἀπὸ πλήθους δουλείας αὐτῆς suggests to some that the Greek translator had as his *Vorlage* מעניה ומרב עברתה (cf. BH³), but while this is possible it is unlikely. It is true that the LXX translator of Lamentations is quite faithful to the original Hebrew, and this fact should encourage us to look carefully at the text in case an emendation is warranted; yet all the other

Versions support MT here. Albrektson has suggested that the anomaly is probably an inner Greek error, that the αὐτῆς after δουλείας is a corruption of αὐτή (=היא MT but omitted in LXX, though elsewhere the translator represents it, e.g. 1.4, 8) and that a later scribe added αὐτῆς after ταπεινώσεως in order to harmonize.[3] This may have been the case; at any rate the presence of αὐτῆς (even if it does not correspond to the absent αὐτή) does not pose a threat to MT. It is just possible that היא is not represented in LXX because the translator felt the pronoun was superfluous, and that the suffix has crept in under the influence of the form עניה (v. 7). If this is the case then our understanding of the LXX of 1.3 may be controlled by the meaning in 1.7.

It should be noted that in this passage we encounter a number of verbs in the perfect tense. Some scholars are inclined to take these to be declarative in nature (cf. v. 1) and hence to be rendered by the English present; others are not so confident that this is intended and render by the English past or by a mixture of the two.

The first and most difficult exegetical problem is in the first line. What does the construction גלה מן mean in this context?

In the Old Testament the verb גלה, when used intransitively, as must be the case here, can mean 'go into exile, emigrate, depart, be away'. The root is used in parallel with סור (Is. 49.21; Amos 6.7). Since the Hiphil can mean either 'to force into exile' or 'to take into exile', and since the terms גולה and גלות came to focus on the Babylonian captivity, not only in the Old Testament but also in post-biblical literature, there has been a tendency among some exegetes, at all stages in the history of exegesis, to interpret גלתה יהודה as referring specifically to the captivity in Babylon. Hence the translation has often been offered: 'Judah is taken into exile', 'is gone into captivity', 'is taken captive' or something similar, as though the verbal form were in the passive, or גלה could take a passive meaning. If the poem had not been an alphabetic acrostic, emendations would certainly have been suggested at this point to confirm that what is meant is the captivity of the Jews, their being taken forcibly to Babylon.

The LXX μετῳκίσθη Ἰουδαία may be the first witness to this interpretation. The translator has given a passive sense to the verb. Whether or not his meaning is 'Judah is forced to move away' or 'Judah is taken into exile' is difficult to say, but the Syro-Hexaplar ܐ ܐܬܓܠܝܬ i.e. the *Ethpaal*, takes it to be the latter, unless the force of this conjugation of the root is different from what Payne

Smith[4] suggests, viz. 'captivus ductus est'. Certainly, the Peshitta ܓܠܠܐ is different, and one suspects that the Syro-Hexaplar is of the opinion that this *Peal* does not carry the required passive meaning here. That the LXX translator may not have had this precise meaning in mind is at least suggested by the occurrence of the verb αἰχμαλωτίζειν, which does refer to the 'captivity of Israel', in the LXX title of Lamentations, and again at 1.18 to translate הלכו בשבי (cf. also 1.5). We shall return to the LXX presently, but we should note that in the history of exegesis the meaning 'go into captivity' or 'taken into exile' is well represented, e.g. Luther: 'Juda ist gefangen', Coverdale: 'Juda is taken prisoner', AV: 'Judah is gone into captivity', Lee: 'La Judée a été emmenée captive' and, more recently, Rudolph: 'Weggeführt ist Juda'.

Having said this, it should be noted that whether or not an exegete or translator will render גלה in the passive, many interpret 'going into exile' as referring specifically to the Babylonian captivity. Thus, while the Targum renders איזלו בית יהודה בגלותא it is likely that the Targumist is speaking of the exiles in Babylon since he goes on to say אנון אתמסרו ביד עממיא . So, too, the midrashic collections Echah Rabbah and Yalkut Shmoni, while Hugo of St. Victor mentions Babylon by name. We should note that neither Rashi nor Joseph Kara refer to Babylon in their comments on this verb, nor indeed to captivity, but Tobia does imply that the word has this denotation.[5] Jerome did not, unfortunately, comment on the book of Lamentations, and the Vulgate's rendering 'Migravit Iuda . . . ' may leave the question unanswered, though it should be noted that in the title to the book in the Vulgate we read 'postquam in captivitatem reductus est Israel', so it might be argued that Jerome was consciously describing something other than the Babylonian captivity here (cf. the above remarks on LXX). In fact he probably meant that Judah had migrated voluntarily, and it is this meaning, and often on the basis of the Vulgate, which is adopted by several scholars. But if we assume that the author of Lamentations had in mind that many people had left the country we should, perhaps, allow for the possibility that the Babylonian exiles are included here. We may reject the statement by the Chronicler that in 587 BC Nebuchadnezzar took captive all those who had not been killed (2 Chron. 36.20). This turns attention on the Babylonian community of exiles at the expense of the many who were left behind in Judah or who had fled to Egypt, Moab, Ammon and Edom, among whom may have been the author of this poem, and has the effect of encouraging us to think of the Babylonian exiles as the continuation of Judah, and that virtually nothing of importance took place in Palestine until this group returned. We should not, however, go to the other extreme and ignore this group, for they were important, and it may be that the author had all these groups in mind when he wrote גלתה יהודה. The translation 'Judah has gone into exile' would, therefore, suffice.

But it is the rest of the first line which perhaps divides exegetes most, and, in particular, the function of the preposition מן; hence in order to understand this line properly we need to look at the construction גלה מן. In this we are in the company of most scholars, though Joseph Kara seems to interpret as though גלה should be treated separately, and Houbigant argues that the punctuation is at fault here and that the first statement is simply 'Migravit Juda'.[6] But it is the difficulty of the construction which has forced these scholars to the position they adopt, and it has not commanded much support.

In the Old Testament the construction occurs ten times, apart from this passage. 1 Sam. 4.21, 22: גלה כבוד מישראל: 'the glory has departed from Israel'; Ezek. 12.3: וגלית ממקומך אל מקום אחר: 'You shall go into exile from your place to another place; Hos. 10.5: על כבודו כי גלה ממנו: 'over its glory which has departed from it'; Mic. 1.16: כי גלו ממך: 'for they shall go from you into exile'; 2 Kgs 17.23; 25.21; Amos 7.11, 17; Jer. 52.27: ויגל יהודה מעל אדמתו: 'So Judah went into exile from his land'.

In each of the above nine cases, although the precise meaning of גלה varies a little, the מן is local. The tenth is at Is. 5.13 גלה עמי מבלי דעת 'my people go into exile for want of knowledge', where the מן is causal. If we look at these instances the pressure is to favour the מן local for our passage, and yet in the history of exegesis it is the causal מן which gets the biggest vote, beginning with the Vulgate 'propter afflictionem et multitudinem servitutis'. Yet even here the doctors differ, and the causal מן takes two different directions, depending on how גלה is understood. In this category, those who see גלה as referring to the fugitives from Judah are inclined to argue that the rest of the line gives the reason for their flight; it is the harsh conditions in Palestine which encouraged many to imagine that life might be more tolerable elsewhere and to scatter to Egypt, Moab, Ammon, Edom etc. This makes sense in the light of Jer. 40.11; 42f. The Babylonian yoke, probably from the year 597 BC and no doubt intensified in 587 BC, is alluded to by affliction (עני) and great servitude (רב עברה). In fact translations which refer to the captivity of Judah and which adopt the causal מן in this way are in danger of making no sense. The AV 'Judah is gone into captivity because of affliction and because of great servitude' does not make sense unless one supposes that captivity was an option freely available to the people of Judah.

A variation of the causal מן is found in Joseph Kara who seems to take the second half of line one with the second line. It is because of the affliction, etc., suffered in exile among the nations that she finds no rest. This view is also detectable in the Targum where we read '. . . she dwells in the midst of the nations and has found no rest because of the harsh servitude wherewith they afflict her'. The other way this line was interpreted while adopting the causal מן, is found in Targum, the midrashic collections and, more recently, in an article by Dahood. To go into exile is certainly seen as punishment and the מן introduces the reasons for the punishment. There is no doubt that the author of Lamentations linked the fall of Jerusalem with the sins of the people (cf. 1.5 etc.), but it is difficult to obtain this meaning from the Hebrew of 1.3. Nevertheless, Midrash Rabbah and Yalkut Shmoni list a number of sins of the people which have a connection with the roots ענה and עבר, and where Judah is accused of afflicting (ענה) the poor (עני), or not eating 'the bread of affliction (עני)', or enslaving the Hebrew slave עברי (משתעברים בעבד עברי) or idolatry (עבורת כוכבים). In spite of the fact that the midrashim offer a number of separate interpretations they can all be reduced to this line of exegesis. The Targum is in general agreement with the latter:

איזלו בית יהודה בגלותא על דהון מענין יתמין וארמלן
ועל סגיאות פלחנא דהוו מפלחין באחיהון

Henderson is a nineteenth century exponent of this understanding of the causal מן. He argues that 'the reference is to the circumstances narrated in Jer. 34, in which the Jews are expressly threatened with captivity, because, in violation of the Mosaic law, and of the covenant into which they had entered, they withdrew the grant of liberty which they had made to their servants and reduced them to their former state of servitude'.[7]

More recently, Dahood has taken up the cause; but he is not altogether happy with MT. He emends the text to read מעוני (from עון, iniquity, plus suffix of third feminine singular, as in Phoenician.) When this is done עברה 'assumes the pejorative sense of serving other gods'. He renders: 'Judah went into exile for her iniquity, and for the diversity of her worship'.[8]

The causal מן has, however, lacked support during the last century, and the majority of scholars would reject it; hence we have Levine saying that the passage 'cannot possibly mean that Judah has gone into exile *because* of poverty and *because* of hard labour';[9] and we may note the confidence with which the causal מן is rejected by Albrektson[10], Meek[11], Gordis[12], Rudolph[13], Kraus[14] and Hillers[15], though these scholars do not all advocate the מן local.

As we noticed earlier, the Old Testament examples of גלה מן are weighted in favour of מן local, yet we have seen that this possibility was given very little scope among commentators until the last century. It *is* present, however, in the LXX translation: μετῳκίσθη Ἰουδαία ἀπὸ ταπεινώσεως αὐτῆς καὶ ἀπὸ πλήθους δουλείας αὐτῆς which should be translated 'Judah is taken (forced) into exile from her affliction and her great servitude . . .', and not 'by reason of her affliction . . .'. That is to say, the Greek translator took the מן in his Hebrew *Vorlage* as מן local. It not only makes good sense to interpret the LXX in this way, but it would seem that if we take ἀπὸ as introducing the reasons for their being taken into exile, the first line in LXX does not add up. For how can the people have been taken into exile because of their affliction? We would, therefore, submit that in LXX we have the earliest example of this line of exegesis. It is probably followed by Peshitta and was later confirmed by Syro-Hexoplar, though, because in Syriac the preposition is similarly ambiguous, the support is less identifiable. Hence the two earliest Versions are in agreement here. The Graecus Venetus ἀπῳκίσται ἰεούδας ἀπὸ ταλαπωρίας ἀπὸ τε πλήθους δουλείας constitutes mediaeval support.

It may be argued that in taking the מן as causal some[16] exegetes and translators would also have had in mind the subsidiary 'local' meaning: the causal and the local cannot be kept completely apart. Again, the exegesis of those who accept מן local is not always the same. We find that some scholars emphasize Judah's *escape* from misery etc. in her own land, whereas those who have understood גלה in a passive sense seem to be depicting Judah as being taken from one miserable situation to another (e.g. Rudolph: 'Weggeführt ist Juda aus Elend und schwerer Knechtung').

A small number of scholars base their interpretation on taking the מן as temporal. The earliest of these seems to have been Hugh Broughton: 'Judah leaveth country after affliction and much bondage . . .'[17] and it is to be found in Hillers' translation[18], in JB and

Fuerst,[19] though Albrektson too observes that there may be 'a temporal shade of meaning combined with the local' here.[20]

There is yet another way in which the מן has been understood. So far, we have noticed that for the most part, the 'misery' and 'hard servitude' have been taken to be that which was experienced at home under the overlords, Egypt and Babylonia. But it is argued that we would expect these words to have been used of the experiences in the Babylonian exile. Luther does not comment on the book of Lamentations, but his translation: 'Judah ist gefangen im Elend und schweren Dienst ...' not only reflects a dissatisfaction with the previous interpretations but seems to imply that מן may be interpreted as 'in'. Other exegetes have felt a need at times to reflect on the hardship suffered by the exiles in Babylon, without ever discussing the syntax of the passage, though we saw that Houbigant and Joseph Kara divided or punctuated the passage in such a way as to achieve an interpretation which allowed the misery to be that which was experienced in exile.

In this connection we should note the French translation:[21] 'La Judée a été emmenée captive, tant elle est affligée, et tant sa servitude est grande ...'; Moffatt: 'To an exile of sad slavery has Judah departed ...'; NEB: 'Judah went into the misery of exile and endless servitude'. Meek makes an attempt to justify such an exegesis, but it is Gordis who argues[22] that we should see here 'the *mem* of condition, which occurs in Rabbinic Hebrew, as, for example, in *Aboth* 4.9 כל המקיים את התורה מעוני סופה לקיימה מעושר "Whoever fulfills the Torah in a condition of poverty will ultimately fulfill the Torah in a condition of wealth."' Gordis finds this *mem* in Biblical Hebrew: Hos. 9.11, 12; Ps. 22.11; Job 3.11. His translation of our passage is: 'Judah is in exile, in a state of poverty and oppression ...'. He further argues that the 'parallelism in our verse (a, b // a', b') also makes it clear that the verse describes Judah's present condition and not its cause'. This latter argument might have been used in support of all those who reject the causal מן, and does not specifically help the question of the '*mem* of condition'. The examples which Gordis gives of the latter are not convincing, though Levine[23] is altogether persuaded.

In the history of exegesis the meaning of היא ישבה בגוים varies according to how the previous line has been interpreted. It would seem that, for the most part, those who take גלה to refer to the Babylonian captivity have to understand this phrase, along with

לא מצאה מנוח, as speaking of the Babylonian exile. The exception
here is perhaps Rudolph who, along with Hillers, sees both these
phrases depicting the pre-exilic Judah—almost a parallel to affliction
and much servitude.[24] Those who interpret גלה to refer to those
fleeing to Moab, etc., take these phrases to refer to the exiles in those
countries.

At this point we might wish for more precision in the Hebrew
language. If we could be certain of the tense of the verbs we could
rule out some interpretations; but we must resist the temptation to
make a decision on this as yet.

The combination of ישב and בגוים does not occur elsewhere in the
Old Testament, so we cannot appeal precisely to other passages for
the meaning of this phrase. However, בגוים does occur many times in
the Old Testament and an examination of other passages where it
appears may be of help. A number of instances might point to a
situation which is threatened in Deut. 4.27 if the settlers in Canaan
do not obey Yahweh: 'Yahweh will scatter you among the peoples
(בעמים), and you will be left few in number among the nations (בגוים)
where Yahweh will drive you'. And again, in Jer. 9.15: 'I will scatter
them among the nations (בגוים) whom neither they nor their fathers
have known . . . '. In particular, Deut. 28.64ff. is worth noting here in
the light of the next phrase in our passage: 'Yahweh shall scatter you
among all the peoples, from one end of the earth to the other; and
there you shall serve other gods, of wood and stone, which neither
you nor your fathers have known. And among these nations (בגוים)
you shall find no ease, and there shall be no rest (מנוח) for the sole of
your foot . . . ' A lot of passages are of this nature, and they lend
support to the view that the author of Lamentations, picking up the
prophetic threat, is describing the plight of the exiles in those very
terms, and in a way which can only mean living among nations such
as Egypt and Moab. The frequent use in these passages of the verb
(Hiphil of פוץ) 'to scatter' adds further weight to the argument.

It is perhaps less natural to take the words בגוים היא ישבה to be a
reference to the captivity in Babylon, though it could be argued that
the words are a poetic way of referring to that experience; but those
exegetes whose interpretation of גלתה יהודה was in those terms are
forced to understand the phrase in this way. A passage which may
support this view is Ezek. 6.8f, especially the phrase בגוים אשר נשבו שם.

Another passage, perhaps more appropriate in that it comes from
the same book, is Lam. 2.9: 'Her king and her princes are among the

nations (בגוים)'. This may refer to Jehoiachin and his entourage in captivity in Babylon, though Rudolph points out that this need not be so.[25] King Zedekiah fled from Jerusalem in 587 BC and headed eastwards, possibly intending to find refuge in Ammon or Moab. This may be in the author's mind here. If the latter knew that Zedekiah had been captured near Jericho and taken to Riblah, then Babylon was not necessarily in his mind.

The view taken by Hillers is that these words היא . . . מנוח refer to the experiences of the pre-exilic period, following on from the reference to affliction and servitude. Hillers acknowledges that this interpretation is not easy here but feels that the reference to pre-exilic conditions is 'preferable as being more in harmony with the whole chapter, which is not otherwise concerned with the plight of the exiles among the heathen'. He supports his position by drawing attention to Lam. 4.20: 'The breath of our nostrils, the anointed of Yahweh, was caught in their traps, the one of whom we said, "In his shadow we will live among the nations"'. This passage, he argues, is 'an unambiguous reference to the pre-exilic period of independent nationhood'.[26] For Hillers, the whole pre-exilic experience is being described as a failure for the people. In Palestine she had 'lived among the nations', but it had all ended in affliction and hard servitude. There is, perhaps, further support for Hillers in Lam. 1.1 where Jerusalem in pre-exilic days had been 'great among the nations (בגוים) . . . queen among the provinces', though this support is tempered when we notice that ישבה in that verse describes the *present* condition of Jerusalem.

The phrase לא מצאה מנוח is an interesting one. The people of God are promised 'rest' on entering the holy land (Deut. 3.20; 12.9); and it might have been argued by Hillers that the phrase laments the fact that Israel's experience in that land was such that the promise was not realized: 'She found no rest'. But a passage already alluded to in connection with 'the nations' is appropriate here. In Deut. 28.64f. we read: 'And Yahweh shall scatter you among all peoples . . . And among these nations you shall find no ease, and there shall be no rest (מנוח) for the sole of your foot; but Yahweh will give you a trembling heart, and failing eyes, and a languishing soul.' This passage supports the view that the people have fled to various countries in the hope of finding conditions less intolerable than in Palestine, but all is in vain. For those who take גלה to refer to the Babylonian captivity this phrase is a problem unless they understand it to refer to pre-exilic conditions. If a people are taken captive they may scarcely expect to find rest in captivity.

The final part of the verse, כל רדפיה השיגוה בין המצרים, is not without its problems, and there is no unanimity among translators and scholars as to its meaning. The verb רדף can mean 'pursue' or 'persecute' though the former is probably the more likely here as it is construed with השיג. It is important to maintain the hunting terminology in translation whatever the exegesis may be.[27]

Although there are other concerns in this line, the crux, as far as translation is concerned, is the phrase בין המצרים. The LXX (cf. also Symmachus) ἀνὰ μέσον τῶν θλιβόντων 'among oppressors' probably had the same Hebrew text but vocalized differently from the Masoretes. The translation probably presupposes a participial form from צרר 'to show hostility towards'; but the sense is not good, since we must surely identify the pursuers with the oppressors.

While the Peshitta is a little ambiguous here, there is no doubt that the Syriac translator took the form to be from צרר, 'to be narrow'; and the Vulgate, which is quite consistent in maintaining the hunting language throughout, renders 'inter angustias', and gives the lead for many later translations. That is not to say that there were not other interpretations in existence (apart from the LXX) alongside the Vulgate's. This can be seen from the very rendering of the Targum: כד היא מתהבאה בין תחומיא ואעיקו לה where we see that המצרים has a double translation, due probably to such varying interpretations.[28]

Neither of these two interpretations corresponds with that of the Vulgate. The second, ואעיקו לה, may be based on that of the LXX, while the first, בין תחומיא, reflects the interpretation given to the entire line, which sees here a reference to the exiles fleeing from their homes and being overtaken by their pursuing enemies as they reached the borders of their land, or in no man's land. The assumption is that מצר, which is uncommon in the Old Testament and which may mean 'narrow place' or 'distress' there, but which in post-biblical Hebrew can also mean 'boundary', has this latter meaning in the Hebrew Bible.

Rashi seems to understand המצרים as 'narrow places'. He refers to height on both sides with no way of escape. The picture is of the hunted being run to ground and cornered. Rashi then offers another meaning, 'boundaries (of fields and vineyards)', a reference to the fugitives in no man's land. Finally, he alludes to the midrashic view that the phrase refers to the 'distresses' between 17th Tammuz and the 9th Ab. The first date is traditionally thought to be the day when the walls of Jerusalem were breached by the Babylonians, and the second, the day on which the Temple was destroyed. Hence the latter view takes the last clause of verse 3 to refer to the destruction of Jerusalem in 587 BC.[29]

Kara is in no doubt that 'borders' is the meaning, and adds 'because they were wanderers and fugitives near their neighbours'. And Tobia ben Elieser, though referring at first to the Tammuz and Ab dates, goes on to interpret the clause as reflecting the incident described in Jer. 52.8 when the Babylonian army pursued (רדף) king Zedekiah and overtook him (וישיגו) in the plains (בערבות) of Jericho.

The Graecus Venetus πάντες οἱ διώκοντες αὐτὸν ἔφθασάν εἰς μέσον τῶν ὁρισμῶν seems to be in the same tradition as Kara.

Hugo of St. Victor, without criticizing the Vulgate on which he comments, keeps alive the hunting imagery, albeit with an anachronistic touch: 'Coarctatus undique locum evadendi invenire non potuit; fugiens Chaldaeos, incidit in Aegyptios; et cum ab Aegyptiis fugaret, occurrit Assyriis'.[30]

Luther's 'alle ihre Verfolger halten sie übel' is an example of interpreting the hunting terminology as referring to general adversity, but it is no more than a guess. Calvin's translation 'apprehenderunt eam inter angustias' maintains the imagery, as does his comment ' . . . it is one of the greatest of evils to fall into the hands of enemies, and to be taken by them when we are enclosed as it were between two walls, or in a narrow passage, as some explain the word'.[31] The tendency nowadays is to maintain the language of the chase, whatever the exegesis, though Moffat 'and in her anguish her pursuers overtook her', RSV 'her pursuers have all overtaken her in the midst of her distress' and NEB 'all her persecutors fell upon her in her sore straits' have compromised somewhat. Whether or not we should understand מצרים as 'narrow places' or 'borders' does not bother Joüon who is convinced that the Masoretes etc. have got it wrong, and that we should vocalize המצרים ('the Egyptians') which is the identification of גוים earlier in the passage. 'Notre "lamentation" suppose la situation historique décrite dans Jér 4.11ff.: les Judéens réfugiés en Egypte sont menacés, par le prophète, du *glaive* et d'autres fléaux (vv. 12, 27). Lam 1.3 parle des Judéens qui ne pouvant supporter la misère qui suivit la ruine de Jérusalem préfèrent s'exiler en Egypte: "Juda s'est exilée pour fuir l'oppression et l'excès de la servitude; elle s'est établie parmi les nations, mais sans y trouver le repos; tous ses persécuteurs l'ont atteinte chez les Egyptiens."'[32]

Conclusion

As has been said already the various problems in this passage are all inter-related, with the result that one can easily find oneself arguing in a circle. Is the author describing more than one category of the people of Judah? Are those who have gone into exile the same as those overtaken by their pursuers? Is he describing different aspects of the desolate situation after the fall of Jerusalem? Is it a reference to three different categories: 'the captured', 'those fled to Moab, etc.' and those caught while escaping'?

There is no doubt that the Babylonian exile was a watershed in the history of Israel; the terms 'pre-exilic' and 'post-exilic' are evidence of that. And because of the importance of this exilic experience for the people of Judah, especially those who were taken captive to Babylon, the terms גולה and גלות which probably, in pre-exilic times, had the general meaning 'exile' or 'exiles', came to refer almost exclusively to the Babylonian captivity. The fact that the Chronicler, describing 587 BC, could omit any reference to fleeing to Egypt, etc, any mention of Gedaliah or indeed any life in Palestine after that date (2 Chron. 36.20) ensured that 'exile' implied 'Babylon';. and when the LXX translators began their work on the 'Prophets' these terms could be rendered μετοικεσία or αἰχμαλωσία, and the verb גלה might be rendered at times in such a way as to obscure its more general meaning.

· It is, therefore, in this early period that the exegesis of this verse begins to be in danger. The ambiguity of the passage, the tense of the verbal forms, the function of מן, the lack of clarity in the allusions, the fact that we are dealing with poetry, not prose, and the consequent lack of confident translation in the Versions, have all contributed to the confusion.

It is the Vulgate which gives us the lead in the exegesis of this passage with its 'migravit Iuda'. Jerome, we know, kept the LXX at hand while translating from the Hebrew, and often was dependent on it, especially on difficult passages, but here he takes an independent stand. We do not know the date of the Peshitta Version of Lamentations. We do know that the Syriac translators were also prone to lean on the LXX especially when in difficulty; but here, we believe, the translator stands his ground, though it might be argued that his rendering remains ambiguous.

The influence of the LXX, however, was enormous, first in Greek-speaking Jewish communities and later among Christian scholars. The result was that its rendering μετῳκίσθη influenced the reader to interpret in terms of the Babylonian captivity.

Rashi is right to break free from this line of interpretation, as is Calvin: 'Interpreters apply this, but in my view improperly, to the captivity of the people; on the contrary, the prophet means that the Jews had been scattered and sought refuge when oppressed, as they were often, by the tyranny of their enemies . . .'[33]

But these words cannot be divorced from the rest of the first line, and those who try to do so (cf. above Kara and Houbigant) force from the passage a meaning which it does not readily bear. The earliest extant interpretation of this first statement is that of LXX which, we suggest, should be translated: 'Judah is taken into exile (or 'forced into exile') from her affliction and from her great servitude'. While we have disagreed with the rendering of גלתה יהודה and while we may question the appearance of αὐτῆς here, the interpretation of מן as 'local' is that which most naturally fits the context. This has been followed by Peshitta. The alternatives open to the people of Judah, or what was left of them, were not attractive. They could either remain at home and be subject to the oppression of the Babylonian occupying power or go into exile in Egypt, Moab, Edom, etc. Hence it could be said that the great many who fled the country did so because of conditions at home which were intolerable, and because they felt that life in exile might just be more bearable. Because, in this instance, the 'movement from' and the 'reason for' are so closely related, the possibility of exegesis on the basis of מן causal was there from the beginning; hence the Vulgate 'propter afflictionem et multitudinem servitutis', which interpretation has had its adherents throughout the history of exegesis.[34]

The fact that the author of Lamentations also discussed the reasons for the disasters of 597 and 587, drawing attention to the sins of the nation and depicting Yahweh as punishing the people in this way (cf. 1.5, 8 etc.), coupled with the subsequent reflection on the cause of the disaster in the light of prophetic statements (cf. Jer. 34 etc.), led exegetes (especially those who would take גלה to be a reference to the Babylonian exile) to interpret the מן as introducing the cause of the disaster, the reason for the punishment. This interpretation of the causal מן need not have replaced the former but might have existed side by side with it.[35]

The subsequent lack of interest among Jewish and Christian scholars in those left behind in Palestine in 587 BC, and the rather exaggerated language used to describe the plight of the exiles in Babylon (cf. Is. 42.22; 47.6f.; Ps. 137.1), were further factors in deflecting attention away from the correct understanding of מן in this passage.

In spite of what Rudolph and Hillers say about the rest of the verse, it is unnatural to interpret these words of the pre-exilic period. 'She dwells among the nations and finds no rest' is a statement by the author that Yahweh has indeed carried out his threat.[36]

There is turmoil and unease in this verse, wherever we look. The people leave their land, when they experience affliction and hard service, to find a less intolerable existence among the nations, but it is an undesirable life which they encounter there. Any equanimity suggested by the verb ישב is negated by the words which follow 'she finds no rest';[37] and the final line depicts fugitives who cannot even put their intended goal (of exile) to the test. Consequently we feel that the final line is not to be interpreted as though we were dealing with a Hebrew idiom for general adversity (cf. Luther, NEB, etc.) but as language describing the scattered fugitives being run to ground. While it may be attractive to read the later meaning 'borders' into מצרים and to picture the fugitives being overtaken as they leave the borders of Judah, it is best to understand the word as narrow place or pass.

'Judah has gone into exile from affliction and harsh service; She sits among the nations but finds no rest; All her pursuers run her to ground in the narrow passes.'

It is both an honour and a pleasure to contribute to this volume. Professor McKane's keen interest in the exegesis of the Hebrew Bible and in the history of interpretation has placed us in his debt.

NOTES

1. D.R. Hillers, *Lamentations* (Anchor Bible), New York: Doubleday and Company, 1972, xix; cf. also P.R. Ackroyd, *Exile and Restoration*, London, 1968, 45.

2. W. Rudolph, *Das Buch Ruth, Das Hohe Lied, Die Klagelieder* (KAT 17), 1-3, Gütersloh, 1962, 193, and on chapter 1.

3. B. Albrektson, *Studies in the Text and Theology of the Book of Lamentations* (STL, 21), Lund, 1963, 57.

4. R.P. Smith, *Thesaurus Syriacus*, Oxford, 1901, 718.

5. J. Nacht (ed.), *Tobia ben Eliesers Commentar zu Threni*, Berlin, 1985.

6. A. Jellinek, *Commentarien zu Esther, Ruth und den Klageliedern*, Leipzig, 1855, 36; C.F. Houbigant, *Biblia Hebraica cum Notis Criticis et Versione Latina ad Notas Criticas Facta*, 1753, Vol. 4, 367, 369; cf. also J.H. Pareau, *Threni Jeremiae; Philologice et Critice Illustrati*, 1790, 65, 91.

7. E. Henderson, *The Book of the Prophet Jeremiah and that of the The Lamentations*, London, 1851, 280.

8. M. Dahood, 'New Readings in Lamentations', *Biblica* 59 (1978), 175. It would be interesting to know what Coverdale had in mind with his: 'Juda is taken prisoner because she was defiled'.

9. E. Levine, *The Aramaic Version of Lamentations*, New York, 1976, 83.

10. *Op. cit.*, 57.

11. T. Meek, 'Lamentations', in *The Interpreter's Bible*, vol. VI, 7.

12. R. Gordis, 'A Commentary on the Text of Lamentations', *JQR* (1967), 273 (The 75th Anniversary Volume).

13. *Op. cit.*, 212.

14. H.J. Kraus, *Klagelieder* (BKAT), 1956, 16, 22.

15. *Op. cit.*, 6f.

16. I.e. the category which takes 'because of affliction . . . ' to refer to that experienced by the Jews.

17. H. Broughton, *The Lamentations of Jeremy*, 1608,. *ad loc.*

18. *Op. cit.*, 1; cf. his remarks on 7.

19. W.J. Fuerst, *The Books of Ruth, Esther, Ecclesiastes, The Song of Songs, Lamentations*, Cambridge, 1975, 217.

20. *Op. cit.*, 57.

21. *Biblia Sacra, Polyglotta Bagsteriana*, London, 1831, *ad loc.*

22. *Op. cit.*, 273.

23. *Op. cit.*, 83f. Gordis might have referred to Tobia ben Elieser's comments on this verse. The latter says, among other things, that we should understand the construction as though it were written בעני. In this connection he cites Lev. 8.32 where בבשר and בלחם must be understood as though written מבשר and מלחם. *Op. cit.*, 6.

24. Rudolph's translation 'Es sitzt unter den Völkern, ohne Ruhe zu finden' differs in tense from that of Hillers because the former understands these pronouns to apply to the situation just before 587 BC. It is his view that the first chapter was written between 597 and 587.

25. *Op. cit.*, 224.

26. *Op. cit.*, 7.

27. Translations which interpret רדף as 'persecute' lose something of this imagery; see AV, NEB etc. The author of Lamentations uses this imagery in two other passages, *viz.* 1.6 and 4.19, to describe the plight of the people after defeat, and it is possible this is a similar allusion. The picture may be an elucidation of 'finding no rest': those who are their enemies seek them out and make life difficult.

28. Cf. Levine, *op.cit.*, 84 n. 5.

29. These last two interpretations of Rashi are present also in Qoheleth Rabbah.

30. Migne, *Patrologia Latina*, vol. 175, 262.

31. J. Calvin, *Commentaries on the Book of the Prophet Jeremiah and the Lamentations* (Translated from the Latin by J. Owen), Edinburgh, 1855, 308.

32. P.P. Joüon, 'Etudes de Philologie Sémitique', *Mélanges de la Faculté Orientale*, 6, Université Saint-Joseph, Beyrouth, 1913, 209. It is interesting to note that this suggestion of Joüon is the first in the history of exegesis. The absence of such a proposal before the twentieth century probably shows that the traditional understanding of the passage—that it referred to the Babylonian captivity—was so strong that 'Egyptians' would have been an unacceptable intrusion.

33. *Op.cit.*, 306. It is interesting to note here Luther's 'Juda ist gefangen . . . ' and to observe that both interpretations are held by scholars today.

34. 'Judah has gone into exile because of misery and harsh oppression.' *The Writings: A New Translation of the Holy Scriptures*, Philadelphia, 1982, 363.

35. It is true that in the midrashic collections the only interpretation of the preposition was that which lists the various sins of the people as the causes for the exile, but in the Targum, while the latter is the main line of exegesis, we may detect another slant on מן in the words ולא אשכחת נייח מפולחנא קשיא דשעבידו יתה.

36. Cf. Deut. 4.27; 28.64f; Jer. 9.15 etc.

37. It is perhaps best to translate ישבה as 'she sits' (cf. Rudolph: 'Es sitzt'; *op.cit.*, 204); 'dwells' and 'settles' have too cosy a connotation.

THE GREAT TREE OF DANIEL 4

Peter W. Coxon

University of St. Andrews

> Behold this troubled tree,
> Complaining as it sways and plies;
> It is the limb of thee.
> ('The Wind Blew Words'—T. Hardy)

Symmetrical patterns of imagery and motif mark the opening chapters of the Aramaic Court Tales of the book of Daniel. The central character in the narratives is Nebuchadnezzar, conqueror of Jerusalem and king of Babylonia and, as head of the Babylonian empire, at the apogee of his career. The apocalyptic imagination of the author of the tales is stirred by the famous empire builder and inspires him to piece together a magnificent prophetic fresco. In chapter 2 Nebuchadnezzar sees in a vision 'a colossal statue ... of exceeding brightness' which unexpectedly keels over when struck on the feet by a stone 'cut out by no human hand'. Possibly inspired by the drama of this vision and certainly flattered that he figured in it as the head of fine gold, Nebuchadnezzar himself, in chapter 3, constructs a statue of gold some sixty cubits high and six cubits broad and erects it 'in the plain of Dura, in the state of Babylon'. In chapter 4 plastic images give way to Nebuchadnezzar's vision of a huge cosmic tree which heaved up from the earth until 'its top reached to heaven and it could be seen from the furthest ends of the whole earth'. In the first and third episodes Daniel appears as statesman and wise man superbly equipped with necessary skills to reveal the uncommon significance of the visions. The intervening episode finds Daniel's three diplomatic colleagues defying the idolatrous *fiat* of the king. But Nebuchadnezzar always remains the central figure and is the catalyst that actively provokes the enunciation of divine oracles.

The figure of Nebuchadnezzar is of central importance because the author subsumes under him not only the entire neo-Babylonian empire but all pagan empires which precede the messianic age. The role of Nebuchadnezzar as king of *Babylon* in the narrative is of seminal importance in that it presupposes a connection between the incident of the tower of Babel and the fall of Jerusalem. The story of Babel in the book of Genesis recorded the paradigmatic defeat of Babylon at the beginning of human history. Now it would appear that the capture of Jerusalem and burning of the temple by Nebuchadnezzar represented a traumatic reversal of that event. The nations once 'scattered abroad upon the face of the whole earth' (Gen. 11.4, 8) with the subsequent confusion and fragmentation of languages (Gen. 11.7) are regathered into the harmonious empire of the king of Babylon. 'All peoples, nations and languages that dwell on the earth' (Dan. 4.1) are brought under his sceptre and the resurgence of Babel seems to have been achieved. But the human Nebuchadnezzar is destined, like the early tower of Babel, to be a crass casualty of time, and an episode of past history becomes the starting point of a detailed panorama to be acted out in the person of the Babylonian king which will detail his fall and fierce ordeal.

At rest in his house and 'flourishing in his palace' a second dream came to trouble him, a dream of a great tree, in which was food for all, and 'the beasts of the field had shade beneath it, and the birds of the heaven dwelt in the boughs thereof'; and then the tree was hewn down, save 'the stump of its roots in the earth'. Daniel interpreted the meaning of the dream and foretold that the king would be mad until 'seven times' had passed. At the end of twelve months Nebuchadnezzar walked through the spacious apartments of his palace, his breast swelled with the consciousness of his own power and achievements. There, below the galleries of his palace, lay Babylon, encircled by its ditched wall and intersected by its great canal. There stood the temples, chief of which was the mighty edifice of Esagila, dedicated to Marduk; and well he knew that each brick used in these stupendous erections had received upon it, in indelible cuneiform markings, the impress of his own illustrious name. And he spoke to himself and said: 'Is not this great Babylon that I have built for the house of my kingdom by the might of my power, and for the honour of my majesty?' His words and vain, babbling reflections floated out over the golden lintels and up through the clear atmosphere of the Babylonian sky, until they came to the hearing of God. And the attention of the Ancient of Days was arrested, and he knew that the Chaldean king was forgetting the limitations, the prescriptions that are set about the earth's inhabitants, and in his wrath he sent insanity upon the king, and he was driven from men that same hour, 'and did eat grass like the oxen, and his body was wet with the dew of heaven, till his hair was grown like eagles' feathers, and his nails like birds' claws and his dwelling was with the wild animals'.

Attempts have been made to find an origin in history[1] for this brilliant apocalyptic story. It seems to me that there is no sound historical basis for them. What is known of Nebuchadnezzar's reign does not admit an episode of this gravity. Forgetting that the author of Daniel is not trying to write history, exegetes have been tempted to explain the origin of the tradition of Nebuchadnezzar's so-called lycanthropy in the strange behaviour of Nabonidus (555–529 BC) the last Babylonian king. A. Lacocque even suggests that the text entitled 'The Prayer of Nabonidus' (4QPrNab) found at Qumran, which contains a description of the king's illness, is a literary source for Dan. 4.[2] L. Hartmann and A.A. Di Lella, on the other hand, argue that there is 'no literary dependence of one story on the other' and that the most that can be posited is that both traditions 'go back to an early folk tale first transmitted in oral form'.[3] A detailed discussion of the problem cannot be undertaken here. However, it must be kept in mind that Dan. 4 is a midrashic composition and as such draws richly on Old Testament literary material and with respect to the tree poem particularly the imagery of Ezek. 31.2-9 and Is. 6.13. Ezekiel's 'parable of the cedar' is appropriated and skilfully welded into a moral tale in no way inferior to those of the magnificent statue of Nebuchadnezzar's first dream (ch. 2), the ordeal of the furnace of burning fire (ch. 3) or the end of Belshazzar (ch. 5). The writer attempts in the manner of the author of the visions in the book of Enoch to depict symbolically the transformation of the world's most powerful human figure into an animal. But if historical foundation for the story is questionable, local colour is certainly present in the parody of the heavy plastic images of Mesopotamian state religion. The ridiculous tableau of the great king on all fours, fed like a bull in a stall, recalls the colossal human-headed royal bulls (and lions) representing divine genii which guarded the great palaces of Khorsabad, Kalḫu, Nineveh and Susa and whose type was propagated throughout the Orient.[4] The transformation and degradation of the king carries with it overtones of monotheistic contempt.

Hellenistic number speculation may have prompted the author to accommodate Nebuchadnezzar's recovery after 'seven times' שבעין עדנין. According to Aristobulus (early 2nd century BC) it is by the principle of the number seven that 'the whole cosmos, with its animals and plants, is moved'.[5] Most interpreters equate the seven periods with seven years,[6] but unless there is a deliberate vagueness in the time span, and this would be in line with the apocalyptic genre, it seems best to see in the number a symbol of the educative process which brought about Nebuchadnezzar's recognition of a divinely approved cosmic order.[7] It is also possible to see here an ironic connection with 3.19. The king who gave the brutal order to heat the furnace 'seven times more than it was wont to be heated' himself becomes the object of a punishment that will last for 'seven times'.

The remarkable conclusion of the narrative in Dan. 4 is the restoration to the king of his royal splendour 'for the glory of my kingdom' (4.33). His former glory made him supreme ruler of the world and sustainer of mankind, but his new position will be entirely different. Hitherto his hubris has made him a symbol of the proud humanity of Babel but now his chastened experience will enable him to become a symbol of the new humanity ready to receive the 'man-like figure' to whom is promised the messianic kingdom. Again it is the exilic prophet Ezekiel who seems to exert an influence on the author of Daniel in the poetic lines which celebrate the re-establishment of the great tree (Ezek. 17.22-24).

Some observations can be made on the literary and mythic background of the description of the great tree in Dan. 4 and the ways in which the author has re-deployed his material for his own purposes. This exercise will start with a brief survey of tree imagery in the Old Testament and will lead into a re-assessment of the tree as a symbol of Nebuchadnezzar, especially when it concerns his restored status at the close of the narrative. In Gen. 2, in the earlier of the two creation stories, after the creation of man the Lord God

> planted a garden in Eden . . . and out of the ground the LORD God make to grow every tree that is pleasant to the sight and good for food, the tree of life also in the midst of the garden, and the tree of the knowledge of good and evil (2.8-9, RSV).

The garden of paradise was lost to man forever when he raided rather than guarded the trees under his charge. The Psalmist suggests that a measure of that primeval bliss could be regained by the man who devoted himself to the study of the Torah:

> He is like a tree
> planted by streams of water,
> that yields its fruit in season . . . (Ps. 1.3, RSV).

Jeremiah reiterates the thought:

> Blessed is the man who trusts in the LORD . . .
> He is like a tree planted by water,
> that sends out its roots by the stream,
> and does not fear when the heat comes
> for its leaves remain green,
> . . . it does not cease to bear fruit (Jer. 17.7-8, RSV).

The preciousness of wisdom is such that she is a 'tree of life' to those who are fortunate enough to locate her and 'lay hold of her' (Prov. 3.18; see also 11.30, 13.12 and 15.4). In Pss. 52 and 92 the righteous man lays claim to be or is likened to three different kinds of tree: a 'green olive' (52.8), a 'palm tree' and a 'cedar in Lebanon' (92.12). The coy maiden of the Song of Songs responds to the tender solicitations of her lover by telling him how special he is:

> As an apple tree among the trees of the wood
> so is my beloved among young men (Cant. 2.3, RSV).

The base pretentions of Abimelech to kingship in the premonarchical period are measured in the delightful plant fable of Judg. 9.8-15 in which the olive tree, the fig tree and the vine recognize their proper function in the natural order by turning down the trees' request to reign over them. The sardonic bramble has conditions of its own if it is to reign:

> If in good faith you are anointing me king over you, then come and
> take refuge in my shade; but if not, let fire come out of the bramble
> and devour the cedars of Lebanon (Judg. 9.15, RSV).

In the last chapters of the book of Isaiah the creation of new heavens and a new earth holds the promise of vigorous growth for the redeemed Israelites:

> like the days of a tree shall the days of my people be . . .(Is. 65.22, RSV).

Even the foreigner and the eunuch, provided they keep justice and do righteousness, will be included in the programme of salvation, and the eunuch will need no longer lament:

> Behold, I am a dry tree. (Is. 56.3, RSV).

Examples like these could be multiplied, but suffice it to mention one more example where human societies are compared to trees. It is a poem that has already been mentioned in connection with Dan. 4

and may be confidently regarded as one of the author's sources. At the close of Ezek. 17 Israel, after many vicissitudes, is vindicated and grows robustly like a cedar tree on a high mountain. Surrounding nations acknowledge the authoritative plan of the Lord God that has accomplished this:

> All the trees of the country-side will know
> that it is I, the LORD,
> who bring low the tall tree
> and raise the low tree high,
> who dry up the green tree
> and make the dry tree put forth buds.
> I, the LORD, have spoken and will do it (Ezek. 17.24, NEB).

From this sample of quotations we can safely deduce that the readers of the great tree narrative in Dan. 4 were thoroughly acquainted with a whole range of images, metaphors, similes, fables, parables and proverbs connected with trees.

The literary form of the chapter is unique in the book inasmuch as it is cast in the form of an official letter. It has the standard mode of address (3.31-33) designating the sender (Nebuchadnezzar), the addressees (all the nations), a greeting ('may all prosperity be yours!') followed by the bulk of the chapter which describes the king's dream, its effects and interpretation (4.1-33) and finally a conclusion (4.34) in which Nebuchadnezzar gives thanks to God and reiterates his introductory utterance. The grandiose salutation sets the tone of the piece and sets in motion the theme of universal sovereignty: 'King Nebuchadnezzar to all peoples and nations of every langue living on all the earth.' The Babylonian monarch seems to have absorbed the lesson of his earlier dream of the composite image (ch. 2) when he had been relieved to discover that despite the ultimate fate of the image, as the head of gold he was destined to live long and prosperously with no diminution of his power and authority as undisputed ruler of the Babylonian empire. Had not the Jewish prophet vindicated his position by declaring that the God of Heaven had placed under his hand 'men and beasts and the birds of the air, wherever they dwell' (2.38)? All seemed well with the king and his household. For the moment there were no signs of revolt in the empire and no military reversals to disturb the peace of the realm.

But the narrator succeeds in casting a shadow across Nebuchadnezzar's path even before his dream experience. The king declares

that he was 'living peacefully at home in the luxury of (his) palace'
(4.1 NEB). The word translated 'luxury' is a loan-word from Hebrew
רענן, an adjective meaning 'green, luxuriant, fresh', commonly used
of the foliage of trees (see, e.g. Hos. 14.8) and in the recurring phrase
תחת כל עץ רענן 'under every green tree', which alludes to sites where
the Israelites indulged in idolatrous rites. D. Winton Thomas has
argued that רען when used of trees or leaves and branches does not
mean 'green' but rather 'thick with leaves, luxuriant'.[8] He draws
support for this view from the evidence provided by the ancient
versions and a proposed new derivation from a root cognate with
Arabic *lġn* which means 'was tangled' (of plants), and in the eleventh
form *'iġġā'nna* 'was long and twisted' (of plants). Just as trees can be
described as 'flourishing', so too in a figurative sense persons share
this condition.

S. Morag prefers to adopt an etymology originally suggested by A.
Schultens (*Liber Jobi*, 1737, 391) which sees in רענן the Arabic root
r'n the meaning of which is 'to be foolish, weakminded' but which
also contains the idea of 'height', 'tallness' (cf. *r'n* 'the peak of a
mountain').[9] This etymology makes good sense and has the advantage
of dispensing with the need to interchange *r* and *l*. If accepted, we
must reckon with a semantic connection between mental (or moral)
traits and physical features which is characteristic of some Semitic
roots. In accordance with this interpretation עץ רענן means 'a tall,
lofty tree', and, when used figuratively, the adjective means 'luxuriant,
strong'. In the context of the Aramaic story רענן describes Nebuchadnezzar's condition as either 'flourishing, prosperous' or 'strong',
'luxuriant'. Morag's derivation is particularly suggestive in view of
the polar contrast in the narrative of the king's 'height' of prosperity
and the bleak condition of 'foolishness' to which he is reduced.

I am not suggesting that the author is playing on the etymological
permutations of רענן which Morag exploits, but it does seem to me
that the term is purposefully deployed in the king's opening speech to
signal a subtle connection with the subject of his dream and that in
the literary structure of the chapter he does achieve an effective
double-entendre. In chapter 2 Nebuchadnezzar had a dream which he
could not recollect when he awoke. In chapter 4 he dreamt again but
on this occasion remembered the dream in every detail. His own
Babylonian professional dream-interpreters and exorcists were unable
to make sense of the dream when he related it to them, and thus the
way is prepared for Daniel, who is now entitled 'chief of the dream-

interpreters', to live up to the brilliant reputation he had acquired earlier in the king's reign.

The first nine verses of the chapter show considerable skill in narrative composition. The content of the vision is not disclosed until v. 7, thus maintaining the tension and momentum of the drama up to the arrival of Daniel. The vision itself is divided into two parts (vv. 7-9, 10b-14), and there is some evidence that they are related but distinctive visionary experiences (NEB translates the intervening v. 10a 'Here is another vision which came into my head . . . '). The first part describes the awesome aspect of the great tree. It can, of course, be taken as a clear paradigm of the sin of pride (cp. ' . . . its top reached to heaven' and ' . . . its top in the heavens' of the tower of Babel in Gen. 11.4), although Daniel does not press this home in the interpretation, which lacks the kind of exegetical pinpointing of the king's condition exemplified in the second part of the vision. Daniel reiterates Nebuchadnezzar's account and identifies the tree ('The tree which you saw grow . . . refers to you') and its meaning:

> You have grown and become strong. Your might has grown so much that it reaches to the heavens; your sovereignty stretches to the ends of the earth (v. 17).

Nebuchadnezzar has not so much exceeded the brief of universal governance granted to him by the Most High as he has allowed himself to be tinctured by the sin of human pride. The heights of power had made him lose his head. The Hebrew scriptures had grudgingly conceded that he was a very special person and had played a God-given role in the harsh education of the people of Judah. Jeremiah had the task of communicating the oracle of the Lord of Hosts to Zedekiah, king of Judah:

> I made the earth with my great strength and with outstretched arm, I made man and beast on the face of the earth, and I give it to whom I see fit. I now give all these lands to my servant Nebuchadnezzar, king of Babylon, and I give him also all the beasts of the field to serve him. All nations shall serve him . . . If any nation or kingdom will not serve Nebuchadnezzar king of Babylon or submit to his yoke, I will punish them . . . (27.5-8, NEB).

The dream indicates that there were beneficial aspects to Nebuchadnezzar's sovereignty. The height and sturdiness of the tree served only to benefit the rest of creation. It gave shelter and protection to wild animals, birds were secure in its branches and from it 'all living beings found nourishment' (v. 9). The tree buttressed nature in all its functions. Taken with the confession in 3.3, in which Nebuchadnezzar acknowledged the over-arching sovereignty of the Most High, the picture of the life-enhancing tree, as in Ezek. 31.3-9, is a positive one and finds harmonious parallels in the Psalms (52.10; 92.12-14).

The sequel to the first scene comes in a further vision (vv. 10bff.), and on this occasion Nebuchadnezzar sees a heavenly visitant, 'a watcher, a holy one', coming down from heaven with the order to devastate the great tree. In the process it is severely pollarded, its branches are lopped off, its foliage stripped away and its fruit scattered. The creatures used to its shelter and provision are startled and bolt from the spot. The final instruction is something of a reprieve in that the destructive process, though severe, falls short of the total destruction meted out to the cedar in Ezek. 31.10-18:

> But leave the stump of its roots in the earth, with a band of iron and bronze, in the grass of the field (v. 12).

A curious feature in the development of the vision is the abrupt shift from the symbol to what is symbolized in vv. 13ff. The change is less readily recognized in the original text because in Aramaic the word for 'tree' is masculine. Thus the purposeful alteration of 'it' to 'him' in v. 13 is not evident in Aramaic, where consistency would expect 'let *it* be wet with dew' referring to the tree rather than 'let *him* be wet with dew' referring to Nebuchadnezzar. To my mind the change, which does have parallels elsewhere (cf. Is. 5.1ff. where the owner of the vineyard, who is spoken of in the third person in vv. 1-2, becomes God who speaks in the first person in vv. 3ff.), is not a smooth one here. It involves a complete change of metaphor in that the king, who has been identified with the tree, is now coupled with one of the animals which had used it as a shelter. The author shifts from the great tree parable to a fable which will more readily reflect the king's mental and physical deterioration, madness and despair. It could be argued that the line which describes the change of mind (Aram. 'heart') is secondary, tacked on to the verse composition to identify with greater precision the miserable fate of Nebuchadnezzar. This element in the prose account of the dream in v. 20 ('Let his mind cease to be a man's mind, and let him be given the mind of a beast') has no counterpart in v. 13a, and neither is the metrically burdensome בעשב ארעי at the end of v. 12b retold in v. 20b. Without these accretions one is left with an account which throughout is consistent with tree imagery:

> . . . leave the stump of its root in the earth, with a band of iron and
> bronze, in the grass of the field; and let it be wet with the dew of
> heaven and let its lot be with the beasts of the field, until seven
> times pass over it.

The 3rd person of the verb and the 3rd pers. suffix will then naturally
refer to the stump of the tree and not as in the EVV be personalized in
the light of v. 13a. Furthermore in the three other accounts (vv. 22,
29, 30) there is no precise equivalent to v. 13a; in the next chapter
only, when Belshazzar is reminded of the event, is the detail of the
change of mind picked up (see 5.21). But these arguments are not
compelling. The difference of wording in the various accounts has
nothing to do with any supposed textual dislocation in the text and is
entirely consonant with the writer's technique in the Court Tales. By
using abbreviations, exploiting the range of synonyms in the language
or simply by judicious modification or expansion of details he rings
subtle changes in the presentation of the tree oracle (cp. 4.12-13, 20,
22, 29, 30; 5.21). A nice example is in 4.30 where in the place of the
prosaic 'until seven times' (vv. 13, 20, 22, 29) one finds 'until his hair
grew like eagles' and his nails like birds''. An omitted detail may be
noted in 4.29 which is the only account not to mention the king's
saturation with the dew of heaven, although this verse, in line with
vv. 22, 30 and 5.21 presupposes the existence of the apparently extra-
metrical בעשב ארעא of the original verse account.

What the author of Dan. 4 has succeeded in doing is to weld
together the well-known myth of the cosmic tree/tree of life, a fitting
symbol of the pride and power of the Babylonian monarch, and the
picture of a shaggy beast-like creature, itself a symbol of humiliation
and despair. In the Syriac version of the *Legend of Aḥiqar* the hero
laments his fall from the favour of Sennacherib, king of the Assyrians:
' . . . the hair of my head had grown down my shoulders and my
beard reached my breast; and my body was foul with the dust and my
nails were grown long like eagles''.[10] The parallelism between the
two passages is quite remarkable and may suggest an acquaintance
on the part of the writer of the Court Tales of Daniel with the
traditional stories and folk tales current in international wisdom
literature. More certain is the background material on Nebuchadnezzar
in prophetic tradition and especially the passage in Jeremiah (27.4-8)
which guaranteed Nebuchadnezzar hegemony over the beasts of the
field. The midrash of Dan. 4 mischievously turns the tables on the
proud king, who is taught a lesson in humility by becoming a 'beast'.

The theme is one of order in the created scheme of things. However great, the human king must concede that only the Most High is sovereign in the kingdom of men and awards it to whom he will.

The response of Nebuchadnezzar to Daniel's discourse is not recorded. A small dramatic touch characteristic of the folk-tale may be noted: the blow that fells Nebuchadnezzar is not immediate but comes a whole year later and is paralleled by the restitution of the first person in the narrative. The change of person is, in fact, carefully charted throughout the story. Imitating the pompous style of the Assyrian and Babylonian royal inscriptions, the first fifteen verses contain the royal address and the directives to the dream-interpreters and Daniel and are composed in the first person. As the details of Nebuchadnezzar's fate are unfolded the focus of attention and authority moves to Daniel. The third person replaces the first, and the king assures him that he can speak freely in the royal presence ('the king said, Do not let the dream and its meaning frighten you' v. 16). A description of Nebuchadnezzar's miserable condition continues in the third person ('He was expelled... his body was bathed in dew...' v. 30), but then the final scene of the story is marked by an abrupt return to the first ('At the end of the appointed time I, Nebuchadnezzar, raised my eyes to heaven...' v. 33) and marks Nebuchadnezzar's restoration to sanity. His confession in v. 31:

> His sovereignty is an everlasting sovereignty
> his reign endures for ages and ages.

forms a poetic *inclusio* (with chiasmus) with 3.33:

> His reign is an everlasting reign,
> his sovereignty endures for ages and ages.

The subject of the great tree which Nebuchadnezzar saw in his vision has an interesting background and is made up of elements drawn from different sources. A number of passages in the Old Testament make use of it as a metaphor of powerful kings but nowhere more persuasively than in the book of Ezekiel. In Ezek. 17 Nebuchadnezzar is an eagle, and the cedar-tree represents the royal house of Judah with its top the young king Jehoiachin who was deported to Babylon (v. 4). The lowly vine planted by the eagle is the regent Zedekiah (v. 5), who is destined to be cut down (v. 9), but Yahweh replants a slip from the lofty crown of the cedar-tree on a tall

mountain (v. 22). There it will thrive and symbolize Judah's universal
prosperity and might:

> It will put out branches, bear its fruit,
> and become a noble cedar.
> Winged birds of every kind will roost under it,
> they will roost in the shelter of its sweeping boughs.
> All the trees of the country-side will know
> that it is I, the LORD,
> who bring low the tall tree
> and raise the low tree high,
> who dry up the green tree
> and make the dry tree put forth buds (17.23-24, *NEB*).

Much closer affinity to Dan. 4 is found in Ezek. 31, which
describes the downfall of Pharaoh king of Egypt, represented by a
stately cedar tree. The author picks up the major theme of this tree
and weaves it into his own midrashic tapestry.[11] The chapter
consists of a poem (vv. 2b-9) and two prose interpretations (vv. 10-14
and 15-18). The prophet finds a prototype of Pharaoh's arrogance
(v. 2) in the absolute autocracy of Assyria which in its heyday was a
'cedar in Lebanon' (v. 3). The strong mythological overtones of the
imagery in the secular poem broaden the picture out to one of a great
cosmic tree whose roots tapped the depths of the subterranean
waters. As in Nebuchadnezzar's vision of the great tree, no pejorative
note is struck in the poem. It towers high but compensates for this in
giving its shade beneficently to mankind (v. 6). The poet reiterates
that it owed its splendour to the life-giving waters of the nether-world
(vv. 4, 7). The incomparable nature of the tree gave it a paradisal
quality (v. 8).

There is general agreement among scholars[12] however, that a
secondary element is introduced in v. 9 which constitutes a theological
qualification to the description of the tree's beauty. 'I, the Lord made
it beautiful' counter-balances v. 7, where the tree's propensities are
associated with life-giving waters. The intrusion is a clumsy one,
since it introduces a Yahweh speech in the first person. The original
poem ended with a reference to the jealousy of the other trees in the
paradisal park, generated by the cedar's outstanding beauty.

The extent of the dependence of the author of Dan. 4 on the
Ezekiel passage may be seen in the appropriation of the major theme
(great height, impressive appearance and universal dominance of the
tree) and in the borrowing of several of the details, as for instance the

picture of the birds at home in the branches and the shelter provided for the animals underneath. There are interesting differences— although the Ezekiel poem introduces the impressive context of Eden as the site of the tree, it stands there solely as an object of grandeur. Dan. 4 in this respect is closer to the primeval Eden myth of Gen. 3 in stressing the tree's abundant food supply ('its fruit was abundant providing food for all' v. 12). The description in Daniel is shorter and less elaborate in its mythological ornamentation. The fate of the tree is also part of Nebuchadnezzar's vision and forms a poetic whole in the chapter. The fate of the tree in Ezekiel is unheralded in the secular poem and forms the substance of the two interpretations spelled out in prose. These are cast in the form of divine oracles introduced by the formula 'Thus has the Lord God said' (vv. 10, 15). In the first interpretation, v. 3 is repeated and made the basis for the ensuing indictment. As in Daniel, the cutting down of the tree is symbolic of the inevitable fall which follows the sin of human pride (cp. Dan. 4.11, 20 and Ezek. 31.10ff.). But in Ezekiel no celestial intermediary acts as a messenger; the word of the Lord God is direct and decisive: 'I have given it over to a prince of the nations' (v. 11). The past tense of the lament is used here, and the injunction anticipates complete disaster for the tree (v. 11b is best taken as a secondary addition; it spells out in pedestrian fashion that the arch-sinner Pharaoh will receive the punishment he deserves). The tree is felled and savaged. Its humiliation is complete when the streams which formerly gave it strength lap by unconcerned, and, like a corpse, the giant tree is trampled down by wild animals and settled on by birds of the sky.[13]

In the second interpretation the fall of the tree is accommodated to the motif of the journey to the nether-world. It incorporates features from 28.1-19, where the myth of a primitive being expelled from Eden is taken up and applied to the king of Tyre. A typical prophetic proclamation of the fall of 'all that is proud and lofty' (Is. 2.12ff.) is joined to the myths of the Eden expulsion and the cosmic tree, and the great reservoirs of the tree's life-supporting waters are withheld by the divine *fiat* as the massive trunk rolls down into the nether-world. The animate forces of nature are stirred in sympathy:

> When it (i.e. the tree) went down to Sheol I made the deep mourn for it . . . On its account I dressed Lebanon in mourning, and on its account all the trees of the field fainted (v. 15).

While the nations on earth are in uproar, feelings of desolation sweep the trees of Eden; situated in the nether-world they are seen to share the fate of the great tree and are 'moved to pity'[14], a pall of sorrow covering them all.

In Dan. 4 and Ezek. 31 the writers identify the cosmic tree with powerful kings. Extra-biblical parallels are not lacking, and scholars have pointed to the dream of Astyages the Mede who, according to Herodotus,[15] saw a vine stock emerging from the stomach of his daughter Mandane and spreading over Asia. That vine was Cyrus. Xerxes also, in the course of military preparation against Greece, saw himself crowned with an olive slip which proliferated until it reached the ends of the earth.[16]

G. Widengren rightly points out that the biblical texts under consideration conflate themes from the cosmic tree and the tree of life, although these are usually distinguished in mythology.[17] In the secular poem of Ezek. 31 the cedar is without peer in the 'garden of God'. The second interpretation (vv. 15ff.) identifies the garden directly with Eden. In Dan. 4 the life-giving propensities of the tree ('it yielded food for all', v. 9) may reflect the same mythological association. The problem here is the extent to which one is prepared to accept the view that the myth of the cosmic tree/tree of life was adopted in Israel. Mythological language has a power of its own and can be used in texts (and especially in poetic texts) for metaphorical enrichment long after it has been detached from the myths which generated it. In common with the Swedish Uppsala School, Widengren (*ad loc.*) argued that Israel, together with her ancient neighbours, regarded the tree as a mythic-ritual symbol of both god and king. He assembled an impressive array of texts from the Mesopotamian area to support this idea, one of which may be cited as an example. The Sumerian King Urninurta is addressed thus in a royal hymn:

> O, chosen cedar, adornment of the yard of Ekur,
> Urninurta, for thy shadow the country may feel awe![18]

The king here is imagined to be the cultic tree growing in the temple precinct, the earthly equivalent of the mythological tree of life. The population is exhorted to be happy and confident in the feeling of awe for the mighty shadow of the divine ruler. Lacocque (*ad loc.*) feels that the human mind attributed to the tree in 4.13 seems to go in this direction. It expresses the close identification of the king with the tree and may be considered with a host of biblical passages in which the king is similarly symbolized as a mighty tree growing in the land.[19] The kind of metaphorical exploitation of the language of myth especially in poetic texts may well apply here, of course, and it could be argued that we are dealing with nothing more than simple metaphorical language of the kind seen in Jotham's fable. O. Plöger noted that when tree imagery is applied to foreign kings it implies their destruction.[20] This is certainly true in Ezek. 31 where the tree is cut down and mercilessly destroyed, but it is not true of Dan. 4 where the destructive process is limited. The stump of the tree is left in the ground with roots undisturbed. Exegetes have found the stump and the iron ring something of a puzzle. Because it occurs in the verse which witnesses the change from the metaphor of the tree to the person symbolized, it is felt that it refers directly to the demented king bound in irons. Rashi argues sensibly that the symbolism extends to the treatment of the king—he should not be removed despite his madness.

A curious feature in connection with the Mesopotamian tree of life and its important function in the temple cult is the fact that this tree is not a real one, but a cult tree, its trunk decorated with metal bands and fillets (Widengren, 7). It is conceivable, especially in view of the authentic Babylonian setting of the story, that the figure of the tree-stump and its metal band in our passage owes something to this phenomenon and preserves the memory of an old Babylonian cult symbol.[21] A comparable architectural design in the Jerusalem temple which may incorporate the image of the tree may be seen in the two free-standing bronze pillars Jachin and Boaz described and named in 1 Kgs 7.15-22. Although he is not prepared to say anything definite about the origin of the pillars, R.B.Y. Scott recognizes their importance in ceremonies in which the king played a central role.[22]

It has often struck me as strange that, although parallels have been drawn with other passages in the Old Testament which describe surviving tree-stumps, the evident potential of the symbol of a new tree emerging from the stump of the old in connection with Nebuchadnezzar has not been fully realized. Perhaps this is because the relevant texts concern Israel and centrifugalize hopes of survival and future existence for the chosen nation. The most notable context is found in the closing verses of Is. 6 where a note of hope follows Isaiah's gloomy forecast of Judah's fall:

Then I said, For how long, O Lord? And he said:

> Until cities lie waste without inhabitants . . .
> until the LORD removes men far away,
> and the land is completely desolate.
> Even if a tenth remains in it
> that too will be burned,
> like a terebinth or an oak which falls away from its *stump*
> (in these trees, the holy seed comes from the *stump*).[23]

Job's affirmation of God's power follows a similar tack, although here the terms are general and the writer does not have Israel in mind.

> For there is hope for a tree,
> if it be cut down, that it will sprout again,
> and that its shoots will not cease.
> Though its root grow old in the earth,
> and its *stump* die in the ground,
> yet at the scent of water it will bud
> and put forth branches like a young plant (14.7-9, RSV).

The Hebrew word for 'stump', גזע appears once more in one of Isaiah's messianic oracles. First divine intervention brings havoc on the nation:

> Behold, the Lord, the LORD of hosts
> will lop the boughs with terrifying power;
> the great in height will be hewn down,
> and the lofty will be brought low (10.33, RSV).

But the wreckage contains a stump, an embryo of potential growth which survives the severity of the chastisement:

> There shall come forth a shoot (חטר) from the stump (גזע) of Jesse,
> and a branch (נצר) shall grow out of his roots (שרשיו) (11.1, RSV).

Other passages deal with the related theme of a transplanted shoot from a lacerated or chopped down tree (see Ezek. 17.22ff.; Is. 61.3). The future king, the scion of David, is described as a 'branch' or 'shoot' from the great root-stock in Jeremiah:

> Behold, days are coming, says the LORD, when I will raise up for
> David a righteous shoot (צמח צדיק).[24]
> He shall rule as king and be successful,
> and shall execute justice and righteousness on earth (23.5)

—a sentiment echoed later in the book in prose:

In those days and at that time I shall
cause to shoot forth a righteous shoot (צמח צדקה) for David,
and he shall execute justice and righteousness on earth (33.15).

A suggestion of remission in the sentence of the celestial watcher
may be seen in the language he uses in Dan. 4.12 'leave (שבקו) the
stump with its roots in the ground'. That we are not dealing with
total abandonment is clear from a suggestive parallel in the so-called
Genesis Apocryphon, an Aramaic text found at Qumran. In the course
of recounting Abraham's wanderings, it describes how Abraham
experiences a premonition of danger shortly before entering Egypt:

> And I, Abram, had a dream in the night of my entering into the
> land of Egypt and I saw in my dream that there was a cedar, and a
> date-palm (which was) very beautiful; and some men came intend-
> ing to cut down and uproot the cedar, but *leave* (ולמשבוק) the date-
> palm by itself. Now the date-palm remonstrated and said, 'Do not
> cut down the cedar, for we are both from one family.' So the cedar
> was *spared* (ושביקו) with the help of the date-palm (1QapGen
> 19.14-16).

The elements of the dream appear to be based on Ps. 92.13, but our
interest lies in the use of the verb שבק in the positive sense of 'sparing,
leaving alive'. Similarly in Dan. 4 the stump of the tree is not left to
rot; it is 'spared, left alive', and the iron ring is secured for the
protection of the root-stock and will ensure its survival.

But the promise of survival does not mitigate the suffering and
humiliation symbolized in the axing of the tree; Nebuchadnezzar on
all fours eating grass like an ox remains a cosmic figure, even though
there may be a comic element in the portrayal. There is no trace of
comedy however in the tree imagery. On the contrary, in the light of
Is. 6.11f., 11.1f.; Job 14.7f., etc. I would argue that the hacked stump
is a potent symbol of the king's tormented spirit in addition to the
latent possibility of eventual resuscitation and regrowth. In Ezek. 31
the second mythological interpretation of the cosmic tree has the
trees reflecting on the gruesome spectacle confronting them in the
nether-world. The great Deep, together with the cedars of the
Lebanon range and all the trees of the field, 'mourned' and 'languished'
for the great tree (v. 15). All the trees of paradisal Eden 'were moved
to pity' (v. 16). In 4 Ezra (2 Esdras) we have evidence that eschatological tradition was familiar with the topos of the suffering tree:

> Blood shall trickle forth from trees ...
> and the people shall be troubled (5.5).

Classical sources know of trees containing the souls of the dead, which bleed and speak if broken. George Eliot refers to this tradition in a superb passage in *Felix Holt*:

> The poets have told us of a dolorous enchanted forest in the under-world. The thorn-bushes there, and the thick barked stems, have human histories hidden in them; the power of unuttered cries dwells in the passionless-seeming branches, and the red warm blood is darkly feeding the quivering nerves of a sleepless memory that watches through all dreams. These things are a parable.[25]

The poets she refers to are Virgil and Dante. In the *Aeneid* 3.22ff., Aeneas makes a propitiatory sacrifice to the gods before setting off on his voyage to Carthage. Cutting wood for the sacrifice he meets the strange sight of a myrtle tree shedding black drops of blood when ripped from the ground. It symbolized the tormented spirit of Polydorus who lay buried beneath. It was here that Dante found the basis for Canto XIII of the *Inferno*:

> Nessus had not yet reached the other side again when we set out through a wood which was not marred by any path. No green leaves, but of dusky hue; no smooth boughs, but knotted and warped ...
> Then I put out my hand a little and plucked a twig from a great thorn, and its trunk died. 'Why dost thou tear me?' And when it had turned dark with blood it began again: 'Why manglest thou me? Hast thou no spirit of pity? We were men and now are turned to stumps' (lines 1-6, 25-37).[26]

The stump of the tree in Dan. 4 is symbolic then not simply of the king's fall from grace but of his consequent suffering and humiliation. The narrative does not explicitly allow the thought of expiation through suffering. The king regains his former status by acknowledging the sovereignty of heaven and by performing good works:

> By this you may know that from the time you acknowledge the sovereignty of heaven your rule will endure. Be advised by me, O king: redeem your sins by charity and your iniquities by generosity to the wretched. So may you long enjoy peace of mind (vv. 23-24, NEB).

But the symbolism inherent in the narrative compels us to link

Nebuchadnezzar's repentance with his humiliation. The 'ritualistic' descent to the level of the animal kingdom (v. 25) and the ascent leading to healing and full recovery (v. 36) incorporate motifs associated with suffering (the stump preserved in the ground) and hark back to the mythic pattern of the dying and rising god-king. The theological framework of the story dilutes the mythopoeic language in the concluding confession of Nebuchadnezzar and puts the Creator safely outside the wheel of myth and destiny:

> He does according to his will in the host of heaven and among the inhabitants of the earth (v. 32, RSV).

In this impressive picture of power politics, Nebuchadnezzar has to learn the basic truth that the complex of human power is always fragile. Civilization is a thin and precarious crust erected by the personality and the will of very few and only maintained by rules and conventions skilfully put across and guilefully preserved. Insane and irrational springs of wickedness exist in most men and bring in their wake inescapable destruction. The overarching dominion of the ethical God is central to the ideas of the writer and constitutes the seminal paradigm by which all totalitarian powers are assessed in his book. But one cannot forget the re-emergence of Nebuchadnezzar from his ordeal. In the stubbornness of human individuality he encountered God and emerged from his experience a symbol of a new humanity ready to receive the 'man-like figure' to whom was promised the messianic kingdom.[27]

The substance of this article was originally prepared as a lecture given at a St Mary's College Summer School of Theology chaired by Principal McKane. In a thoroughly revised form it is presented to him as a token of admiration and friendship.

NOTES

1. See e.g. W. Dommershausen, *Nabonid im Buche Daniel*, Mainz, 1964.

2. See A. Lacocque, *The Book of Daniel*, ET: London, 1979, 74.

3. See L.F. Hartmann and A.A. Di Lella, *The Book of Daniel*, New York, 1978, 179.

4. In the neo-Assyrian period the guardians of the palace gates were usually winged *Mischwesen* having bodies of oxen and human heads with ox ears appearing beneath the divine tiara. Nebuchadnezzar, depicted in the book of *Daniel* as a lover of statues and images is made to feed on grass 'like the ox'. Cartoonist elements in this depiction are amusingly paralleled in the

March 2, 1978 number of *Punch* where A.H. Layard, distinguished archaeologist turned politician, appeared as an Assyrian bull in a diplomatic china shop; see G. Waterfield, *Layard of Nineveh*, London, 1963, 40. For the Mesopotamian iconography see J.B. Pritchard, *The Ancient Near East in Pictures*, New Jersey, 1954, 212ff., and H.W.F. Saggs, *The Greatness that was Babylon*, London, 1962, 313ff. and plate 53.

5. See Eusebius, *Praeparatio Evangelica* 13.12.13.

6. See e.g. J.A. Montgomery, *A Critical and Exegetical Commentary on the Book of Daniel* (ICC), Edinburgh, 1927, 234.

7. Compare the apocalyptic idea that in the great apostasy at the end of time the elect will be assembled together to receive 'sevenfold teaching about the whole of creation' (1 Enoch 93.9f.).

8. D. Winton Thomas, 'Some Observations on the Hebrew Word רענן', *Hebräische Wortforschung* (Festschrift W. Baumgartner) (SVT 16), 1967, 387-97.

9. S. Morag, 'ומתערה כאזרח רענן (Ps. 37.35)', *Tarbiz* 41 (1971-72), 14-23.

10. See J. Rendel Harris, *The Story of Ahikar*, London, 1898, 73.

11. For a full discussion of the image of the tree in Ezekiel see W. Zimmerli, *A Commentary on the Book of the Prophet Ezekiel, Chapters 25–48*, ET: London, 1983, 150-53. Cited as Zimmerli.

12. See e.g. Zimmerli, 143.

13. A number of scholars think that the first oracle closes at this point and that v. 14 is a later parenetic extension of vv. 15-18. It points up the fate of the cosmic tree as a gruesome example to all other trees; see Zimmerli, 151.

14. Heb. וינחמו; cf. Ezek. 24.14 לא אנחם 'I will not be moved to pity' (parallel to ולא אחום and the LXX rendering (παρεκάλουν αὐτόν 'gave it comfort'). Zimmerli understands this differently and translates 'they comforted themselves' seeing here a scene of 'contented observation of a similar fate' (152).

15. Herodotus, *The Histories*, 1. 108.

16. Herodotus, 5. 11, 19.

17. See G. Widengren, *The Tree of Life in Ancient Near Eastern Religion*, Uppsala, 1951, 57ff. Cited as Widengren.

18. Widengren, 43.

19. Cf. Is. 4.2; 11.1; Jer. 23.5; 33.15; Zech. 3.8; 4.3 and especially Lam. 4.20: 'The breath of our nostrils, the LORD's anointed, was taken in their pits, he of whom we said, *Under his shadow we shall live among the nations*' (RSV).

20. See O. Plöger, *Das Buch Daniel* (KAT, 18), Gütersloh, 1965, 74f.

21. A number of proposals have been made to account for the mythological material that informs so much of Jewish apocalyptic literature. Some see in it a survival of old Canaanite traditions which were absorbed in the earliest Israelite sources (see J.A. Emerton, 'The Origin of the Son of Man Imagery',

JTS n.s. 9 [1958], 225-42). The strong local flavour of the Court Tales of Dan. 2–7, however, impels the recognition of the forceful impact of language, religion and culture on the Jewish imagination during the Babylonian exile.

22. Cf. R.B.Y. Scott, 'The Pillars Jachin and Boaz', *JBL* 58 (1939), 143-49. In post-exilic Zech. 4.11ff. the two olive trees on the right and left of the lampstand are understandably given a priestly interpretation.

23. Verse 13 is beset with textual and philological problems. My translation presupposes the reading משלכת ('falls away') for MT בשלכת ('in the felling') in accordance with 1QIsᵃ, and the repointing of מצבת as from מן צבת ('from its base or stump'). The last line appears to be a gloss and represents a later theological protest against the unrelieved gloom of the original oracle. The corrected picture sees in the stump a symbol of perpetual hope and assurance in Israel's future existence. See G.R. Driver, 'Isaiah i-xxxix: Textual and Linguistic Problems', *JSS* 13 (1968), 38 and H. Wildberger, *Jesaja 1–12* (KAT 9/1), Neukirchen, 1972, 258.

24. The imagery here conveys the idea of an undisputed claim to David's throne. In this context the term צדיק might best be rendered 'legitimate'. A clear parallel may be seen in the corresponding phrase צמח צדק (= 'legitimate shoot') in a Phoenician text of the third century BC found in Cyprus. See J.C.L. Gibson, *Textbook of Syrian Semitic Inscriptions*, Vol. 3, Oxford, 1982, 136.

25. See the final paragraph of Eliot's Introduction to the novel.

26. See *The Divine Comedy of Dante Alighieri I: Inferno* (tr. J. Sinclair), Oxford, 1939; revised ed. 1948, 166-69.

27. See J. Steinmann, *Daniel*, Paris/Bruges, 1960, 71.

GUILT AND ATONEMENT:
THE THEME OF 1 AND 2 CHRONICLES

William Johnstone

University of Aberdeen

I

It is clear that the books of 1–2 Chronicles[1] represent a highly ideological work. That this is so is apparent from a number of considerations.

1. Even if it were 'only' a work of historiography, it is obvious that any treatment of the entire history of Israel against the background of mankind as a whole, from Adam (1 Chron. 1.1) to the edict of Cyrus (2 Chron. 36.22-23) in 538 BC, within the compass of two books of the Bible must be using ruthless principles of selection of the material available and must be arranging these materials according to some preconceived pattern.

2. The relationship of Chronicles to other works in the Old Testament, which deal with Israel's history, Samuel—Kings on the one side, especially, and Ezra—Nehemiah on the other, raises the question of the Chronicler's ideology still more sharply.[2]
(a) The relationship between Chronicles and Samuel—Kings is exceedingly complex: the Chronicler adds much, omits more and incessantly modifies material even where he reuses it.[3] It is obvious that principles of selection have been operated with added stringency and that, to a limited extent, materials have been rearranged.[4] It is unlikely, however, that the Chronicler has made these modifications of his underlying source for purely, or even mainly, historiographical reasons. In comparison with Samuel—Kings, circumstantial detail revealing human motive and intrigue has been still further reduced; e.g., the rivalries for the succession to David recorded in 2 Sam. 13–21 have been entirely suppressed by the Chronicler. Where his work can be checked against an underlying source, it can be seen that the Chronicler has consistently simplified the presentation of historical events (compare, e.g., the accounts of the raising of the siege of Jerusalem in 2 Kgs 19.35-37 and 2 Chron. 32.21-23). Elsewhere, his

material includes theological comment either on his own part (e.g. 1 Chron. 10.13-14) or placed on the lips of a prophet (e.g. the series of prophetic interventions in 2 Chron. 12ff.). There can surely be little doubt that the Chronicler's selection of material and his incorporation of such comment are motivated by some ideological purpose.

(b) Further indications of the motive and character of the Chronicler's work may be gathered from a couple of parallel passages in Chronicles and Ezra—Nehemiah, that other corpus commonly regarded as historiography. It has been widely held that Chronicles—Ezra—Nehemiah is, in fact, a single work by a single author, 'The Chronicler'. Those familiar with the sequence Chronicles—Ezra—Nehemiah in the Christian Bible may be already predisposed to this view. It is seemingly confirmed by the overlap between the two works in the edict of Cyrus (2 Chron. 36.22-23 // Ezra 1.1-4), which links the earlier historical episodes of Chronicles with the later ones of Ezra—Nehemiah. There seems, however, to be a growing number of interpreters[5] who would subscribe to a view perhaps already implied by the sequence in the Hebrew Bible, Ezra—Nehemiah—Chronicles: Chronicles is not primarily conceived as the historical account which provides the necessary preamble to Ezra—Nehemiah; it is a later and independent work, which, strangely enough, despite its being later, ends back at the point at which Ezra—Nehemiah begins. I should argue that, while Ezra—Nehemiah depicts 'The Return from the Exile' (see n. 2), Chronicles grapples with the mystery that, despite 'The Return', Israel is still 'in Exile', still poised on the eve of the definitive 'Return'. It may be that already the true lineaments of Chronicles as religious and theological writing, using historical materials in symbolical fashion and not composed primarily for historiographical purposes, are beginning to appear.

In my view, one of the clearest indications of the priority of Ezra—Nehemiah is provided again by parallel passages, in this case 1 Chron. 9.2-17 and Neh. 11.3-19. That dependence is on the side of Chronicles is particularly clear from the lameness of 1 Chron. 9.2: 'The original settlers, who were *in their [Neh.: 'his'] holding in their cities, were the Israelites, the priests, the levites and the n^{e}tinîm.*' The harshness and apparent redundancy of the statement (but see below at the end of the article), which pull the translator up sharp, can be explained by the fact that the Chronicler by his usual scissors-and-paste method has conjoined his own material, 'The original settlers, who were', which continues from his own previous verse summarizing the list of tribal genealogies and territories itemized in the preceding chapters (1 Chron. 2–8), with material borrowed from Neh. 11.3, which makes fluent sense in the Nehemiah context: 'These are the chief men of the province, who resided in Jerusalem, while in the cities of Judah there resided, each one *in his holding in their cities, the Israelites, the priests, and the levites and the n^etînîm....*' (parallel phrases italicized). The Chronicler, with scant attention to the particularities of the Nehemiah passage (the disapproving comparison between the nine-tenths of the population, who with heedless hedonism settled into their landed possessions, and the pioneering one-tenth, who altruistically gave up such pleasures in order to repopulate the capital), blandly turns the material to his own purposes.

It is not perhaps so clearly demonstrable that the edict of Cyrus material in 2 Chron. 36.22-23 is similarly derived from the parallel in Ezra 1.1-4. Nonetheless, in a couple of features it would be entirely characteristic of the Chronicler as dependent. Chronicles as the shorter text could well be another example of the Chronicler's regular practice of abbreviation and the excision of material redundant for his purpose. By a subtle change in reading (unless it is merely an instance of textual corruption!), the Chronicler alters the tentative greeting of the pagan emperor in Ezra, 'Let his God be with each among you, who is one of all his people...', to the triumphant affirmation, 'Yahweh his God is with each among you...'

3. The reference just made to 1 Chron. 9.2 introduces another indication of the Chronicler's intention of providing not a merely historical but a suprahistorical interpretation of his people's existence. Already in the genealogies in 1 Chron. 2–8 he has used eclectically lists from a great variety of historical periods, as if they were all on the same time-plane, in order to complete his muster of the people of Israel.[6] Now in 1 Chron. 9.2-17 he borrows as his source for the inhabitants of Jerusalem a post-exilic list from the time of Nehemiah (Neh. 11.3-19). The effect is that individuals of widely differing historical periods are brought into association with one another: these men of Nehemiah's time in vv. 3-17 rub shoulders with David and Samuel's appointees (the inversion of the historical Samuel and David is further evidence of the Chronicler's suprahistorical thinking!) in vv. 18-22. The Chronicler is not now interested in the historian's discriminations of time and epoch; rather, his purpose is to gather together in a global manner the fulness of Israel past and present in timeless contemporaneity. He is concerned to portray an ideal Israel

in all-inclusive terms, not to reconstruct the actual population at some point in time.[7]

Perhaps such indications are sufficient to make the necessary preliminary point that Chronicles is better understood as primarily a theological essay than as a work of historiography. Without accepting any of the negative implications sometimes attaching to the term, I should be happy to call it 'midrash'.[8] This definition of genre is of the utmost importance in shielding the reader from false expectations and the Chronicler himself from misguided reproaches that he is not fulfilling a function, which he never intended to fulfil.

II

If the Chronicler's work is primarily a theological essay, with what purpose has it been written? A not unreasonable place at which to start one's inquiry into the Chronicler's distinctive purpose is surely provided by those materials without parallel in Samuel–Kings, especially those where he offers an evaluation of a historical incident, borrowed or adapted from Samuel–Kings, to which he has just referred. Within the narrative section of Chronicles, which begins with 1 Chron. 10, the first such comment is to be found in 1 Chron. 10.13-14. In the preceding verses he recounts, with significant changes in detail, the narrative of the last, fatal, campaign of Saul against the Philistines at Gilboa, which is to be found in 1 Sam. 31.1-13. On this debacle he offers the following independent evaluative comment:

> Thus Saul died for the *ma'al* (מעל), which he *ma'aled* against the Lord: for the word of the Lord which he did not keep even to the extent of resorting to necromancy. He did not resort to the Lord; therefore, he put him to death and passed the monarchy over to David, son of Jesse (1 Chron. 10.13-14).

The use of root מעל in such an evaluative context becomes all the more striking when it is realized that this same root is used at key points in similar evaluative comments throughout the Chronicler's work. Already in the genealogies it occurs three times (1 Chron. 2.7; 5.25; 9.1). After 1 Chron. 10.13 there is a long gap, but there are a further twelve occurrences in 2 Chronicles (12.2; 26.16, 18; 28.19 [twice], 22; 29.6, 19; 30.7; 33.19; 36.14[twice]).[9]

An examination of these passages shows that this distribution of the root מעל can hardly be accidental. By means of it the Chronicler punctuates the decisive periods of Israel's history; from first to last, on West Bank and on East, in North and in South, Israel in its occupation of the land has been characterized by מעל. 1 Chron. 2.3ff. begins the genealogies of the tribes of Israel with Judah. Almost immediately, the incident recorded in Josh. 7.1ff. is alluded to: at Jericho, in the very first campaign of the conquest of the West Bank, Achar, the 'troubler' of Israel (the form of his name here is derived from Josh. 6.18; 7.24-26), committed an act of מעל (1 Chron. 2.7). The first phase of Israel's settlement of the land is already vitiated. What is true of the West Bank is equally true of the East (1 Chron. 5.25): the Chronicler, in free reminiscence of Josh. 22, where the root occurs seven times, records how the two-and-a-half tribes of Reuben, Gad and Half-Manasseh committed מעל against their ancestral God.[10]

In the summary on the genealogies in 1 Chron. 9.1, מעל is singled out as the significant factor leading to the Exile. After the occurrence, which has already been noted, in 1 Chron. 10.13 in the evaluation of the reign of Saul, the first episode in the history of Israel recounted in any detail by the Chronicler, the root does not reappear until 2 Chron. 12.2. The reason for this gap is clear. The reigns of David and Solomon (apart from the highly significant episode of 1 Chron. 21, to be noted below, where, however, not מעל but the associated root אשם is used) do not add to the fateful entail already announced in the genealogies. It is only with the Judaean king Rehoboam, son of Solomon and instrument of the break-up of the United Monarchy, that the deadly course of מעל is resumed and continues down through the reigns of Uzziah (2 Chron. 26.16, 18), Ahaz (2 Chron. 28.19, 22; 29.19) and Manasseh (2 Chron. 33.19), until it issues in the shared מעל of the whole community under their last king, Zedekiah (2 Chron. 36.14). The pleas of the pious Hezekiah, urged precisely on the basis of this past history of מעל, are unavailing (2 Chron. 29.6; 30.7). The Chronicler's message is clear: his explanation for why Israel is 'in Exile' is that from beginning to end of her occupation of the land, whether on West Bank or on East, whether in Northern Kingdom or in Southern, Israel has been guilty of מעל and has paid the penalty for it. Confirmation that the concept is indeed of distinctive significance for the Chronicler's thinking may be found in the fact that in all its occurrences from and including 1 Chron. 9.1 the root is not to be found in the Chronicler's underlying sources but belongs exclusively to his own material.[11]

What, then, is מעל? The meaning of the term the Chronicler has already begun to make clear contextually. In Achar's case, it consisted in violation of the חרם, i.e., of the spoils of battle, the fruits of victory, which ought to have been devoted wholly and exclusively to God in virtue of the fact that the victory had been won by him alone and that he is the sole giver of the land and of every gift which Israel possesses. The reminiscence of Josh. 6–7 is so clear, that it is surely legitimate to assume that the concepts associated in Josh. 6–7 are also presupposed by the Chronicler. The חרם infringed by Achar is there defined as that which is holy (קדש) to the Lord and which ought to be deposited in 'the Lord's storehouse' (אוצר יהוה) (Josh. 6.19, 24). Terms synonymous with violating the חרם are 'to sin' (חטא), 'to transgress the covenant' (עבר את הברית, Josh. 7.11), 'to commit folly in Israel' (עשה נבלה בישראל, Josh. 7.15). The double-sided nature of the offence is also recognized: מעל is not only to deprive God of that which is rightfully his; it is also to misapply what has thus been wrongfully gained to one's own profit (Josh. 7.11, 'They have stolen, dissembled and put among their own goods'). The penalty for the individual guilty of מעל is stoning to death by the whole community of the culprit, his family and all living creatures within his household and the burning of the corpses. The whole community thus has a hand in extirpating the wrongdoer from their midst and in purging the effect of his wrongdoing.

The model case of the individual guilty of מעל is then writ large in the life of the nation as a whole. Here again, מעל is failure to accord God what is his due (חטאת is used in 2 Chron. 33.19 in conjunction with it as in Josh. 7.11). The duty owed to God is, in particular, exclusive obedience and utter reliance (1 Chron. 10.13), the ancestral faith of Israel being sometimes stated as the ground for such trust (1 Chron. 5.25). מעל is evidenced in turning to other gods (2 Chron. 33.19), a particular irony since Israel's God had exposed their powerlessness at the conquest (1 Chron. 5.25). Thus Israel reduces itself to the level of the nations in a way that is as inexplicable as it is inexcusable, even to the extent of polluting and profaning its own sanctuary or of abandoning it altogether (2 Chron. 28.22; 36.14). The double fault of מעל, of defrauding God and misapplying that which is holy, is seen in the activities of Ahaz (2 Chron. 28.24). Uzziah is roundly informed that he is trespassing in the sphere of the holy (קדש), to which only those duly consecrated (המקדשים) have access, and that he had better depart from the sanctuary (המקדש) forthwith

(2 Chron. 26.16-18). The penalties of מעל are recognized to be incapacitating illness (Uzziah, 2 Chron. 26.19), death (Saul, 1 Chron. 10.13f.), or exile (the people, 1 Chron. 9.1; 2 Chron. 30.6, 9), and the devastation of the land (2 Chron. 30.7); in a word, forfeiture of status, life, or land.

The account in 2 Chron. 29 of Hezekiah's rededication of the temple after Ahaz' מעל provides a convenient summary of the Chronicler's view of the significance of מעל and the range of concepts associated with it, and of the institutions ordained to deal with the situation caused by it. מעל is expounded in vv. 6-7:

> Our forebears have committed מעל, have done what is evil in the estimation of the Lord our God and have forsaken him: they have disregarded the dwelling-place of the Lord and have abandoned it; they have locked the doors of the porch; they have extinguished the lamps; they have not burned incense; they have not sacrificed holocaust in the sanctuary to the God of Israel.

The penalties are grimly recorded: the men have been slain in battle, and their widows and orphans have been carried off as captives (v. 9). God has made of them an awesome object-lesson for all to see (v. 8). What is the remedy? Hezekiah proposes a covenant (v. 10). The prerequisite is the rededication of the sanctuary by the removal of defilement (הנדה, v. 5; הטמאה, v. 16) and the performing of the appropriate rites of atonement. Holocausts of bulls, rams and lambs are offered by the priests and goats for a sin-offering (חטאת, v. 21), with which the king and the whole community identify themselves by the imposition of their hands (v. 23). All is done to the accompaniment of the liturgy intoned by the levites and as approved by the prophets (v. 25). When the focus of community life has thus been reinaugurated, the round of ideal normal life can recommence. Thus in one incident the Chronicler lays bare profound forces underlying and unifying the disparate elements of Israel's life: king, priests, levites, prophets and people are harmoniously integrated with one another in a national act of atonement.[12]

III

It is hardly surprising, then, that beyond the confines of the books of Chronicles this circle of ideas and institutions related to מעל is primarily associated with priestly theology and practice. For a full appreciation of the term it is, therefore, necessary to consider its place in priestly theories of atonement, so far as these can be determined, especially in the book of Leviticus. In principle, it would be relevant to consider the significance of all rites connected with the sin-offering (חטאת, Lev. 4.1–5.13; cf. 2 Chron. 29.21 referred to above) and the Day of Atonement (יום הכפרים, Lev. 16; 23.26-32; cf. לכפר in 2 Chron. 29.24). In practice, the regulations concerning מעל itself in Lev. 5.14-26 serve to impose some limitation on the discussion: the sacrifice to be offered on the occasion of מעל is the אשם ('guilt-offering'). The rites of the אשם are similar to those of the חטאת (so Lev. 7.1-7). Indeed, that the אשם is regarded as the sacrifice for the graver offence is indicated by the offering required: whereas for the חטאת a female goat or female lamb was the most required in the case of the individual (Lev. 4.27ff.), for the אשם only a ram sufficed (Lev. 5.18).

A number of the elements in Lev. 5.14-26 appear to be of particular significance for the Chronicler's argument.

1. מעל may be defined as the act of defrauding (cf. the examples listed in Lev. 5.21-24 of the ways in which one may wrongfully gain possession of another's property). It is always in principle committed against God. Even where it is an act of defrauding of one fellow-Israelite by another, e.g., by embezzlement, extortion or theft (Num. 5.2, 27 adds adultery), it is regarded as an offence against God (Lev. 5.21), because it involves violation of an oath taken in the name of God,[13] who is, in any case, the framer of Israel's entire social order. But the primary act of מעל specified is when an individual is guilty of defrauding God of some of the sacred dues (הקדשים: Lev. 5.15); a convenient list of such sacred dues is to be found in Num. 18.8ff., which includes tithes, firstlings and firstfruits, as well as prescribed portions of sacrifice (the Mishnah tractate on the subject, *Me'ilah*, provides a much fuller list). The double guilt of מעל is again clearly in evidence: it is not merely the denying of another his rights; it is also the misappropriation of goods belonging to another for one's own use and benefit. Where God is the party wronged, as he always is in principle, the wrong-doer must be guilty of sacrilege.

2. It should not be thought that the קדשים belong merely to the externals of religion. Inasmuch as they are offered from the produce of the land, they are tokens of Israel's acknowledgment that God is the giver of the land, indeed of the life which that produce sustains. Deut. 26.1-15 gives classic expression to these concepts. מעל is,

consequently, greatly extended in meaning: it is not simply failure to offer הקדשים, the symbols of Israel's submissive obedience to the one on whom they totally depend for all they have and are; it is an expression of defiant disobedience and failure to acknowledge the source of their being and possessions. מעל extends beyond the symbol to the whole of life represented by the symbol. The point is made explicitly in the continuation of the discussion in Lev. 5: 'If anyone sins and does any one of the things which ought not to be done in all the commandments of the Lord . . . ' (v. 17).[14]

It is thus that מעל, as failure in rendering הקדשים and sacrilegious use of them, provides the Chronicler with a powerful category by which to explain Israel's predicament. Not surprisingly in the light of their Pentateuchal background, as מעל is a key root in the Chronicler's vocabulary, so also is קדש.[15] The two are brought together in the same contrast as in Lev. 5.15 in the Chronicler's summary on the climactic occurrence of מעל under Zedekiah:

> Indeed all the leaders [of Judah],[16] the priests and the people committed as much מעל as the nations abominably practised: they polluted (ויטמאו) the house of the Lord, which he had consecrated (הקדיש) in Jerusalem (2 Chron. 36.14).

The holiness, which Israel has profaned, is typically understood by the Chronicler in terms of the temple, its personnel, rites and furnishings, and also of the sacred dues and, significantly in view of Achar's מעל בחרם, the spoils of war (e.g., 1 Chron. 18.10f.). Yet the wider implications of the term are included. The account of Hezekiah's reformation can again suffice for illustration (not least since more than half of the occurrences of the root קדש in Chron. [44 out of 80] are to be found in that section [2 Chron. 29–31]). Behind the idyllic picture of the sanctuary restored, the cult reinaugurated in accordance with the most punctilious observance of the law, the land purged, and the people fulfilling all their obligations in the payment of the sacred dues, stands the larger reality of the restoration of an ideal and wholly sanctified common life, on which blessing showers down in abundance (2 Chron. 31.10). It is equally recognized that beyond the temple and its cult lies the heavenly dwelling-place of God, of which the earthly is but the local physical counterpart (2 Chron. 30.27; cf. 1 Chron. 28.29). The roots מעל and קדש are understood in their widest sense: the 'holy things' are not merely sacred dues, which are but the externals of religion, ends in themselves; rather, their dedication symbolizes and expresses the consecration of Israel's entire life to God the giver of all. Israel is guilty of מעל, because it has failed both in the symbol and in the reality behind the symbol. Where God required consecration and sanctity, Israel responded with desecration and sacrilege.

3.   Lev. 5.15-26 specifies the necessary remedial action for מעל. Where the fraud involves goods, the guilty person has, naturally enough, to restore in full the amount due. In addition, he has to pay 20%. The Old Testament does not make clear the reason for this 'added fifth', whether it is conceived in terms of compensation to the wronged party, or the surrender of value illegitimately enjoyed by the guilty, or punishment aimed at deterring further similar acts by himself or others within the community, or, indeed, all of these.

But the fact that the מעל is, in principle, committed against God raises the matter to an altogether more problematical level. How can God, the giver of all, be compensated? On what terms can the relationship with him, disturbed by the individual's unilateral act of faithlessness, be restored? Can atonement for the sacrilegious act be made? The legislation in Lev. 5.15ff. required the sacrifice of a ram as a guilt-offering (אשם) along with the restitution and the 'added fifth'. The rite of the אשם is described in Lev. 7.1-7. Again the significance of the details of the rite is never explained in the Old Testament. As in all other Israelite sacrifices, the victim was selected from among the domesticated animals. It was an integral part of the householder's own possessions; indeed, as presumably a breeding ram, and in any case fit for human consumption, upon it in part at least the support of the household might be said to depend. By its very nature, the victim was also a representative part of the household and its life. It is not clear whether the imposition of hands by the offerer on the head of the victim was a further symbol of its representative function; whether, indeed, there was implied an identification of the offerer with the victim, a substitution by the victim for the offerer, or an imparting to the victim of the guilt of the offerer, or, again, whether there are elements of all included. What is clear is the emphasis on the grace of God. The guilty is aware that restoration of the relationship with God is not worked mechanically but depends upon God's gracious choice; man cannot coerce God into forgiveness, nor can he wrest favour from him. Despite sacrifice, forgiveness may be withheld (cf. Hos. 8.11-14). All that the individual can hope for is the gracious acceptance of God, symbolized by the smoke of the burnt

portion of the sacrifice ascending into the heavens, consumed by the
fire, which is, in principle, God's own gift (Lev. 9.24; the point is
made by the Chronicler in 2 Chron. 7.1, 3; cf. 1 Kgs 18.24, 38).

It is against this background of the guilt of מעל and its expiation
that the fundamental purpose of the great central section of the
Chronicler's work on the reigns of David and Solomon (1 Chron. 11–
2 Chron. 9) can be appreciated. If Israel's life from start to finish is
riddled with מעל, then the rearing of the altar of sacrifice, where
atonement is effected, is cardinal for the continued life of Israel.

The Chronicler's design is heightened by the function of 1 Chron.
21 in the overall structure of his work. The chapter concerns the
reason for the ultimate choice of location for the altar of sacrifice,
where the guilt of the Israelites may be expiated. It is the guilt of
David himself, the king and cult-founder, which determines the
selection. As David's adultery with Bathsheba is the hinge of the
presentation of the reign of David in 2 Samuel (2 Sam. 11f.), so
David's census of the people in 1 Chron. 21, the presumptuous act of
numbering the people of God, is the pivot of the presentation of the
reign of David in 1 Chronicles. Before the census, David with
immediacy of access to God functions as high priest, clad in ephod
and linen garments, before the ark (1 Chron. 15f.). But with the
census all is changed: David himself incurs guilt, as is explicitly
stated in 1 Chron. 21.3, in the words of Joab, again not in the
Chronicler's underlying source in 2 Sam. 24, 'Why should my lord
the king bring guilt (אשמה) upon Israel?' The aftermath was the
terrible plague. But the angel of the Lord stayed his hand at the
threshing-floor of Ornan, and there David reared the altar of burnt-
offering, which thenceforward was to be the place of sacrifice, where
atonement between God and people was to be effected. But the result
of David's guilt was loss of immediacy of access to God. As the
Chronicler notes in 1 Chron. 21.29ff., in sentences which inaugurate
the Chronicler's independent account of David's measures to found
the cult in Jerusalem in 1 Chron. 21.27–29.30:

> The altar of holocaust was at that time at the high place at Gibeon.
> But David could not come before it to consult God because he was
> afraid of the sword of the angel of the Lord. So he said, '*This* is the
> house of the Lord God; *this* is the altar of holocausts for Israel.'

The Chronicler could scarcely have more eloquently stated his
theme: at the centre of Israel's guilt-laden life, as supremely indicated

in the very life of David the ideal king himself, there is raised the altar where that guilt itself may be expiated. Where guilt occurs, there God himself graciously provides the means of atonement. The Chronicler does not neglect, therefore, to note, in words which are again his own, that, when David had built the altar, the Lord 'answered him with fire from heaven' (1 Chron. 21.26), the symbol of the Lord's gracious acceptance. It is hardly surprising that in 2 Chron. 3.1, with reference back to 1 Chron. 21, the Chronicler alone in the Old Testament picks up from the story of Abraham's sacrifice of Isaac in Gen. 22 the name of Moriah for the temple mount, the place where the Lord provides.

4. The Chronicler is, however, aware that the problem of the guilt of Israel is altogether more serious than the situation envisaged in Lev. 5.15ff. There are two features in the legislation on מעל and its expiation, which make it not directly applicable to Israel's case: firstly, Lev. 5.15ff. concerns only the individual, not the nation; secondly, and even more seriously, it concerns inadvertent מעל. By contrast, Israel on the Chronicler's argument is guilty of corporate and deliberate מעל. The inexcusability of Israel's national, wilful guilt is emphasized by the Chronicler's theory of the centrality of the levites, to be noted below, and of the role of the prophets (in summary in 2 Chron. 36.15-16). If the condition of the individual inadvertently guilty of מעל is precarious, entirely dependent on the gracious decision of God, how much more must Israel's be? If the fate of the individual, who, like Achar, was guilty of defrauding God deliberately ('with a high hand', Num. 5.30), was summary extirpation from the community, what then was to become of Israel?

The Chronicler is not the first in the Old Testament to grapple with this problem of the punishment, survival and restoration of Israel, corporately and wilfully guilty of מעל. He stands in the tradition pioneered by the priestly writer of Lev. 26 (where מעל explicitly occurs in v. 40) and by the priest-prophet Ezekiel (see n. 9). The penalty for such deliberate מעל in the case of the individual is summary extirpation to expiate the sacrilege in the holy things, and to restore and preserve the sanctity of the community symbolized by the precise rendering of the duty owed to the giver of the land. Where the whole community is guilty of such מעל, the total profanation of the community leaves no margin of sanctity for the rendering of the holy things, which are the tokens of Israel's dutiful response, let alone fit material for the payment of the 'added fifth'. The consequence

must be the forfeiture by the entire community of the land for which
they have so totally failed to show gratitude. In Lev. 26 this forfeiture
is interpreted in terms of the sabbatical years of which the land has
been deprived, while in Ezek. 20 Israel is represented as reverting to
its condition before the conquest of the land of wandering in the
wilderness, now understood typologically as the 'wilderness of the
nations'.

It may be doubted whether the Chronicler advances much the
thinking already found in Leviticus and Ezekiel on Israel's predicament as guilty of national, premeditated מעל. What the Chronicler is
doing is to apply these ready-made categories as 'hermeneutical key'
to the interpretation of Israel's past history and understanding of her
present state: the Chronicler matches Ezekiel's typological 'wilderness of the nations' with his own typological 'Exile', in which he
perceives Israel still to languish. Using the materials of Israel's past
history in a suprahistorical way, the Chronicler expounds in narrative
form the teaching of both law and prophets on the guilt of Israel and
its destructive consequences. If one were to be bold, one would say
that, as the 'Deuteronomistic History' from Deuteronomy to 2 Kings
constitutes an aggadic midrash on the levitical doctrine of the
blessing and curse of the covenant, so Chronicles constitutes an
aggadic midrash on the complementary levitical (including priestly)
doctrine of guilt and atonement.[17] In the contemporary phase of
scholarship, when much attention is being directed to Deuteronomy,
the 'Deuteronomistic History' and the 'Deuteronomistic School', it is
not inappropriate to redress the balance by drawing attention to this
complementary presentation of Israel's history in the work of the
Chronicler.[18]

There is a further analogy between the work of the 'Deuteronomistic School' and that of the Chronicler. As in the end of the day the
'Deuteronomistic School' found itself constrained to transcend its
doctrine of covenant and await a final act of God himself, when God
would 'both will and do of his good pleasure' by circumcising the
heart of his people and writing the covenant code on that heart
renewed (Deut. 30.6; Jer. 31.31-34),[19] so the Chronicler, the latest
representative of the levitical-priestly school, is forced to look beyond
the limits of his theological category, not to the destruction of Israel,
fully required though that would be for its colossal fraud, inherited
and compounded generation by generation, but to its restoration
through an act of the free grace of God already implied in the אשם for

individual, inadvertent guilt, now prevailing immeasurably more for Israel's corporate, wilful guilt. He does not see that this restoration has yet taken place, any more than the Deuteronomist sees the fulfilment of his expectation of the new covenant. Meantime, though the return from the exile is, historically speaking, long past, theologically speaking, Israel is still 'in Exile', still poised on the verge of 'the Return' proper (just as Deuteronomy leaves Israel poised on the verge of the settlement in the Promised Land). As Israel awaits the dawning of that day, it must seek to realize that total sanctity of life, untainted by any מעל sacrilege, which is its divinely willed destiny.

IV

The argument up till now has largely concerned the narrative section of Chronicles from 1 Chron. 10. In conclusion it may be appropriate to consider something of the function in the Chronicler's purpose of the genealogical section, 1 Chron. 1–9, which presents such a formidable obstacle to the reader.[20] As has been noted above, the thematic term מעל has already been enunciated in the genealogical section; indeed, it binds the whole together. From start to finish, on West Bank and on East, Israel's history has been blighted by מעל (1 Chron. 2.7; 5.25; 9.1).

Four major themes are handled in 1 Chron. 1–9: the universal context of Israel's life; the divinely ordained ordering of Israel's life so that its destiny as God's people can be realized; the ideal vitiated by Israel; the necessary remedial action.

1. The work opens by setting the descendants of Abraham within the context of the whole family of mankind. The genealogical material, which the Chronicler freely quarries from Genesis, is wholly congenial to the Chronicler's developing theme (it is safe to assume that, throughout, he presupposes the narrative material in Genesis as well; e.g., 1 Chron. 1.27 clearly alludes to the narrative of Gen. 17.4-5). The history of mankind as a whole is characterized from the beginning by a pattern of false starts and abortive restarts, as God's original plan is vitiated by rebellious man and his new arrangement, by which his intention may yet be fulfilled, is again thwarted. Already in the first two names of the work in 1 Chron. 1.1 there is a premonition: Adam, the primal man, is succeeded by his third son Seth, whose very name means 'the substitute one' (cf. Gen.

4.25). In the tenth generation, Noah, the second father of mankind, is reached (1 Chron. 1.4). In 1 Chron. 1, the Chronicler allows himself four evaluative comments on the character of this emerging world of the nations: in their pursuit of war (v. 10) and nationalism (v. 19), they are the origin of the powers, which threated Israel both physically (v. 11) and ideologically (v. 43). After a further ten generations there springs, from one of the three branches of Noah's descendants, Abraham, and, in turn, from one of the three branches of his descendants, Israel. Out of the broad mass of humanity, a single family has now been chosen; Israel is to realize on behalf of mankind what mankind as a whole cannot. But lurking in the background stands the world of the nations, from which Israel springs and to which it is kin. Israel's pursuit of the ideal is constantly threatened by reversion to that 'wilderness of the nations', from which it took its origins, or by invasion from these destructive nations. It is notable how often in Chronicles Israel's מעל is visited by the incursion of a foreign force (already in 1 Chron. 5.26). The ideal relationship between Israel and the world of the nations is portrayed in 1 Chron. 14, where the gathering of all Israel to David (1 Chron. 11–13) is crowned by the recognition and pacification of the nations of the world (1 Chron. 14.17, yet another of the Chronicler's original statements).

2. The Chronicler then proceeds in 1 Chron. 2–8 to portray Israel in its ideal tribal structure. The recurrent verb התיחש, 'to enrol by families' (1 Chron. 4.33; 5.1, 7, 17; 7.5, 7, 9, 40; 9.1, 42), expresses his concern to give a complete muster of those eligible to be counted among the people. The organization of the tribal lists by 'father's houses', i.e., by households in their hereditary succession through the male line, in which every member has his place, whether specified by name or not, enables the range and width of God's people to be indicated without the presumptuousness of such a census as David conducted in 1 Chron. 21, which seeks to number them precisely.

He begins, conventionally enough in 1 Chron. 2.1-2, with a list of the twelve tribes in the order familiar from Gen. 35.23-25; Exod. 1.2-4 (except that Dan is now placed between the 'Leah' and 'Rachel' tribes, instead of following the latter). But thereafter (1 Chron. 2.3–8.40), he follows an entirely different sequence. Again its uniqueness may be taken to confirm that it reflects his specific purpose. The intention behind it becomes relatively clear, when it is tabulated as follows:

Judah Simeon	Reuben Gad Hal-Manasseh	Levi	Issachar Benjamin Naphtali Half-Manasseh Ephraim Asher	Benjamin

The reason for this singular disposition of the tribes of Israel[21] is presumably that Judah (with Simeon incorporated) and Benjamin, the two tribes of the Southern Kingdom of Judah, were the elements of the whole nation, which endured the longest in their territories, surviving until the exile of 587 (but see also below under paragraph 4). They form the enclosing bracket whereby the more vulnerable elements, Reuben, Gad and Half-Manasseh on the East Bank, and the remaining tribes in the North, are enclosed and thus have their status as permanent members of the Israelite tribal system, though 'in Exile', preserved, at least ideologically, if not practically.

The major point of interest is, however, the centrality of Levi. The role of the levites is, in the Chronicler's view, quite literally, central to Israel's life.[22] In what way they are central is indicated by his treatment of them in 1 Chron. 5.27–6.66. After noting the descent of the priests through Aaron from Kohath son of Levi (5.27-41) and the descent of the remaining levites in the conventional order of the sons of Levi, Gershom, Kohath and Merari (6.1-15), the section culminates in the specification of the chief duties of the levites in the sanctuary (the music of the liturgy and the service at the altar, 6.16-38) and the settlements assigned to the levites throughout the other tribes. Clearly for the Chronicler, the means whereby Israel is to maintain its identity and sanctity as the people of God is the central ministry of the levites, both as priests and officiants at the central altar, and as teachers of the law in the forty-eight levitical citites dispersed throughout the entire body of Israel. It is through the ministrations of the levites, living in the midst, that all the duty which Israel owes to God will be performed.

Again the Chronicler points up his meaning by a characteristic addition to his underlying source. He begins his list of levitical settlements in 1 Chron. 6.39 with a phrase not present in the parent list in Josh. 21.10ff.: 'The following are their settlements according to their טירות throughout their territory.' By the comparatively rare word טירות, 'dwellings', used only seven times in the Old Testament, typically in connection with nomadic populations (e.g., Ishmael, Gen. 25.16; Midian, Num. 31.10; 'sons of the east', Ezek. 25.4), the Chronicler stresses that the levites remain as pastors of flocks with grazing-grounds (מגרשים) in the midst of the tribes settled in their agricultural lands and are, therefore, dependent like the other landless ones on the tithes (part of the קרשים!) rendered by the community. As such, the levites would become immediately aware of מעל, any shortfall in the payment of the sacred dues, on the part of Israel.

The ideal constitution of Israel has thus been stated: the community lives clustered round the levites living in the midst, both centrally and in dispersion throughout the length and breadth of the land. It is to be remarked how comparable this system of the Chronicler's is to other equally ideological systems of the levites in the midst in the priestly materials in Num. 2, 7 and 10 and in the priest-prophet Ezekiel (ch. 48). In 1 Chron. 5.20b, 22a, the Chronicler gives an example of the ideal trusting obedience of Israel to God, which he has in mind.

3. But Israel, chosen to realize on their behalf what the rest of mankind cannot, immediately vitiates the divinely ordained ideal order. Even within Israel, the same vicious pattern of false start and abortive restart is amply in evidence. Beyond the familiar examples of overreaching and supplanting of Esau by Jacob, or of Manasseh by Ephraim, the Chronicler has others to cite. He begins his muster of the tribes with Judah (1 Chron. 2.3–4.23). But he is well aware that Reuben should come first by right of primogeniture, but had forfeited that right by a deplorable act of incest. He knows, too, the tradition that, subsequently, the birthright was allotted to the House of Joseph. Nonetheless, he elevates Judah to first place in virtue of its military strength, as evidenced above all in the leadership of the House of David (1 Chron. 5.1-2). But, even after all these adjustments, the same pattern of the failure of the favoured first choice and his replacement by a secondary repeats itself. Judah's first three sons spring from a disastrous liaison with a Canaanite woman (one may recall that in Ezra–Nehemiah מעל is used above all of intermarriage between Israelite and non-Israelite, which is condemned as the contamination of the 'holy seed' [Ezra 9.2, 4; 10.2, 6, 10; Neh. 13.27]). The two oldest ones mark the false start and are eliminated; the third is relegated to the end of the Chronicler's account of Judah's progeny (1 Chron. 4.21-23). Even then, the replacement

main line springs from the most dubious of circumstances. The
Chronicler presupposes the narrative of Gen. 38 (1 Chron. 2.3a is
freely composed from Gen. 38.1-5; v. 3b is virtually identical with
Gen. 38.7), which records the irregular birth of Judah's two later sons
by his daughter-in-law, twins who, like Jacob and Esau, are to be
contentious from the womb, with the younger, Perez, from whom
David is descended, ousting the originally intended elder, Zerah. It is
from Achar, a scion of the latter branch of the house of Judah, which
is itself the replacement leader of Israel at several removes, that
immediately the first, trend-setting act of מעל arises (1 Chron. 2.7).

There are a number of details in 1 Chron. 2–8 which stress Israel's
מעל and its deadly effects. As has just been noted, 1 Chron. 5.20b, 22a
provides an example of the ideal trusting obedience which Israel
ought to have accorded God. The same passage continues to show
how such reliance upon God was soon abandoned in the perfidious
turning to other gods, whose powerlessness before the Lord had first
been exposed and acknowledged. The consequences of such treachery
are that the East Bank tribes languish in exile from their forfeited
land 'until this day' (v. 26). This act of מעל is then brought into
immediate juxtaposition with the role of the levites as officiants at
the altar and as teachers throughout the land in 1 Chron. 5.27ff. But,
by recording the names of Nadab and Abihu, the two eldest sons of
Aaron, the archetypal chief priest descended from the central son of
Levi, who were extirpated from the priesthood because of their
irregular practice (Lev. 10.1-3), the Chronicler does not flinch from
acknowledging that even among the levites, the fulfillers of the
central role for the hallowing, and, therefore, for the wellbeing, of
their people, the same pattern of false start is reproduced. It is
perhaps, then, not accidental, that the line of the priesthood is traced
in 1 Chron. 5.26-41 only as far as Jehozadak, the high-priest carried
off into exile by Nebuchadnezzar. Nothing could emphasize more
clearly that the mere rites of the altar as such can neither suffice nor
avail to expunge the guilt even of its own officiants.

Another detail which may expose the fatal power of מעל is the
omission of any mention of the tribe of Dan in the Chronicler's tribal
system in 1 Chron. 2.3–8.40. While Dan is mentioned in 1 Chron.
2.2, in material derived from Gen. 35 and Exod. 1, as noted above, it
fails to recur in the subsequent detailed genealogical lists.[23] The
omission is not likely to be accidental: in 1 Chron. 6.46, there is a
barely comprehensible text, 'And to the remaining Kohathites there

were assigned by lot ten cities from the clan of the tribe, from the half of the tribe of the half of Manasseh', while Josh. 21.5, the parent text from which this verse is derived, records with total intelligibility, 'And to the remaining Kohathites there were assigned by lot ten cities from the clans of the tribe of Ephraim and from the tribe of Dan and from the half of the tribe of Manasseh.' The reason for the elimination of Dan is surely not far to seek: unlike the East Bank tribes, whose מעל according to Josh. 22 consisted in their erecting an altar not for sacrifice but only as a reminder of their devotion to the Lord, the Danites were the originators of a sanctuary of their own self-conceiving, in which a full-scale and idolatrous cult was practised (Judg. 17–18) and which was eventually to become the focus of the schismatic and apostate kingdom of the North.[24] The one who is guilty of מעל must suffer forfeiture and elimination, so that the community can be protected from the contagion of uncleanness.

4. But the ideal vitiated is not the end of the matter. By his layout of the genealogical material, the Chronicler indicates the divinely intended remedy. It is thus that the oddity of the repetition of the genealogy of Benjamin can be fully explained. The repetition of Benjamin is only part of a series of interweavings of material in 1 Chron. 7–10, which may be most conveniently presented diagrammatically (overleaf).

An immediate, unambiguous point, which can be made about this table, is that there is repetition of material: 8.28b = 9.34b; 8.29-38 = 9.35-44. The reason for this repetition is, surely, not difficult to infer. The repeated material concerns, on the one hand, the population of Jerusalem, and, on the other, the family of Saul. Both are in origin Benjaminite (for Jerusalem as a Benjaminite city, cf. the definition of tribal boundaries in Josh. 18.11-28; apart from the Chronicler's genealogies, the Benjaminite origin of Saul is recognized in 1 Sam. 9.1ff.); both are, therefore, appropriately included in connection with the genealogies of Benjamin in 1 Chron. 8. But both receive a supra-Benjaminite significance. In the immediately ensuing chapters (1 Chron. 10ff.), in which the Chronicler begins his historical narrative proper, tracing the theme of guilt and atonement, it is Saul, the Benjaminite, who provides the Chronicler with his first example of מעל. But by this interweaving of materials, the Chronicler associates with that, namely the first breakdown of the ideal order intended by God for his people, the new supratribal significance of the old Benjaminite city of Jerusalem, the place where the new centralized

7.6-12	genealogy of Benjamin
7.13-40	genealogy of the northern tribes
8.1-27a	genealogy of Benjamin
8.28b	opening of list of inhabitants of Jerusalem
8.29-40	the Benjaminites of Gibeon (family of Saul)
9.1a	conclusion of the ideal tribal muster
9.1b	the ideal marred
9.2	the primal ideal
9.3-9	the inter-tribal population of Jerusalem (Judah, Benjamin, Ephraim, Manasseh)
9.10-13	the priests resident in Jerusalem
9.14-34a	the levites resident in Jerusalem
9.34b	= 8.28b
9.35-44	= 8.29-38 (*sic!*)
10.1-14	the reign of Saul
11ff.	the accession of David; Jerusalem the capital

atonement cult will be introduced. The intention is expressed with great clarity: where Israel falls into guilt, there God provides the means of atonement. The reason that Benjamin appears last in the tribal genealogies is, therefore, not merely that Benjamin, as one of the last survivors, constitutes an enclosing bracket around the more vulnerable northern tribes; rather, it is that Benjamin provides the Chronicler with the double link of both guilt and atonement forward into his account of Israel's history.

Had the old model of the constitution of Israel (decentralized tribal life, hallowed by the presence of the levites indwelling in the midst) remained intact, the tribal muster could well have ended at 1 Chron. 7.40, before the second appearance of Benjamin. The tribal muster would then have been sufficiently complete to justify the statement in 1 Chron. 9.1a, 'So all Israel was enrolled by genealogical descent' and the ideal portrayed in 1 Chron. 9.2, 'The original settlers, who were in their holdings in their cities, were the Israelites, the priests, the levites and the *nᵉtînîm*.' But the ideal has been destroyed by מעל; Judah is in exile (1 Chron. 9.1b).[25]

Within the new context of the ideal marred, the climax to the genealogical section is now the new population of Jerusalem. The citizens are now drawn from several tribes, not merely from Benjamin (1 Chron. 9.3-9). The list passes swiftly to the chief inhabitants of the city, the priests, who officiate at the altar in the new House of God, at which atonement can be effected (1 Chron. 9.10-13). At first sight, it then seems a crass anticlimax that the portrayal of the new centralized order, through which the crisis provoked by Israel's מעל is to be handled, should culminate in the families and duties of the non-priestly levites, in particular in their role as custodians of the temple storehouses (1 Chron. 9.26ff.). In fact, however, this conclusion exactly fits the Chronicler's theme. מעל, in the legislation of Lev. 5.15ff., concerns precisely the violation of the holy things, the supreme, tangible token of Israel's rendering of its duty towards God as the giver of the land and the possibilities of life within it. It is to the storehouses of the temple that such holy things were brought to the levites to confirm that Israel's duty towards God had been completely fulfilled.[26] Atonement for sacrilege is not an end in itself: it is the necessary means whereby Israel, made for sanctity, can regain its status as holy. Atonement was made for Israel, not Israel for atonement.[27]

As a postscript, it may be commented that the Chronicler's thesis is hardly unexpected. After the excitements and disappointments of the 'Zionist' phase of Israel's history from Second Isaiah to Ezra/Nehemiah, it is hardly surprising that, faced with the apparently meagre achievements of the restoration period, the Chronicler, in a way no doubt representative of many within the community, looks for a more ultimate 'Return', not only for the thousands still in the Diaspora but even for those physically present in the land. But this 'Return' and the ending of the present 'Exile' depend upon atonement, an act in which the initiative lies always and only in God himself. Meantime, in waiting for that day, at the dawning of which Israel stands poised, it is levitical instruction on man's duty toward God and the levitical custodianship of the rendering of that duty, which must stand at the heart of the community's life. Beyond the scrupulous rendering to God of every obligation due to him, the community waits in quiet expectation for the restoration, which God alone can accomplish.[28]

It is with great pleasure that this article is dedicated to William McKane, whom I have known for many years as teacher and colleague.

NOTES

1. Chronicles is here sometimes construed in the singular as a single work. 'The Chronicler' refers to the author(s) of the work, without prejudice to critical decisions which might be reached concerning his (or their) identity, or the process of the composition or compilation of the books.

2. I should be prepared to subscribe to the view that already both Samuel–Kings and Ezra–Nehemiah are highly ideological. In broad terms, 'covenant' is the 'hermeneutical key' (to use the term of P. Buis, *La notion d'alliance dans l'ancien testament* [Paris, 1976]) in the former, whereby the history of Israel from Sinai to exile is interpreted by the criteria of the blessing and curse of the covenant: e.g., the 'blessing' narrative of the conquest in Josh. 1-12 and the 'curse' narrative in Judg. 1.1–2.5; or the way in which the histories of David, Solomon and Hezekiah are hinged round pivotal points (the Bathsheba incident in 2 Sam. 11–12, the trafficking with Egypt in 1 Kgs 10.28-29 [cf. Deut. 17.16], and the 'fourteenth year' in 2 Kgs 18.13ff., respectively). Ezra and Nehemiah are constructed in such a way as to present the 'Return from Exile' as a single concerted event, as the lay-out of the books makes clear:

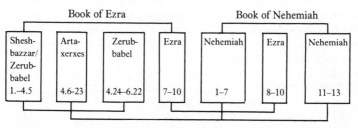

The fact that the time-scale from Sheshbazzar to Nehemiah spans at least one hundred years (whatever conclusion one may reach about the historical relationship between the activities of Ezra and Nehemiah) is apparently of little concern to the writer/editor of Ezra–Nehemiah.

3. It is surprisingly difficult to compile accurate statistics of the relationship between the two corpora. Apart from the quite external factor of the occasional variation in verse numbering, the Chronicler intervenes so constantly in his Samuel–Kings source that at times it is almost arbitrary whether one regards the texts as parallel or whether the Chronicler's modification of a phrase should be counted as a plus to the Chronicler and a minus to Samuel–Kings. My assessment would be somewhat as follows: 1 Chron. 11.1–2 Chron. 36.21 contains 1341 verses; the parallel 2 Sam. 1.1–2 Kgs 25.30 contains 2229 verses; Chronicles in this part contains some 530 verses with parallels to Samuel–Kings; i.e., some 2/5 of Chronicles (from 1 Chron. 11 on) has parallel material in Samuel–Kings, while some 3/5 is independent of Samuel–Kings. Contrariwise, Chronicles uses only about 1/4 of the material available in Samuel–Kings (again from 1 Chron. 11ff.).

4. E.g. the sequence of materials derived from 2 Samuel in 1 Chron. 11ff., where the order begins:

1 Chron. 11.1-9	cf. 2 Sam. 5.1-3, 6-10
1 Chron. 11.11-41a	cf. 2 Sam. 23.8-39
1 Chron. 13.6b-14	cf. 2 Sam. 6.2b-11
1 Chron. 14.1-16	cf. 2 Sam. 5.11-25
1 Chron. 15.25–16.3	cf. 2 Sam. 6.12b-19a.

5. See, e.g., H.G.M. Williamson, *1 and 2 Chronicles* (New Century Bible), London, 1982. It should perhaps be explained that the present article has been written entirely independently of the substantial secondary literature on Chronicles (though, as one tries to do one's own map-making, it is hard to avoid altogether coming across tales that earlier travellers have had to tell of their pioneering explorations in this rugged terrain). It represents part of the preliminary thinking of what, it is hoped, will be a larger-scale work (in the *International Theological Commentary* series) and the development of an earlier contention that the work of the Chronicler is 'an essay in the preservation of Israel's identity by the unification of her streams of

tradition ... the uniting focus ... is the Temple in Jerusalem' (W. Johnstone, 'Chronicles, Canons and Contexts', *Aberdeen University Review*, 50 (1983), 1-18, above quotation from p. 13). I am concerned here to try to identify the basic centripetal force, by which Israel's disparate traditions are brought into relationship with one another.

6. E.g., the descent of the House of David is traced for some 38 generations in 1 Chron. 2.10-16; 3.1-24, whereas the obscurer branches of the Calebites are fobbed off with a couple of generations and are then indicated by the names of the places which they populated (e.g. 1 Chron. 2.19f., 50-55; 4.1-8). Lineal descent and lateral spread are thus placed side by side in order to achieve the most ample presentation of the descendants of Israel. Statistics obtained under David in the tenth century (1 Chron. 7.2) stand alongside data from Jotham in the eighth century (1 Chron. 5.17).

7. The RSV translation of 1 Chron. 9.2 (cf. also GNB), 'Now the first to dwell *again* [my italics] in their possessions ... ', is conditioned by the knowledge of the parallel with Neh. 11.3, the reasoning being, presumably, that, since Neh. 11 is about the fifth century, 1 Chron. 9 must be about the post-exilic repopulation of Jerusalem. This conclusion is simply symptomatic of the captivity of the modern mind to historicism. There is no word in the Hebrew corresponding to the RSV's 'again'; the RSV translation also ignores the fact that 1 Chron. 9.2ff. resumes 1 Chron. 8.28 and that the sequel to 1 Chron. 9 is the early monarchy. Even more serious is its misconstruing, in my view, of the Chronicler's intention.

8. In applying the term 'midrash', I am thinking of some such understanding of it as that of J. Neusner: '*Midrash* represents ... creative philology and creative historiography. As creative philology, the *Midrash* discovers meaning in apparently meaningless detail. It ... uses the elements of language not as fixed, unchanging categories, but as relative, living, tentative nuances of thought. As creative historiography, the *Midrash* rewrites the past to make manifest the eternal rightness of Scriptural paradigms. What would it be like if all people lived at one moment? ...*Midrash* thus exchanges stability of language and the continuity of history for stability of values and the eternity of truth' (*Between Time and Eternity*, Encino, 1975, 52). The only two occurrences of the word מדרש in the Old Testament are in Chronicles (2 Chron. 13.22; 24.27).

9. The distribution of the remaining 47 occurrences of מעל throughout the rest of the Old Testament may be noted: Lev. 5.15 (2x), 21 (2x); 26.40 (2x); Num. 5.6 (2x), 12 (2x), 27 (2x); 31.16; Deut. 32.51; Josh. 7.1 (2x); 22.16 (2x), 20 (2x), 22, 31 (2x); Ezek. 14.13 (2x); 15.8 (2x); 17.20 (2x); 18.24 (2x); 20.27 (2x); 39.23, 26 (2x); Job 21.34; Prov. 16.10; Dan. 9.7 (2x); Ezra 9.2, 4; 10.2, 6, 10; Neh. 1.8; 13.27.

10. Incidentally, one notes again the Chronicler's lack of interest in historiographical accuracy: while there may be other factors in his elevation

of Judah to pre-eminence among the tribes (e.g. the emergence of David from Judah) besides the notoriety of their early history, his dealing with the West Bank before the East reverses the sequence familiar from the Hexateuch.

11. Contrast, e.g., 2 Chron. 12.2 with 1 Kgs 14.25; 2 Chron. 26.16-21 with 2 Kgs 15.5; 2 Chron. 28.16-20 with 2 Kgs 16.7-9; 2 Chron. 33.18-20 with 2 Kgs 21.17-18; 2 Chron. 36.11-14 with 2 Kgs 24.18-20.

12. With what degree of acceptability to the parties involved is, of course, quite another matter.

13. Cf. B.M. Bokser, 'מעל and blessings over food', *JBL* 100 (1981), 561.

14. Cf. the comment by J. Milgrom, *Cult and Conscience*, Leiden, 1976, 80: 'The increased importance of the asham at the end of the second Temple bespeaks a development whose significance cannot be overestimated. Heretofore, man tended to dichotomize the world into the sacred and the profane, the discrete realms of the gods and man... With the promulgation of Lev. 5.17-19... whereby the unwitting violation of any of the Lord's commandments required expiation for sancta desecration, the boundaries of the sacred and profane are obliterated for ever. Henceforth the sacred is unbounded; it is coextensive with the will of God. It embraces ethics as well as ritual, the relations between men and not just those between man and God. In short, the violation of any of the Torah's prohibitions constitutes sacrilege, *ma'al*, the expiation of which is essential for Israel to remain in divine grace.'

15. The distribution of the root קדשׁ in the Old Testament is instructive. Not counting the eleven occurrences of קדשׁ (m. and f., sg. and pl.), or proper names derived from the root, it occurs some 775 times in the Old Testament. The major concentrations are in Ex. 25–31, 35–40 (77x), Lev. (except H) (76x), H (63x), Num. (72x), Is. 1–39 (32x), Is. 40–66 (40x), Ezek. (93x), Pss. (65x), and Chronicles itself (80x). The 16x in Dan. and 14x in Neh. are also proportionately significant. At the intermediate level are the rest of Exod. (17x), Deut. (15x), Josh.–Kgs (41x), Jer. (19x). The statistics for the remainder are Gen. (1x), Hos. (2x), Joel (7x), Amos (4x), Obad. (2x), Jonah (2x), Mic. (2x), Nah. (2x), Hab. (3x), Zeph. (3x), Hag. (2x), Zech. (6x), Mal. (1x), Job (6x), Prov. (2x), Eccl. (1x), Lam. (4x), Ezra (5x) (statistics on the basis of Mandelkern's *Concordance*).

16. Reading with BHS.

17. Cf. J. Milgrom's identification of an 'aggadic Midrash' on the law of sancta desecration in Jer. 2.3 (*Cult and Conscience*, pp. 70f.).

18. A straw in the wind is the recent appearance of M. Noth, *The Deuteronomistic History* (JSOT Supplement Series, 15), Sheffield, 1981, which translates only the first part of his original *Überlieferungsgeschichtliche Studien. Die sammelnden und bearbeitenden Geschichtswerke im Alten Testament* and omits the second part on Chronicles. (However, I understand that the translation of the second part is in preparation for JSOT Press.)

19. My indebtedness to W. Thiel, *Die deuteronomistische Redaktion von Jeremia 26–45* (WMANT 52), Neukirchen, 1981 is obvious.

20. Thus *The Reader's Bible*, London, 1983 retains only fragments of some 20 of the 407 verses of 1 Chron. 1–9. Lord Coggan writes in the Foreword (p. xi) that the book, 'shorn of . . . such things as long genealogies, . . . just because of this, is more likely to convey the essence of what the Bible is really about.' If my interpretation is right, it is precisely this 'shearing' that will condemn Chronicles to continued misunderstanding.

21. The absence of Dan and the repetition of Benjamin will be discussed below.

22. This device of central location to indicate prominence and leadership is used quite widely by the Chronicler, e.g., the House of David (1 Chron. 3.1-24) within Judah (1 Chron. 2.6–4.23), Solomon within David's sons, even to the extent of the Chronicler's making up the number of 19 to get the pattern 9-1-9 (1 Chron. 3.1-8). So also, as in the Pentateuch, in the case of the sons of Levi (see text below).

23. There may be a vestigial trace in 1 Chron. 7.12: Hushim appears as a Danite in Gen. 46.23. Aher may then not be a proper name but the adjective 'another', an oblique reference to Dan avoiding mention of the accursed name (so already Bertheau, according to BDB).

24. N.H. Snaith, *Leviticus and Numbers* (NCBC), London, 1967, on Lev. 24.11, points out that Dan is omitted from the list of the twelve tribes of Israel in Rev. 7.5-8.

25. It is tempting to propose a transposition of the *'athnaḥ* in 1 Chron. 9.1 and to translate: 'So all Israel was enrolled by genealogical descent. They are recorded in the records of the kings of Israel and Judah [for which see 2 Chron. 27.7; 35.27; 36.8]. They [i.e. Israel, understood collectively] were exiled to Babylon for their מעל.'

26. The אצרות, 'storehouses', are specified in 1 Chron. 9.26. The occurrence of the אוצר יהוה in Josh. 6.19 in the context of the חרם, in connection with which Achan/r was guilty of מעל, is striking.

27. There may be added relevance, then, in the fact that Chronicles was one of the works read out to the High Priest on the eve of the Day of Atonement (*m. Yoma* 1.6. See H. Danby, *The Mishnah*, Oxford, 1933, 163).

28. For an analysis of the rhythms of Zionism and the study of Torah in contemporary Judaism, see J. Neusner, *Between Time and Eternity*, 171ff.

PART B

POST-BIBLICAL STUDIES

BEN SIRA—A CHILD OF HIS TIME

James D. Martin

University of St. Andrews

In a recent monograph on the 'didactic speeches' in Sirach,[1] Martin Löhr has indicated not only the special place which the 'Hymn to the Fathers' occupies in the book as a whole but the fact that its special nature and the special problems which it throws up ideally demand a separate study.[2] There has, over the past twenty or so years, been a series of important monographs on different aspects of Ben Sira, his work and his cultural milieu.[3] Only one has dealt exclusively with the Hymn to the Fathers.[4] The series in which that monograph appeared, however, already indicates something of its nature and style. One of its main concerns is with the way in which the author regards Ben Sira, especially in the Hymn to the Fathers, as a half-way point between the Old Testament and Judaism on the one hand and Christianity on the other. This, then, is for the most part a Christian spiritual guide through Ben Sira's Hymn, and, although there are some valuable insights in this monograph, it is not the definitive study of the Hymn to the Fathers. This article is by way of prolegomena to such a study.

At first sight the book of Ecclesiasticus, or Sirach, is a perfectly orthodox wisdom book. The single-line proverb which predominates in the book of Proverbs has here been developed into the short essay, and the various topics of wisdom instruction are dealt with more or less extensively by this wisdom-school teacher from second century BC Jerusalem, e.g. filial duty (3.1-16), attitude to women (9.1-9), the art of government (9.17-10.18). Ben Sira does not forget matters such as table etiquette (31.12–32.13), to our minds perhaps apparently more trivial, but necessary for the right conduct of life by the rich upper-class young men who were his pupils and students. Ben Sira also pushes further the kind of theological thinking about wisdom which we find in Prov. 8. This he does primarily in his great Hymn to

Wisdom in chapter 24 but also in various other parts of his book:
16.24–17.14; 39.16-35; 42.15–43.33. In all of these passages his
concern is with God and creation and the nature of the world created
by God and in which men live. But although in these respects Ben
Sira might mark an advance with regard both to form and to content
on the book of Proverbs, he nevertheless continues to affirm the
traditional doctrine of reward and punishment. In 4.10, for example,
he reaffirms the doctrine that the doing of good works will bring its
reward, though the language does suggest that such reward is beyond
death. Similarly, 11.27-28 suggests that a man's true fate, the real
assessment of his life, comes only after his death. God is described as
a 'God of recompense' (35.13), and this idea is expounded more fully
in 17.15-24. In spite of his late date, Ben Sira seems completely
ignorant of the so-called 'Crisis of Wisdom' to which the authors of
Job and Ecclesiastes are often thought to be reacting. There is in
Sirach no sign of the heart-searching about the meaning of life that
we find in Qoheleth, no anguishing over the suffering of the righteous
such as we find in Job. The book, then, seems firmly in the line of
traditional wisdom teaching and thinking. Yet one of the major
characteristics of the wisdom movement in Israel and of the literary
products of such thinking is that they make no reference to Israel's
history. Wisdom is essentially ahistorical. Yet in Sirach, that apparently orthodox wisdom book, we find a major section, chapters 44–
49,[5] devoted exclusively to Israel's historical past. Two questions
immediately suggest themselves. What is the reason for the inclusion
of such historical material and what function does it serve in a corpus
of traditional wisdom material?

In their introductions to this particular section of Ben Sira's book,
a number of commentators refer to a larger or smaller number of
supposedly similar treatments, in the Old Testament and the inter-
testamental literature, of God's acts in history.[6] The passages most
often cited are in the Psalms, Pss. 78; 105; 106; 135 and 136. To these
have been added the prayer in Neh. 9 and the historical survey in
Ezek. 20. In some of these—Pss. 105, 106, 135 and 136—the
historical range covered is from the Egyptian bondage to the Settlement in Canaan, a much smaller period than that covered by Ben
Sira. In all of them, the purpose of the historical recital is reasonably
clear. Pss. 105, 135 and 136 are hymns of praise for Yahweh's saving
activity in his people's history. Ps. 106 presents the obverse of the
coin, depicting the people's rebelliousness even in Egypt and at the

Red Sea. It ends with a prayer for Yahweh to save his people now, as, in spite of their unfaithfulness, he has done in the past. So he can be praised by a psalmist confident of Yahweh's deliverance. Neh. 9 is somewhat similar, with its account of the people's repeated infidelity and Yahweh's repeated merciful forgiveness. The prayer culminates in their confession of their present sinfulness (v. 33), with its concomitant suffering of hardship and oppression. Sure in the knowledge of God's repeated forgiveness in the past, the people confidently renew the covenant in the expectation of his forgiveness in the present. Ps. 78 has a slightly different purpose, in that its description of the people's repeated past apostasy, in spite of Yahweh's continued guidance of them, culminates in the rejection of the Joseph tribes—the reference probably being to the ultimate rejection of the northern kingdom—and the establishment of Judah and the Davidic dynasty. The review in Ezek. 20 is again confined in the main to the Exodus–Settlement period, but the historical element here is largely secondary. What is emphasized is Israel's continued unfaithfulness, especially in the cultic sphere, and the context in which this is set is one of judgment.[7]

In these examples from the Old Testament, what we have for the most part is a history of the people as a whole. It is Israel that is faithless, not individual Israelites. Occasionally, it is true, individuals are mentioned in these historical reviews, but they are usually mentioned with some specific characteristic in mind, and the references to them rarely exceed one or two verses.[8] When individuals are cited, it is often those who are the objects of divine judgment.[9] But these individuals—those who figure in a positive light and those who figure as objects of God's punishment—appear against a background of more or less continuous historical narrative, even though that narrative is confined, for the most part, to the Exodus–Settlement period. In Sirach, on the other hand, there is no continuous narrative and little or no reference to the people as a whole. What we have, rather, are more or less elaborate cameos of individual figures in Israelite history. These occur, to be sure, in chronological order, but they are not portrayed against a background of salvation history, as are the examples cited from the Old Testament.

The function of the historical recital in the Old Testament contexts is, as we have seen, reasonably clear, but there is no such obvious function for Ben Sira's gallery of famous figures from the past. The opening verse of the Hymn might suggest that what follows is nothing but praise: Let us now praise men of piety (40.1), and this might seem to be borne out by the heading, which may or may not be a secondary element in the text: Praise of the Fathers of Old (שבח אבות עולם).[10] Praise certainly seemed to be the function of the historical recitals in Pss. 105, 135 and 136. But it was Yahweh who was praised there for his saving activity in his people's history. Here in Sirach the objects of praise seem to be, again, the individual heroes of old. The fact that what we have here is a gallery of individuals should not surprise us unduly, for this Hymn is, after all, part of a wisdom book, and it is the individual who is essentially the object of wisdom instruction. Wisdom admonitions are generally addressed to a single pupil (בני) and the commands and prohibitions are expressed by means of singular verbs. Since the Hymn is part of a wisdom book and since this is essentially didactic literature, it is likely that the Hymn will have some didactic function. But such a function, if it exists, is not immediately obvious nor explicitly expressed.

Let us turn now, briefly, to look at those passages from the non-canonical books which are also sometimes cited as parallels to the use of history by Ben Sira. The earliest of these[11] is in Judith 5.5-21 where Achior, the Ammonite leader, is pointing out to Holofernes why the Israelites have the audacity to resist him. Their history, he says, shows that it is their God who is their strength and that when they rely on him they are invincible. Only when they abandon their God are they subject to defeat (especially vv. 17-18). This historical recital in Judith is still very much in the Old Testament tradition. It is a history of the people as a whole, but it is an unbalanced historical picture. From the nation's origins to the patriarchs occupies four verses (6-9); from the descent to Egypt to the Exodus–Settlement events occupies seven (10-16); the long period from the Settlement to the Exile is dealt with in two verses (17-18), while the restoration is dealt with in one (19). We have noted already how several of the Old Testament 'histories' go no further than Moses. This one in Judith is little different, with only a perfunctory glance at post-Settlement history. There is also the fact that the purpose of this historical recital is made very plain in its demonstrating to Holofernes that as long as the Israelites remained, and continue to remain, faithful to their God, they have been, and will continue to be, invincible.

In the Wisdom of Solomon 10.1–11.4 we have another historical recital, the purpose of which is to show how the 'good man' is the one who is guided by wisdom. Here we have a catalogue of individuals (Adam, Cain, Noah, Abraham, Lot, Jacob, Joseph and Moses),[12] but none of them is mentioned by name. This section is almost a kind of midrash on the 'good man' motif in chapter 4, where already Enoch, again anonymously, has figured by way of example (4.7ff; Enoch in vv. 10-15). But the focal point here is the role of wisdom in guiding and guarding these men down through the ages. In 1 Macc. 2.51-60 we again have a catalogue of individuals, this time clearly identified by name: Abraham, Joseph, Phinehas, Joshua, Caleb, David, Elijah, Hananiah–Azariah–Mishael, Daniel. Each is encapsulated in a sentence underlining their fidelity and zeal even in the face of great trials and tribulations. The purpose of this categorization is expressed initially in the introductory verse 51: Remember the deeds they did in their generation, and great glory and eternal fame shall be yours.[13] The fact that 'remembrance' alone is not enough is brought out clearly by the concluding verse 61: As generation succeeds generation, follow their example; for no one who trusts in Heaven shall ever lack strength. There is a final example in 3 Macc. 6.4-8 where a number of individuals are cited as instances where God has intervened on behalf of his people. But two of those listed are foreign rulers who were conquered in the course of the divine deliverance of Israel (Pharaoh in verse 4, Sennacherib in verse 5). The remainder are somewhat legendary characters ('the three companions in Babylonia', that is Hananiah, Azariah and Mishael again in verse 6; Daniel in verse 7; Jonah in verse 8) who are scarcely part of the core of Israel's history.

Of these examples of historical recollection from the non-canonical Jewish literature only two, Wisdom and 1 Maccabees, are at all similar to what we find in Sirach. In them we have personal categorization, even though anonymously in Wisdom. Both of them, however, must be dated later than Sirach,[14] so can in no sense be thought of as Ben Sira's models. Again, both in Wisdom and in 1 Maccabees, these lists have fairly clear functions within their respective contexts, illustrative of wisdom's guiding and guarding hand in the case of Wisdom and examples to be imitated of fortitude in tribulation in the case of 1 Maccabees. It may be that the function of the list is also what is intended by Ben Sira, but nowhere does he make it explicit that his intention is that we should 'follow their example'.[15]

There is, however, another literary genre which has an interest in

history, namely apocalyptic. In a recent book[16] Christopher Rowland
has stressed two points. One is that in apocalyptic there appears to be
'an interest in history for its own sake'[17] and not just as a prelude to
the eschatological element which we often consider to be the
characteristic of apocalyptic literature. The second is that 'the
presence of such an interest in history is ... not a distinguishing
mark of apocalyptic alone'.[18] In other words, there is, in the period
in which apocalyptic literature was being produced in Judaism, a
genuine interest in history for its own sake, and that interest is not
confined to apocalyptic literature. Without going into detail, it is
possible to locate the beginnings of apocalyptic in the middle of the
3rd century BC. The earliest parts of the Enoch literature, 1 Enoch 1–
36, were certainly in existence before Ben Sira, and shortly after him
we have Daniel (c. 165 BC) and further material from the Enoch
tradition (1 Enoch 83–90, 91–105).[19] Even if Ben Sira's book is not
apocalyptic literature as such, it may be that his interest in history is
part of the general trend in this period towards an interest in history
for its own sake.

We can perhaps even go a little further than that. In an article
published in 1978 Graham Davies makes a number of interesting
points in this connection.[20] At one point in his article Davies is
concerned to forge links with earlier Israelite literature, particularly
with Israelite historiography. The Old Testament works with the
most obvious parallels to apocalyptic's interest in history, from the
point of view of their systematic and chronologically ordered approach,
are the Priestly Work and that of the Chronicler, in other words
'historical works which are strongly committed to and interested in
the maintenance of the Jerusalem cult'.[21] Now one of the prominent
characteristics of Ben Sira, one which, like his interest in history,
tends also to set him apart from the general tenor of the wisdom
movement, is his interest in the cult. This may be seen in his high
regard for the priesthood generally (7.29-31), in his singling out of
special festival days as being of particular importance (33.7-9) and in
his extolling of cultic practice (35.4-11). It is clear also from the
particularly prominent position given to both Aaron and Phinehas in
the Hymn (45.6-22, 23-26). It is perhaps most obvious in chapter 50,
his great eulogy of Simeon ben Johanan, most probably the High
Priest Simeon II (c. 218-192), with its description of him offering the
Daily Whole-Offering.[22] Davies makes the point that 'the extensive
treatment of past history which appears in apocalyptic'[23] is not to be

found among those elements in the prophetic literature such as Joel, Zechariah 9–14, Isaiah 24–27 which are most often thought to be the sources from which apocalyptic sprang. Apocalyptic's historical expression, then, may well have its origins in cult-centred historiography. Ben Sira, too, has a strong interest in cult and priesthood. We have already noted the difference between Ben Sira's treatment of history in the Hymn to the Fathers and those passages in the Old Testament and in the apocryphal literature with which it is most often compared. It may be, then, that Ben Sira's historical expression, too, has origins similar to those posited for that of apocalyptic literature.

Davies goes on to point to two 'more recent' (recent, that is, in 1978) theories on the origins of apocalyptic which may prove to be of interest in a consideration of Ben Sira. The first is that of Hengel who suggests that the origins of apocalyptic are to be found in priestly circles of Hasidim.[24] We have just noted Ben Sira's cultic interests as these are expressed in different parts of his book and how this may suggest links between Ben Sira and the 'cult-centred historiography' that we find in the Priestly Work and in Chronicles. The other theory to which Davies refers is the suggestion put forward by J.J. Collins that the book of Daniel, the most substantial example of apocalyptic writing to have found its way into the Hebrew canon, originated among those wisdom circles in which stress was laid on the interpretation of dreams, signs and visions.[25] Collins makes a very sharp distinction between this 'mantic' type of wisdom and what he calls 'proverbial wisdom', when he says that 'the *maśkîlîm* of Daniel have very little in common with the scribes of the Ben Sira type'.[26] Whether such a sharp division is justified might be questioned. Both of Collins' types use largely the same range of vocabulary, both about themselves and about the world in which they live, and while, from our vantage point, we seem to see sharply divergent concerns and interests, these two types of 'wise men' may not have regarded themselves as so very different from each other.[27] Collins is suggesting, then, the origin of apocalyptic in wisdom circles, though not, in his view, the same wisdom circles as those suggested by, for example, von Rad. Ben Sira clearly belongs to wisdom circles even though these are not the same wisdom circles as those to which Collins is referring. There are, then, some connections between wisdom circles and an apocalyptic work like Daniel which has a marked interest in history. Davies thinks that it is 'a not unreasonable assumption' that such 'wise men' would be familar with and devoted to the study of history.[28]

A final point from Davies' article is worth picking up. He is concerned to make the point that apocalyptic is not concerned solely with eschatology[29] and that history was a major concern of the authors of this type of literature. He goes on to say, in his final paragraph, that 'the order immanent in the cosmos was another'.[30] This, too, is a feature which may be found in several places in Sirach. Chapter 24, with its personal appeal to men by Wisdom (verse 19), is clearly in the same line as Prov. 8 (and, perhaps less clearly, as Job 28), but the idea that Wisdom was the first of God's creations (Prov. 8.22-26) and his partner in the creation of the cosmos (Prov. 8.27-31) is not present in Sir. 24, though it may well be presupposed.[31]

In 16.24-17.14 we have a passage which deals explicitly with God's creative activity. It falls broadly into three sections: 16.24-28; 16.29-17.10; 17.11-14. The second of these deals specifically with the creation of the world, including the latter's inherent goodness, and with the creation of man. Throughout this section there are a number of direct reminiscences of Gen. 1, but in his account of the creation of man (17.1-10) Ben Sira deals much more expansively with man's nature and abilities than does the Genesis writer. Both of these aspects, the taking up of and the expanding of elements from the Old Testament account of creation, are found in apocalyptic works. One thinks particularly of the account of creation in Jubilees 2, which is based on the Biblical text but which expands on it where the writer, in the light of his own particular interests, feels that it is incomplete.[32] If Jubilees is correctly dated to the second century BC, it is a work which is not far removed from Ben Sira in time.[33] More significantly, however, in the light of Davies' statement about 'the order immanent in the cosmos', the first of these sections, 16.24-28, deals specifically with that 'order':

> When the Lord created his works in the beginning,
> and after making them defined their boundaries,
> he disposed them in an eternal order
> and fixed their influences for all time.
>
> (16.26-27a)

Here an 'order' is imposed upon the cosmos ('his works'), in that the various elements which it comprises are delimited as to their extent and their sphere of influence. The latter may not extend unpredictably into a different area but is established and delimited 'for all time'. The final section of this larger passage, 17.11-14, following on from the expanded account of the creation of man, indicates how God gave to the people thus created 'the law of life' and 'an everlasting covenant' (verses 11-12). The terms 'law' and 'covenant' clearly indicate that it is God's chosen people that are the objects of his attention here. It is 'Israel' who has been created. This 'nationalistic' element is discernible also in chapter 24 where the created 'wisdom' finds a home in Israel (24.8-12) and where the same wisdom is equated with 'the book of the covenant' and 'the Law' of Moses (24.23). What had once been international wisdom is now an Israel-orientated wisdom and is equated with that specifically Israelite channel of revelation, the Torah. So here, too, in 16.24–17.14 creation is also Israel-orientated.

33.7-15 asks why some days are different from others when the light of the same sun illuminates all of them. The answer is that the world is full of opposites: Two and two, one over against the other (33.15b), but all are created thus by God; they are 'all the works of the Most High' (33.15a). What appears as random chance is within God's control. The idea of 'order' is not explicit here, but it is clearly implicit. The same may be said of another passage, 39.16-35,[34] where emphasis is laid on the purposefulness of creation. In both verses 16 and 33 the goodness of the divine creation is emphasised. More particularly, what is underlined in verse 21 is the 'order immanent in the cosmos': Everything has been created for its own purpose. In verse 17b the Hebrew text emphasises the same idea: Everything in its own time is excellent, and in verse 34b the expression is: All things prove good at their proper time. All of these phrases 'its own time', 'its own purpose', 'their proper time' are again expressive of the concept of cosmic 'order'.

Perhaps more significantly still, however, in view of its location in close proximity to the Hymn to the Fathers, is Ben Sira's 'Hymn on Creation' in 42.15–43.33. This passage, too, falls into three sections. In 42.15-25 we have praise of God's power and emphasis on the purposiveness of his creation of apparent opposites:

> All things go in pairs, one the opposite of the other;
> he has made nothing incomplete.
>
> (42.24)

We have an echo here of the thought of 33.15, and in verse 21a 'He has set in order the masterpieces of his wisdom', we have the same thought as in 16.27a.[35] Here, again, the contrasting diversities of the world are part of God's purposive plan for a cosmos which is 'set in order', and regulated by his controlling power. In the second section, 43.1-26, we have a series of very delicate descriptions of a range of natural phenomena. There are here a number of reminiscences of Gen. 1 but also an expansion in some breadth of the creation of the celestial phenomena—sun, moon, stars, rainbow, storms. It ends with a brief reference to the creation of the oceans with their islands and 'all kinds of living things'. This recalls the identical phenomena to be found in 16.29–17.10, especially the expansionist element in the account of the creation of man in 17.1-10. We have already observed the occurrence of similar features in a nearly contemporary apocalyptic work, Jubilees 2.[36] The third section, 43.27-33, rounds off this Creation Hymn by highlighting the inexhaustible nature of the poetic theme:

> We have seen but a small part of his works,
> and there remain many mysteries greater still.
>
> (43.32)

In this Hymn on Creation, then, we find reiterated once again the motif of the 'order immanent in the cosmos' and the reference to and expansion of the Genesis creation account which can be observed in, for example, Jubilees.

This emphasis on order in the created world is not, of course, unique either to Sirach or to apocalyptic literature. It is, in fact, exactly what has already been expressed in earlier wisdom literature, which has always rightly been regarded as a principal repository of the Old Testament's creation theology.[37] It is observable already in parts of Proverbs 10–29; it is expressed in hymnic form in Ps. 104 and in Pss. 89.10-14 and 93; it reaches a certain climax in the Yahweh speeches in the book of Job (Job 38–41) from where its 'perfect expression'[38] is attained in Prov. 8. Obviously Sirach and, indeed, apocalyptic literature too, in this respect at least, follows on this line which leads from Israel's early wisdom literature through to the later expressions in Job and Prov. 8. But we have already observed above[39] a nationalistic element in Sir. 24 which is not discernible in Prov. 8 but which is discernible also in Sir. 17.11-14. This is a development beyond what is found in Old Testament wisdom literature strictly speaking, though it is perhaps to be associated with the fervent expression given to a Torah-orientated piety in those late, so-called 'wisdom' Psalms such as 19.7-10 and 119. In Sirach, too, we find a much greater and more explicit insistence on 'order' in the cosmos. This aspect, then, distances Ben Sira somewhat from his wisdom predecessors and reveals a certain affinity with the concerns of those of his contemporaries or near contemporaries who are giving expression to their thought in the form of apocalyptic.

One verse in this Hymn on Creation perhaps leads us on to yet another area where Ben Sira may be linked with his apocalyptic contemporaries.

> He discloses the past and the future,
> and uncovers the traces of the world's mysteries.
>
> (42.19)

We have observed his interest in the past, and we have noted his insistence on cosmic order, on the uncovering of 'the traces of the world's mysteries'. Does he perhaps also have an interest in the future? One passage which fairly clearly seems to be expressing a future hope is 36.1-17 which has been described by Siebeneck as 'Sirach's vision of the future messianic kingdom'[40] and by Hengel as 'his prayer for the eschatological liberation from heathen and Seleucid rule'.[41] Even Caquot, who adopts on the whole a negative attitude towards the idea of messianism in Ben Sira, would accept that in 36.1-17 we have an expression of eschatological hope combined with nationalism.[42] The passage may well be nationalistic in its expression of antipathy towards the Seleucid rulers and their Jewish supporters who are described by terms such as 'adversary' and 'enemy' (v. 7), 'the oppressors of thy people' (v. 9) and 'hostile princes' (v. 10). There is also clearly an eschatological element in it with its looking forward to the 'end' (קץ) and the 'appointed time' (מועד) (both terms in verse 10 of the Hebrew text; the Greek text, v. 8, is slightly different)[43] when the destruction of these enemies will be accomplished. Indeed, the final verse of what is essentially a prayer:

> Hear the prayer of Thy servants
> According to Thy favour towards Thy people
> That all the ends of the earth may know
> That Thou art the Eternal God
>
> (Hebrew 36.22; Greek 36.17)

is described by Hengel as displaying 'that universal breadth which becomes typical of Jewish apocalyptic in Hellenistic times'.[44] Now while Davies, in the article cited earlier, is at pains to show that a preoccupation with the future is not the sole mark of apocalyptic literature, he is not, of course, denying that such a preoccupation is a common characteristic of the literary genre and of that particular mode of thought.[45] Rowland is more cautious when, speaking of 'the relationship between apocalyptic and eschatology', he says 'that we are dealing with two separate issues in Jewish religion'.[46] In other words, while some apocalyptic writers are concerned with eschatological matters, not all of them are. But the combination in Sirach of 42.19 with its reference to 'the future' and 36.1-17 with its nationalistic eschatology does again serve to suggest a link between Ben Sira and those of his contemporaries who were writing in different literary genres.

Some would go further still. While Rowland would deny 'that the apocalypses have any profound interest in messianism',[47] Siebeneck, in his article, has a final section entitled 'Messianic Perspective'.[48] He takes 36.1-17 as his starting point, but he refers also to what is said in the Hymn to the Fathers about Elijah as the one who is 'written as ready for the time ... to restore the tribes of Israel' (48.10). The language of that verse strongly echoes that of Mal. 3.23 (EVV 4.5) which in due course leads to the idea of Elijah as the messianic precursor.[49] Siebeneck also believes that Ben Sira's recurring references to the Davidic covenant in 45.25 and 47.11, 22 might be 'the expression of a hope for a new Davidic king' and that the idea of the 'perpetual covenant with Aaron and his family (45.15, 24) too might be read as having an eschatological orientation'.[50] Caquot, on the other hand, thinks that there is no real evidence in Sirach to warrant such conclusions. Caquot's article makes no reference to Siebeneck; his criticism is directed against J. Klausner who finds that there is enough in Sirach to testify 'to the vitality of the Messianic idea in the storm-heralding time that preceded the Hasmonean uprising'.[51] Caquot's arguments against Klausner and against the existence of any real messianic current of thought in Sirach would lead us into a more detailed study of the text of the book than there is a place for here. Suffice it to say at this point that it is possible to argue for or against the concept of 'royal messianism' in Sirach and that there is also the possibility that in his eulogy particularly of Aaron and Phinehas (45.6-22, 23-26) Ben Sira is coming close to what one might call a 'priestly messianism'.[52] It is perhaps significant that, at a time and in a place not too far removed from Ben Sira's Jerusalem of c. 190 BC, the doctrine of a double messiah did in fact emerge.[53] Here again, then, Ben Sira is perhaps to be illuminated by the writing and thinking of those who were his near contemporaries.

Two other factors are worth noting briefly at this point, since they, too, serve to associate Ben Sira with those contemporaries whose thinking was along apocalyptic lines. In 33.7-9, part of a passage which we looked at earlier in connection with Ben Sira's concept of 'order' in the cosmos, we find him saying that days are differentiated one from the other 'by the Lord's decision', and that it is he who ordained 'the various seasons and festivals'. This is amplified in another creation passage, 43.6-8, where the purpose of the creation of the moon is not only 'to mark the divisions of time' but to serve as the norm by which feast-days are reckoned.[54] Ben Sira also notes the marvel of its waxing and waning and how it serves as the indicator for the division of the year into months. Here we have an interest, perhaps not a very developed one, but an interest nonetheless, in the calendar and, if we look at a slightly wider canvas in that chapter, perhaps in verses 1-10 (or 1-12), in matters astronomical. This, too, is one of the significant aspects of some of the apocalyptic literature. We find it in Jubilees, a work to which we have already had occasion to refer in association with Ben Sira's interest in creation, in 6.32ff. We find the same concern in 1 Enoch 72–82, a section of the Enoch literature which may be dated as far back as the middle of the third century BC.[55] Here, too, there is a Qumran connection, in so far as one of the main areas of disagreement between the Qumran community and the Jerusalem establishment was the calendar.[56]

The second of these factors involves the choice of those who are included in Ben Sira's Hymn to the Fathers. This is a broad area, for a discussion of which there is no room at the moment. The point which I wish to bring out very briefly here is that the list is bracketed by Enoch at the beginning (44.16) and by Enoch again and Adam at the end (49.14-16). Enoch was a subject of apocalyptic speculation right from the earliest times, probably, as we have just noted, from the middle of the third century BC. This interest in Enoch was undoubtedly fuelled by the fact that he was not, according to Gen. 5.24, subject to death but 'walked with God; and he was not, for God took him'. The pseudepigraphical works which deal specifically with Adam[57] can, in their present forms at least, scarcely be dated earlier than the turn of the era.[58] Edmond Jacob, however, goes so far as to speak, in relation to Ben Sira, of 'une eschatologie adamique'[59], and Siebeneck, acknowledging here explicitly his debt to Maertens, suggests that Ben Sira 'has concretized traditional messianic ideas in the heroes of the past' and cites as an example the specific case of Moses (45.1-5) with a quotation from Maertens to the effect that the descriptions applied to Moses by Ben Sira carry so many eschatological overtones that what Ben Sira has to say there can be construed only as a prophecy of the new Moses.[60]

Clearly we cannot carry any association between the work of Ben Sira and second century BC apocalyptic thought and literature too far. Indeed, he himself probably felt in some ways that the realm of apocalyptic was a strange and potentially dangerous one. There is a passage in 3.21-24 in which Ben Sira warns his readers of the dangers of prying into 'things too hard' for them and of examining 'what is beyond (their) reach'. This is often interpreted as referring to the speculative approach of Greek philosophy, to which many in Jerusalem and Judea has been introduced with the advent of Hellenism in the post-Alexander period.[61] But an equally possible interpretation, one which is perhaps more apposite in view of those associations with apocalyptic which we have been observing, is that Ben Sira is warning his readers against idle speculation and of the dangers of possible apocalyptic 'excesses'.[62]

We began with two questions, the reason for the inclusion of historical material in a wisdom book and the function that such material serves there. I have tried to point out the many areas in which Ben Sira, in so many ways an orthodox wisdom teacher, has affinities with those of his contemporaries who are thinking and writing in apocalyptic terms. Like so many of them Ben Sira, too, is interested in history. His interest in history is, as we have seen, quite different from that of those Old Testament passages which are normally cited by way of comparison. The only similarities we have observed are in two works which are of a later, though not much later, date than Sirach, namely Wisdom and 1 Maccabees. One major difference between Ben Sira's approach to history and that of the Old Testament passages cited is that, while they are dealing with 'Israel' as a unit and with a continuous narrative, he is concerned with individual figures with no on-going narrative background. Apocalyptic's presentation of history is often in terms of ages and epochs, as, for example, in Dan. 7–12, and this aspect almost certainly has its origins in those Old Testament historical works which also betray a systematic and chronologically ordered approach, the Priestly Work and Chronicles. While Ben Sira's presentation is not in terms of ages and epochs, his decision to concentrate on a succession of individuals may be his particular version of this same general approach.

The Priestly Work and Chronicles are examples of what has been called 'cult-centred historiography', and this aspect is almost certainly present in Ben Sira's Hymn to the Fathers as well. There is a concentration there on two figures who are secondary in terms of 'saving history', but primary in the sphere of 'cult history', namely Aaron and Phinehas. In the post-Solomonic monarchical period, apart from Solomon's immediate successors, only Hezekiah and Josiah are singled out for special mention, the same two figures who receive unqualified praise from the Deuteronomist for their cultic reforms in Jerusalem. In the post-exilic period it is Zerubbabel and Joshuah the High Priest who feature, the two who were the principal agents of the rebuilding of the Jerusalem Temple and of the re-establishment of its cult. Nehemiah is praised for his part in the rebuilding of the city and its walls, but there is, undoubtedly significantly, no mention of Ezra, the prototype of the Pharisee.

But it seems probable that Ben Sira had an interest not only in the past for its own sake but for its eschatological significance as well. We have seen the distinct possibility that in his Hymn he gives expression to a royal and/or a priestly messianism in his eulogies of the figures of David, on the one hand, and of Aaron and Phinehas, and even perhaps the High Priest Simeon, on the other. The fact that the Hymn begins and ends with Enoch would also appear to link Ben Sira with those of his contemporaries whose interests were more overtly concentrated on that figure from Israel's remotest past. All of these considerations require a more detailed study of the text of the Hymn than we can enter upon here, but, in view of the clear links between Ben Sira and other intellectual movements of his day, it is with these apocalyptic and eschatological and even messianic possibilities in mind that we should approach a more detailed study of his Hymn to the Fathers.

It is with pleasure that I dedicate this 'torso' to William McKane who was my first teacher of Hebrew and who has been a friend and colleague over the years since. His interests in wisdom are well known, and I trust that he will accept, as a token of my regard for his scholarship, this contribution to the study of one who felt himself to be both prophet and wise man.

NOTES

1. Martin Löhr, *Bildung aus dem Glauben: Beiträge zum Verständnis der Lehrreden des Buches Jesus Sirach*, Bonn, 1975. In this paper, we refer to the book as Sirach, and to the author as Ben Sira.

2. *Ibid.*, 11: 'Diesem wichtigen Stück würde man durch eine selbständige Untersuchung eher gerecht werden'. This by way of excuse for excluding the Hymn entirely from his field of study.

3. A.A.Di Lella, *The Hebrew Text of Sirach. A Textcritical and Historical Study*, The Hague, 1966; J. Haspecker, *Gottesfurcht bei Jesus Sirach* (Analecta Biblica, 30), Rome, 1967; H.P. Rüger, *Text und Textform im hebräischen Sirach* (BZAW, 112), Berlin, 1970; Th. Middendorp, *Die Stellung Jesus Ben Siras zwischen Judentum und Hellenismus*, Leiden, 1973; O. Rickenbacher, *Weisheitsperikopen bei Ben Sira*, Göttingen, 1973; M. Löhr, *Bildung aus dem Glauben*, Bonn, 1975; G.L. Prato, *Il problema della teodicea in Ben Sira* (Analecta Biblica, 65), Rome, 1975; H. Stadelmann, *Ben Sira als Schriftgelehrter* (WUNT 2nd Series, 6) Tübingen, 1980; P.C. Beentjes, *Jesus Sirach en Tenach*, Nieuwegein, 1981.

4. Dom Th. Maertens, *L'Eloge des Pères (Ecclésiastique XLIV-L)* (Collection Lumière et Vie, 5), Bruges, 1956.

5. Or possibly 'chapters 44–50'. Commentators differ as to whether chapter 50, with its description of the High Priest engaged in cultic activity in the Temple, belongs with the Hymn to the Fathers or stands apart from it. Certainly 49.14-16 seems to round off the Hymn by returning to some extent to its starting point (see below), but the eulogy of a High Priest who was almost certainly dead when Ben Sira wrote his poem about him is looking to a past, even if a very recent one, and picks up an emphasis on cultic and priestly matters which is discernible not only in the book as a whole but also in the Hymn itself with its extended 'praise' of Aaron and Phinehas (45.6-26).

6. The standard commentaries are as follows: I. Lévi, *L'Ecclésiastique ou La Sagesse de Jésus, fils de Sira*, Texte original hébreu, édité, traduit et commenté (Bibliothèque de l'Ecole des Hautes Etudes. Sciences Religieuses, 10), Paris, Pt.1, 1898, Pt.2, 1901; R. Smend, *Die Weisheit des Jesus Sirach*, Berlin, 1906; W.O.E. Oesterley, *Ecclesiasticus* (Cambridge Bible for Schools and Colleges), Cambridge, 1912; N. Peters, *Das Buch Jesus Sirach* (Exegetisches Handbuch zum Alten Testament, 25), Münster, 1913; G.H. Box and W.O.E. Oesterley, 'Sirach' in R.H. Charles (ed.), *The Apocrypha and Pseudepigrapha of the Old Testament*, Vol. 1, Oxford, 1913; M.S. Segal, *Sēpher Ben Sira hāshālēm*, Jerusalem, ³1972; J.G. Snaith, *Ecclesiasticus* (CBC), Cambridge, 1974.

7. See esp. verse 4 and Zimmerli's description of this section as 'a history of Israel's disobedience, deserving of judgement' (Walther Zimmerli, *Ezekiel* I [Hermeneia], Philadelphia, 1979, 405).

8. Abraham (Ps. 105.9-10, along with Isaac and Jacob as partners in the covenant with God; Ps. 105.42; Neh. 9.7); Moses (Ps.105.26, along with Aaron; Ps. 106.16; Ps. 106.23, Moses on his own with the designation 'his chosen one'; Neh. 9.14); Phinehas (Ps. 106.30f; he figures largely in Ben Sira's Hymn, 45.23-26).

9. Pharaoh (Ps. 135.9, 136.15; Neh. 9.10), Dathan and Abiram (Ps. 106.17), Sihon and Og (Ps. 135.11; 136.19f; Neh. 9.22).

10. See Martin Hengel, *Judaism and Hellenism*, London, 1974, 194, who refers to the Hymn to the Fathers as simply 'the glorification of the past'.

11. The date of the book of Judith is variously located from the late Persian period down to that of the Hasmoneans. The latter seems the more likely. See, e.g., G.W.E. Nickelsburg, *Jewish Literature between the Bible and the Mishnah*, Philadelphia and London, 1981, 108-9 and S. Zeitlin, *The Book of Judith* (Jewish Apocryphal Literature, 7), Leiden, 1972, 26-31.

12. Not all of these are 'good men'. Cain certainly appears by way of contrast. Lot is perhaps also rather unexpected, though his rescue from Sodom clearly classified him as a 'righteous' man.

13. The Greek actually has a double imperative: Remember... and receive... Dancy (J.C. Dancy, *A Commentary on I Maccabees*, Oxford, 1954, 87), following Fairweather (Fairweather and Black, *Commentary on I Maccabees*, 1897), suggests that the double imperative is a Hebraic form of conditional: If you remember... you will receive... Cf. A.B. Davidson, *Hebrew Syntax*, Edinburgh, [3]1901, §132 (b), 181.

14. Wisdom is dated variously from the mid second century BC to the early first century AD. See, e.g., J.A.F. Gregg, *The Wisdom of Solomon*, Cambridge, 1922, who suggests 125–100 BC; John Geyer, *The Wisdom of Solomon*, London, 1963, 'during the first century before Christ'; E.G. Clarke, *The Wisdom of Solomon*, Cambridge, 1973, 'mid second or early first century BC'; Nickelsburg, *op.cit.*, 184, 'the first decades of the Common Era', possibly even 'during the reign of Caligula (37–41 CE)'. The date of 1 Maccabees can be fixed as prior to 63 BC and probably around 100 BC. See, e.g., F.-M. Abel, *Les Livres des Maccabées*, Paris, 1949, xxviii-xxix; Nickelsburg, 117; J.A. Goldstein, *I Maccabees* (Anchor Bible), New York, 1976, 63.

15. In 1 Macc. 2 the purpose of the list is made plain in the verse immediately preceding it (verse 51) and in the verse immediately following it (verse 61). The only possible parallel in Sirach is 44.15, the final verse of the prologue to the Hymn. This verse appears only in the margin of MS B of the Hebrew text but is found, with its first half fragmentary, in the Masada scroll. See Y. Yadin, *The Ben Sira Scroll from Masada*, Jerusalem, 1965, 37.

16. *The Open Heaven. A Study of Apocalyptic in Judaism and Early Christianity*, London and New York, 1982.

17. P. 137. Cf. also 142, 'There seems here (in Syrian Baruch), and for that matter in the similar reviews in other apocalypses, an interest in history in its own right'.

18. P. 141. Rowland makes this point because we find such an interest in history also in the Assumption of Moses where there is no 'apocalyptic framework of divine revelation' (140). See also 140: 'The retelling of biblical history is not confined to the apocalypses'.

19. See the section in Rowland 'Dating the Apocalypses', *op.cit.*, 248-67, with the summary table 266-67.

20. 'Apocalyptic and Historiography', *JSOT* 5 (1978), 15-28.

21. Pp. 23-24.

22. Such is the view of Fearghas O'Fearghail, 'Sir. 50:5-21—Yom Kippur or the Daily Whole Offering?', *Biblica* 59 (1978), 301-16. Most commentators believe that what Ben Sira is describing in chapter 50 is the High Priest functioning in the ritual of the Day of Atonement.

23. P. 25.

24. Davies' article, 25 and its reference in n. 26 to Hengel, *Judaism and Hellenism*, 189. P.R. Davies, 'Hasidim in the Maccabean Period', *JJS* 28 (1977), 127-140, doubts the existence of a group or party known as the Hasidim. Note also Hengel's reference (also 189) to 'the stress on priestly privileges' in the Testament of Levi which he describes as being both Hasidic/proto-Essene *and* apocalyptic in style. R.T. Beckwith, 'The Earliest Enoch Literature and its Calendar', *RQ* 10 (1979-81), 365-403, calls Sirach 'a pre-Pharisaic work' (367). He points also to its several anti-Sadducean features (belief in angels and a future life) and calls it 'distinctly anti-Essene' in view of its acceptance of the lunar calendar. For this last in Sirach see below. In a later article, Beckwith argues that the antecedents of the three main Jewish schools of thought 'need to be sought in a period before, not during, the Hellenizing crisis of 175 BC'. ('The pre-history of the Pharisees, Sadducees and Essenes: A tentative reconstruction', *RQ* 11 (1982f.), 3-46; the quotation on 3).

25. Davies, 25 and the reference in n. 27 to J.J. Collins, 'The Court-Tales in Daniel and the Development of Apocalyptic', *JBL* 94 (1975), 218-34, esp. 232-34.

26. Collins, 232.

27. Collins criticizes V. Tcherikover, *Hellenistic Civilization and the Jews*, New York, 1970 for his attribution of the book of Daniel to the scribal class of wise men. Such an attribution is nowhere explicit in the page references to Tcherikover which Collins gives, namely 125-26, 196-8, nor does it even seem to be implicit there.

28. Davies, 25. The 'wise men' he refers to are those 'mantic wisdom circles' of Collins' theory. If, however, one thinks of wisdom circles generally as the core of ancient Israel's educational system, there is certainly a very strong probability that history, and especially the history of their own nation, would be one of the subjects of study.

29. This is the popular misconception which Davies' article is mainly intended to counter.

30. Davies, 25.

31. It is clear from Sir. 24.3 that Wisdom is *a* creation of God's but not necessarily the first, as the Proverbs passage makes quite explicit. Nor is there any explicit indication in Sir. 24 that Wisdom was God's partner in the creation of the rest of the cosmos.

32. Rowland, 146f.

33. For a discussion of the date of Jubilees see, e.g., Nickelsburg, 78f and, in more detail, James C. VanderKam, *Textual and Historical Studies in the Book of Jubilees*, Chico, 1977, 207-85, who opts for a date between 161 and 152 BC (284). Similar features, the reproduction and occasional expansion of the biblical text, are to be found in 4 Ezra (6.38-54), see Rowland, 147f., but this is, of course, a much later work, belonging to the first century AD. See Nickelsburg, 287-94. On the dating of the various apocalypses see again Rowland, 248-67.

34. It is possible that a slightly wider context should be considered here, namely 39.12-35. The section which I have delineated is introduced in 39.15 as if it were a hymn, and v. 35 takes up that motif again. There are in addition certain refrain-like elements in the body of the 'hymn'. Verse 16 is echoed to some extent by v. 33, and, more significantly, vv. 17, 21 and 34 are couched in the same question and answer form. Perhaps Snaith's heading for this passage in his Cambridge Bible commentary (192) is the neatest description of it: 'A Doctrinal Hymn of Creation', underlining both its hymnic chracter and its theological content.

35. And the same verb, κοσμέω. The Hebrew text of 16.27a is not extant. The verb in 42.21a is תכן, the Piel 'regulate, measure out', which the Greek translation renders as ἐκόσμησε, 'he set in order'.

36. See above, p. 148 and notes 32 and 33.

37. See, e.g., H.-J. Hermisson, 'Observations on the Creation Theology in Wisdom', in *Israelite Wisdom. Theological and Literary Essays in Honor of Samuel Terrien*, ed. J.G. Gammie and others, Chico, 1978, 43-57.

38. Hermisson, 44.

39. P. 149.

40. R.T. Siebeneck, 'May their bones return to life!—Sirach's praise of the fathers', *CBQ* 21 (1959), 411-28, citation on 425.

41. M. Hengel, *Jews, Greeks and Barbarians*, London, 1980, 47.

42. A. Caquot, 'Ben Sira et le Messianisme', *Semitica* 16 (1966), 43-68. Reference is to p. 49.

43. 36.1-17 of the Hebrew text appears in the Greek translation as 33.1-13a + 36.16b-22. For an account of the dislocation of the Greek text see, e.g., Di Lella, *Hebrew Text of Sirach*, 49-51, with his quotation on 50 from Swete, *The Old Testament in Greek*, vi-vii. Different editions of the Hebrew text seem to follow different verse numberings. The best edition for comparison here is that of F. Vattioni, *Ecclesiastico*, Naples, 1968, 188f., where it can be

clearly seen that the relevant verse here is 36.8 in the Hebrew text and 33.10 in the Greek.

44. Hengel, *Jews, Greeks*, 48.

45. G.I. Davies, *art. cit., passim*.

46. Rowland, *op. cit.*, 47-48.

47. *Ibid.*, 176.

48. Siebeneck, 424-28.

49. According to Hermann L. Strack and Paul Billerbeck, *Kommentar zum Neuen Testament aus Talmud und Midrasch*, Munich, 1926, Vol. IV, 2, 779-80, Sir. 48.10 is the earliest written source to refer to Mal. 3.1, 23f. in this way and to refer to Elijah as a Messianic figure. See, too, the article 'Ἠλ(ε)ίας by J. Jeremias in *TDNT*, II, 928-41, esp. 931-34.

50. Siebeneck, 427.

51. J. Klausner, *The Messianic Idea in Israel*, London, 1956, 252-58, citations from p. 258.

52. See E. Schürer, *The History of the Jewish People in the age of Jesus Christ*, rev. and ed. by G. Vermes and others, Edinburgh, 1973f., Vol. II, 499: 'He was much more concerned about the renewal of the Davidic dynasty (45.24f.)'. The expression '*messianisme sacerdotale*' is used by Caquot, *art. cit.*, 63, but just as he rejects the idea of royal messianism so, too, he rejects the idea that Ben Sira gives expression to any priestly messianism, because the family in which the priesthood is legitimately enshrined currently holds the position of head of state. There can, therefore, be no question of 'restoration', and it is that which Caquot regards as an essential element in the concept of 'messiah'. For a slightly different conception and for the use of the expression 'priestly messianism' he refers to an article by P. Zerafa, 'Priestly Messianism in the OT', *Angelicum* 42 (1965), 318-41, which I have not seen.

53. At Qumran. See, e.g., Schürer, II, 550-54. See also J. Priest, 'Ben Sira 45, 25, in the Light of the Qumran Literature', *RQ* 5 (1964-66), 111-18.

54. The Hebrew text of 43.6 is obscure, but the Masada text throws some light at least on 43.6a. Even with its obscurities, the Hebrew text does seem to be speaking of the moon's function in delimiting 'times' עתות and 'festivals' (חג in 43.7aM). See Yadin, *The Ben Sira Scroll from Masada*, 29f., 45f.

55. See, e.g., Nickelsburg, 47f. For a discussion of this astronomical aspect of apocalyptic literature see Rowland, 120-23.

56. For a discussion of this topic at Qumran see G. Vermes, *The Dead Sea Scrolls. Qumran in Perspective*, London, 1977, 175-78, 191f. For the importance of the topic in the Enoch tradition see the first article by Beckwith cited in n. 24.

57. The Apocalypse of Adam, the Testament of Adam and the Life of Adam and Eve, the last with its variant recension known as the Apocalypse of Moses.

58. See, in summary, J.H. Charlesworth, *The Pseudepigrapha and Modern Research*, Chico, 1976; [2]1981, 72-75, 91f.

59. Edmond Jacob, 'L'histoire d'Israël vue par Ben Sira', in *Mélanges bibliques rédigés en l'honneur de M. André Robert*, Paris, 1957, 288-94, citation from 294. Jacob's view is, of course, questioned by Caquot, 64-67.

60. Siebeneck, 426 n. 28 with reference to Maertens (above n. 4), 95. The terms referred to occur in 45.1-5, and the specific terms cited are 'beloved by God', 'showed him His glory' and 'caused him to hear His voice'. More telling than either of the last two might have been the phrase in verse 2 'made him equal in glory to the angels' (so NEB) or 'made him glorious as God' (so Box and Oesterley in Charles, *APOT* I, 485).

61. See, e.g., Smend, 31; Snaith, 23.

62. Rowland, 75; Nickelsburg, 67 n. 53, 'a warning against apocalyptic speculation'; so also possibly Peters, 34: 'Die Warnung wird sich vornehmlich gegen die in Israel eindringende kosmogonische und theosophische Spekulation richten . . . insbesondere nach rabbinischer Auffassung gegen das allzu tiefe Sichversenken in das Schöpfungswerk von Gen c.1'. This last is, of course, precisely one of the common subjects of apocalyptic speculation, one in which Ben Sira himself to some extent indulged.

THE PROPHETIC-SAPIENTIAL ORIGINS OF APOCALYPTIC THOUGHT

James C. VanderKam

North Carolina State University

During the last decades a number of scholars have investigated the problem(s) of apocalyptic origins. Their attempts at isolating the biblical and extra-biblical traditions which were the dominant influences on Jewish 'apocalyptic' have resulted in several different proposals. There continues to be widespread agreement that Persian dualism was one of the most significant foreign influences, although dating problems have perennially complicated use of Iranian sources.[1] Among the biblical traditions, contemporary scholars have usually defended either prophecy or wisdom as the major precursor of 'apocalyptic'.[2] The present essay is not intended as yet another survey of modern scholarly opinions in this field nor as an apology for any of them. Its primary aim is rather to suggest lines along which further research might profitably proceed. In the first part of the paper some terminological distinctions will be made, and these will be followed by short sketches of the arguments which have been adduced for both the prophetic and the sapiential theories of apocalyptic origins. Finally it will be maintained that these two options may not be as different as one might think. It is a special pleasure to be able to present this essay to Professor William McKane, some of whose perceptive words in his *Prophets and Wise Men* stimulated the line of thought which is here developed.

I. *Terminological Distinctions*

As several experts have lamented, the search for apocalyptic origins has been hindered by use of the vague term *apocalyptic* to refer to more than one entity.[3] It functions as a noun or adjective and can refer to a kind of literature or type of thought. The situation has been clarified in recent times by more precise delimitations of these

entities and by a tendency to avoid the word *apocalyptic* except
perhaps as an adjective (hence the quotation marks around the word
in the preceding paragraph). Paul Hanson, for instance, has proposed
the following terms and meanings: *apocalypse* designates a genre of
literature; *apocalyptic eschatology* refers to a system of thought; and
apocalypticism denotes an ideological phenomenon.[4] The first two
distinctions have been suggested by others as well and have proved
especially helpful.[5]

The most thorough treatment of the genre *apocalypse* has appeared
in the fourteenth volume of *Semeia*, entitled *Apocalypse: The
Morphology of a Genre*. The editor, J.J. Collins, defines the genre
thus:

> 'Apocalypse' is a genre of revelatory literature with a narrative
> framework, in which a revelation is mediated by an otherworldly
> being to a human recipient, disclosing a transcendent reality which
> is both temporal, insofar as it envisages eschatological salvation,
> and spatial insofar as it involves another, supernatural world.[6]

There is a perhaps unavoidable element of circularity about such
definitions in that the characteristics of texts which are intuitively or
traditionally regarded as apocalypses constitute the definition which
then determines the texts that are to be included in the genre.
Nevertheless, there is a group of documents or parts of texts which
are widely recognized as apocalypses and whose traits distinguish
them from other sorts of revelatory literature.[7] Apocalypses, understood in this generic sense, have formal precursors in accounts of
prophetic visions in the first part of Zechariah, although no biblical
vision report other than those in Daniel 7–12 deals with the subject
matter that one finds in apocalyptic dreams or visions.

It has proved more difficult to characterize apocalyptic thought.
Understanding the nature of this sort of thinking is essential if one is
to search for antecedents, but not all students of the subject agree
about what constitutes the heart of apocalyptic thought. Two recent
books illustrate the disagreement. Hanson found the core of apocalyptic doctrine in the special eschatology which comes to expression in
apocalypses and related works. In apocalyptic eschatology salvation
is awaited in a transformed cosmos rather than in more normal
historical conditions.[8] Christopher Rowland has more recently
countered that the central feature of apocalyptic thought (what he
calls 'apocalyptic') is '. . . the revelation of the divine mysteries

through visions or some other form of immediate disclosure of heavenly truths'.[9] These mysteries include more than just eschatological data; for Rowland they can be summarized in the words of *m. Ḥagigah* 2.1: ' . . . what is above, what is beneath, what was beforetime, and what will be hereafter'.[10] Rowland's thesis accounts for a broader range of material in apocalyptic works, but he has extended the category to include more than some others would allow. He thinks, for example, that all of 1 Enoch and Jubilees are apocalypses.[11] If both documents are included among the apocalypses, then clearly apocalyptic thinking must involve more than eschatology—a subject on which Jubilees and the Astronomical Book of 1 Enoch (72–82) are rather restrained. So Rowland's view is a helpful corrective to the narrower focus on eschatology, but it does entail a questionable expansion of the genre apocalypse and an unnecessary downplaying of the importance of eschatology in apocalyptic thought.

II. *The Antecedents of Apocalyptic Thought*

It seems reasonable to say that the revelation of secrets—especially eschatological ones of many varieties—is crucial to apocalyptic thinking. As one searches for biblical influences that may have stimulated these ways of thinking, one should attempt to find one or several in which the future plays a significant role. As noted above, contemporary scholars have regularly found the requisite antecedent either in biblical prophecy or in the sapiential traditions of Israel. Both obviously made contributions to apocalyptic thought, but the experts have opted for one or the other as the more dominant one while in almost every case recognizing that it is 'both/and' rather than an 'either/or' situation.

Prophecy
Advocates of prophecy as the major formative influence on apocalyptic teachings usually concentrate on eschatological themes which figure in prophetic books but which undergo greater development or elaboration in the apocalyptic texts. D.S. Russell, for one, quotes with approval H.T. Andrew's claim that 'apocalyptic arose out of prophecy by developing and universalizing the conception of the Day of the Lord'.[12] And, before him, H.H. Rowley had affirmed: 'That apocalyptic is the child of prophecy, yet diverse from prophecy, can hardly be disputed.'[13] He did admit that 'apocalyptic' owed ' . . . more

to the circumstances that gave it birth in the Maccabean age' than to prophecy or foreign influences, but for him prophecy was the most important traditional factor.[14] That prophetic heritage was heavily eschatological. In words that others have echoed, he wrote that, 'speaking generally, the prophets foretold the future that should arise out of the present, while the apocalypticists foretold the future that should break into the present'.[15] Within biblical prophetic literature segments such as Second and Third Isaiah, Isaiah 24–27, Ezekiel, and Zechariah are frequently cited as compositions which reveal varied aspects of the transition from prophecy to 'apocalyptic'. If eschatology of one or, more likely, several kinds is characteristic of apocalyptic writings and thought, then biblical prophecy, in which eschatological themes play significant roles, seems a plausible and indeed likely source of influence.

It is worth adding that ancient writers of apocalypses often called their works prophecies or named their apocalyptic seers prophets. The Revelation of John terms itself a prophecy (1.3; 22.18-19), and several of the writings that circulated under the name of Ezra refer to him as a prophet (4 Ezra 1.1; the Greek Apocalypse of Ezra 1.3; and the Questions of Ezra 1.1). Moreover, Enoch prophesies according to Jude 14, while the efforts of the Jewish Sibyl are also regularly called prophesying (e.g. Book 1, line 2; 3, lines 3, 163, 298, 401, 491, 811-12, etc.). Then, too, there has been a long debate about whether the book of Daniel should be classified among the prophets (as in the LXX and the Lives of the Prophets) or the Writings (as in the MT).

There is ample reason for concluding that the prophetic teachings had a strong impact on the authors of the Jewish apocalyptic books, especially in eschatological matters. Some ancient writers expressed this special connection by naming their apocalyptic works prophecies or the seers prophets. Prophetic texts and motifs find echoes throughout the apocalyptic literature, and in some cases the seer had the text of a prophetic book before him as he pondered (Daniel 9 is an obvious example).[16]

Wisdom

Among those who have rejected prophecy as the major native influence on apocalyptic thought, the most prominent and radical was Gerhard von Rad. He not only saw another tradition—wisdom—as more important but completely excluded a prophetic connection.

> In view of its keen interest in the last things and of the significance
> it attaches to visions and dreams, it might seem appropriate to
> understand apocalyptic literature as a child of prophecy. To my
> mind, however, this is completely out of the question ... The
> decisive factor, as I see it, is the incompatibility between apocalyp-
> tic literature's view of history and that of the prophets. The
> prophetic message is specifically rooted in the saving history, that
> is to say, it is rooted in definite election traditions. But there is no
> way which leads from this to the apocalyptic view of history, no
> more than there is any which leads to the idea that the last things
> were determined in a far-off past.[17]

Once he had rejected prophecy as the traditional source of apocalyptic
thought, von Rad turned to Israel's sapiential traditions which, he
thought, offered a more convincing background. Knowledge was, in
his words, the 'nerve-centre of apocalyptic literature', which was
further characterized by the sorts of 'figurative discourses' which
were traditional in wisdom. And, of course, the great seers are wise
men (Daniel, Enoch, and Ezra).[18]

Von Rad's thesis has aroused strongly negative reactions which
have centered on the lack of eschatology in the wisdom traditions.[19]
In later editions of his *Theologie des Alten Testaments*, von Rad
attempted to cope with this objection by arguing that not all wisdom
traditions continued into apocalyptic literature, '... sondern nur
einige ihrer Sektoren, also vor allem die alte Traumdeutungswissen-
schaft und die Wissenschaft von den Orakeln und den "Zeichen"'.[20]
This was an important concession, though it still has not led to wide
acceptance of his view. H.P. Müller has subsequently refined von
Rad's approach by demonstrating that the type of wisdom which
exerted strong influence on apocalyptic thought was not the courtly-
pedagogical but the mantic or divinatory kind. He focused his
investigation on the figure of Daniel who was, of course, both a
diviner and seer. Müller suggested that if one saw the roots of
apocalyptic thinking in divination, then four features of the apocalyptic material that do not come from classical prophecy can be
explained: determinism, claim to inspiration, use of symbolic imagery,
and pseudonymity.[21] Daniel is a parade example, but Enoch, too,
embodies a number of mantic traits as he evolves into a seer.[22]

One could object that the highly negative manner in which the
Hebrew Bible pictures divination argues against it as a major
influence on apocalyptic writers who were greatly concerned with

understanding the sacred writings. Moreover, the kinds of predictions which mantic specialists usually made seem to have little in common with the eschatological visions of the seers. The remainder of the paper will in part be a response to the former objection but here it should at least be noted that there always seem to have been officially acceptable types of divination in Israel. The *Urim* and *Thummim* and the ephod are well-known examples. There is reason to think that biblical opposition to certain mantic arts was based less on qualms about divination itself than on the pagan milieu within which Israel's neighbors and conquerors practiced them. The latter objection can now be faced in a new way because of the Akkadian prophecies. These texts share some central features with the Jewish apocalyptic works that include historical surveys—e.g. *vaticinia ex eventu* regarding the fate of nations and kings.[23] The Akkadian prophecies, which W.W. Hallo wanted to call apocalypses,[24] also appear to have some connection with the language and concepts of divination.[25] If this is true, then it raises the interesting possibility that in Mesopotamia, as in Israel, texts of this sort were shaped by mantic influences. It may not, therefore, be at all unlikely that apocalyptic visions represent a development of divinatory predictions. It is also highly likely, though, that the predictive side of prophecy has made an impact in this regard.

III. *A New Suggestion*

Though the experts have arrived at differing conclusions about the origins of apocalyptic thought, it may be that they are actually pointing in largely the same direction. It becomes evident, when one examines the data, that prophecy and divination were rather similar phenomena, not sharply contrasting entities. When scholars claim that apocalyptic thought developed from prophecy, they actually mean the work of that handful of prophets whose names are attached to biblical books, not the total phenomenon of Israelite prophecy. When one narrows the field to those few, who seem the exception and not the rule, one can more easily miss some of the mantic sides of prophecy. That prophecy and divination overlap to a surprising degree will be argued on the basis of specific texts below, but first it will be useful to note some of the general similarities between the two. Some of them are more obvious and will simply be mentioned while others will require additional explanation.

Similarities between prophecy and divination

1. Both were possible only because the deity or deities chose to reveal themselves, it was believed, to certain select individuals. The media chosen for these divine disclosures often differed (the word of the Lord is stressed in biblical prophecy, while Mesopotamian diviners, for example, characteristically examined sheep livers, etc., for omens), but both appealed to revelation. (In some cases the medium was the same; see no. 4 below.)

2. Both by their very nature dealt with the future and with learning its course in advance. Prophets may generally have operated within a covenantal framework and have addressed their oracles to their contemporaries, but the blessings and curses which rewarded obedience and punished disobedience pointed toward the future—usually one that would arrive soon. The deuteronomist certainly understood prophecy in this sense when he wrote that the criterion for a true prophecy was whether the word came to pass (Deut. 18.21-22). The diviner would read omens of many kinds and make predictions based on the patterns and traits that he saw. Both prophets and diviners at times made prognostications for individuals and at other times for larger groups or entire nations.

3. Both *late* prophecy and divination concerned themselves with deciphering messages which were encoded in ominous media. Cracking codes in which revelatory messages were concealed was the stock in trade of the mantic sage, while late prophecy in Israel involved a parallel decoding although the medium in question seems to have been the text of earlier prophetic books. Scholars who have studied the phenomenon of late biblical prophecy have observed that it was strongly interpretative in nature. As Joseph Blenkinsopp has recently put the matter:

> Increasing reference to former prophets, occasional laments for the absence of prophetic guidance and, not least, the well attested practice of adapting earlier prophetic sayings to new situations— e.g., in Zech. 1–8—are symptomatic of this new situation. With the availability of prophetic material in writing, the emphasis was less on direct inspired utterance and more on the inspired interpretation of past prophecy. Correspondingly, there was an increasing sense that, in the normal course of events, God does not communicate directly but has revealed his will and purpose in past communications whose bearing on the present situation remains to be elucidated.[26]

David L. Petersen has reached similar conclusions from his analysis of Second and Third Isaiah; Jer. 23.33-40; Zech. 13.2-6; Joel 3.1-5; and Malachi.[27] In the later prophetic corpus it appears, then, that prophecy has shifted from fresh proclamation to studied exegesis. The same feature is found, of course, in the apocalyptic texts as well. Daniel 9, for instance, tells how the seer divined the meaning of Jeremiah's 70 years of exile and based predictions on it.[28]

4. Prophets and diviners at times resorted to the same media for their revelations. Dreams or night visions are the principal example. As is well known, oneiromancy was a popular divinatory field in many cultures, including that of Israel where Joseph and Daniel were the most famous experts. Dreams were generally thought to be a means for divine communication (Job 33.14-18), but they apparently had a special connection with prophecy. This fact emerges clearly from Num. 12.6: 'And he said, "Hear my words: If there is a prophet among you, I the Lord make myself known to him in a vision, I speak with him in a dream."' Jeremiah makes a number of references to prophetic dreams but always in a negative sense (23.23-32; cf. 27.9; 29.8-9). Deut. 13.1-6 juxtaposes the prophet and the dreamer, while Zech. 13.4a declares that 'on that day every prophet will be ashamed of his vision when he prophesies; . . . ' As noted earlier, however, it is the night visions of Zechariah that in form most nearly resemble the literary accounts of apocalyptic dreams or visions. Moreover, the interpreted visions of Amos and other analogous ones in the prophetic books exhibit mantic traits.[29]

5. Both prophets and diviners brought divine messages to bear on political and military issues. It is well known that the prophets did so (e.g. Isaiah 7), but Mesopotamian diviners also advised on matters of war and state.[30]

Overlap between prophecy and divination
The general similarities listed above show that there was a definite overlap between the worlds of prophecy and divination. Naturally they could be distinguished in many instances, but their practitioners seem to have operated in generally the same sphere, to have used similar media at times, and to have performed analogous functions. This noteworthy degree of resemblance is not merely something that can be deduced through a modern critical approach; it was perceived by ancient writers as well. Two different kinds of passages make the point: those which juxtapose prophecy and divination apparently

because of their near kinship, and those which say that prophets divine or diviners prophesy.

1. Deuteronomy and 2 Isaiah bring the arts of divining and of prophesying into close contact with one another.

a. Deuteronomy 18, the well-known chapter which deals with a prophet like Moses (18.15-22), ranges diviner and prophet next to one another. 18.9-14 offers a warning to Israel that when it arrives in the land it is not to 'learn to follow the abominable practices of those nations' (18.9b), that is, diverse mantic arts. In fact, 18.10-14 provides instances of most items in the biblical vocabulary of divination. For the present purposes the most significant feature of Deut. 18.9-22 is the fact that it juxtaposes divination and prophecy. The author explains why: 'For these nations, which you are about to dispossess, give heed to soothsayers and to diviners; but as for you, the Lord your God has not allowed you to do so. The Lord your God will raise up for you a prophet like me from among your brethren— him you shall heed . . . ' (18.14-15). The issue here is one of obedience (note the repeated 'Heed'): the prophet is to be obeyed, not the diviner. But why contrast prophet and diviner rather than, say, prophet and priest? S.R. Driver correctly saw the point:

> The position assigned in this law to the prophet is a noticeable one. He appears in it as the representative in Israel of the heathen diviner; he is presented as the appointed agent for satisfying, in so far as they are legitimate, those cravings of humanity to unlock the secrets of the future, or to discover in some critical situation . . . the purpose of Heaven, which gave birth in other nations to the arts of the diviner, and kindred superstitions.[31]

Conveying messages from the divine side to the human was supposed to be the work of both; they are distinguished by the fact that the Lord has chosen to relay his word through the one and not encoded predictions through the other. That is, it seems that the religious context within which the two operate (the religion of Israel and that of Canaan) is the decisive factor and the basis for the condemnation of the latter. Prophets are apparently specialized diviners who serve the Lord and have the advantage of hearing his word rather than prying messages from omens.

b. Second Isaiah also places prophets and diviners side by side. In 44.25-26 the Lord identifies himself as the one

who frustrates the omens of liars,

and makes fools of diviners;
who turns the wise men back,
and makes their knowledge foolish;
who confirms the word of his servant,
and performs the counsel of his messengers . . .

The two functions are unmistakably contrasted to the disadvantage
of the diviners, but the decisive difference resides in the action of the
Lord, not necessarily in the nature of the disciplines. A related series
of verses figures in Isaiah 47–48. In 47.12-13 the prophet offers
mocking encouragement to the Babylonian diviners, whereas in 48.3-
8 he contrasts them, as prognosticators, with the Lord who declares
things '. . . from of old, before they came to pass . . . ' (48.5ab).
Prediction takes place but only in the manner chosen by God.[32]

2. A more specific way in which biblical writers indicate the
similarities between prophecy and divination is by asserting that
prophets divine or diviners prophesy.

a. Micah offers the earliest evidence for this usage. In the third
chapter the prophet delivers a divine indictment of his fellow
prophets (הנביאים [3.5]): 'Therefore it shall be night to you, without
vision,/ and darkness to you, without divination (מקסם [3.6]).' In the
following lines prophets, seers, and diviners (הקסמים) figure in a
poetic sequence, but 3.11 illustrates the point under consideration
with the greatest clarity:

> Its heads give judgment for a bribe,
> its priests teach for hire,
> its prophets divine for money (ונביאיה בכסף יקסמו). . .

The simple fact that what a prophet—even a 'false' one—does can be
expressed by the common word for divining shows that for the writer
the two were intimately related.

b. The book of Jeremiah offers related information. At 14.14 the
Lord responds to Jeremiah's report about the prophets who have told
the people that they would enjoy peace: ' . . . The prophets are
prophesying lies in my name; I did not send them, nor did I
command them or speak to them. They are prophesying to you a
lying vision, worthless divination (קסם), and the deceit of their own
minds.' In Jeremiah 27 the prophet directs a message to the envoys of
neighboring kings who had come to Zedekiah (27.3-4) and were
organizing against Nebuchadnezzar. Jeremiah threatens those who
will not submit to the Babylonian king (vv. 8-11); later in the chapter

the same address comes to Zedekiah (vv. 12-15). 27.9-10 reads as follows:

> So do not listen to your prophets, your diviners (קסמיכם), your dreamers, your soothsayers, or your sorcerers, who are saying to you, 'You shall not serve the king of Babylon.' For it is a lie which they are prophesying to you.

(The parallel in 27.14-15 mentions only prophets, not the mantic specialists.) Later, in his letter to the exiles, Jeremiah echoes his previous counsel:

> For thus says the Lord of hosts, the God of Israel:
> Do not let your prophets and your diviners (וקסמיכם) who are among you deceive you, . . . for it is a lie which they are prophesying to you in my name; I did not send them, says the Lord (29.8-9).

c. Ezekiel is the third prophetic book that adds to this body of evidence. According to 13.1-9, Ezekiel opposed Israel's prophets and, in the Lord's name, charged that 'they have spoken falsehood and divined a lie (וקסם כזב); they say, "Says the Lord", when the Lord has not sent them, and yet they expect him to fulfill their word. Have you not seen a delusive vision, and uttered a lying divination (ומקסם כזב) . . . ?' (vv. 6-7a). 13.9 continues the denunciation by quoting the Lord as saying: 'My hand will be against the prophets who see delusive visions and who give lying divinations . . . ' Later in the same chapter, prophetesses are also charged with seeing misleading visions and practicing divination (vv. 17-23).[33] Ezek. 22.28 repeats these charges against the prophets.

These passages which come from three prophetic books—one dating from the eighth century and the other two from the time of the exile—express something important about the way in which biblical writers understood prophecy. If it was acceptable for them to credit prophets with divining and diviners with prophesying, then there must have been a significant measure of overlap in what these religious figures did. It is no doubt important that mantic efforts are attributed to prophets only in negative contexts, but it is probably as noteworthy that Ezekiel at least consistently adds the word כזב to קסם thus indicating that there may have been a kind of divination that he regarded more favorably. If one wishes, then, to learn from the sources themselves about the activities of Judean prophets, he is bound to conclude that their labors had a divinatory side to them.

Conclusion

The foregoing data from the Hebrew Bible have some important implications for the issue of the origins of or leading influences on apocalyptic thought. First, given the divinatory aspects of prophecy in Israel, one ought to avoid drawing a sharp distinction between mantic wisdom and biblical prophecy as candidates for the leading influences on apocalyptic thought and procedure. Second, in these discussions the term prophecy should not be limited to what the few great literary prophets taught or did. Israelite or Judean prophecy was a far broader phenomenon that included not only their efforts but also late prophecy, of course, and an unavoidable mantic element. Prophecy in this wider sense was probably the decisive stimulus in the evolution of apocalyptic thought.

NOTES

1. See, for example, the comments of P. Vielhauer, 'Apocalypses and Related Subjects. Introduction', in E. Hennecke and W. Schneemelcher, *New Testament Apocrypha*, 2 vols., Philadelphia and London, 1965, 2.594-95; and D.S. Russell, *The Method and Message of Jewish Apocalyptic* (OTL), Philadelphia and London, 1964, 19, 266, 270f., etc.

2. The most detailed account of scholarship in this area is J.M. Schmidt, *Die jüdische Apokalyptik: die Geschichte ihrer Erforschung von den Anfängen bis zu den Textfunden von Qumran*, 2nd ed., Neukirchen-Vluyn, 1976. In the last few years, several surveys of recent publications have also appeared, among which are Klaus Koch, *The Rediscovery of Apocalyptic* (SBT 2/22), Naperville and London, 1970, 18-35; J. Barr, 'Jewish Apocalyptic in Recent Scholarly Study', *BJRL* 58 (1975), 9-35; M.A. Knibb, 'Prophecy and the Emergence of the Jewish Apocalypses', in R. Coggins, A. Phillips, and M. Knibb, eds., *Israel's Prophetic Tradition: Essays in Honour of P. Ackroyd*, New York/Cambridge/London, 1982, 155-80; and J.C. VanderKam, 'Recent Studies in "Apocalyptic"', *Word and World* 4 (1984), 70-77.

3. See M. Stone, 'Lists of Revealed Things in the Apocalyptic Literature', in F.M. Cross, W.E. Lemke, and P.D. Miller, eds., *Magnalia Dei: The Mighty Acts of God*, Garden City, 1976, 439-43.

4. 'Apocalypticism', *IDBSup*, 29-31; cf. also the important terminological discussion of E.P. Sanders, 'The Genre of Palestinian Jewish Apocalypses', in D. Hellholm, ed., *Apocalypticism in the Mediterranean World and the Near East: Proceedings of the International Colloquium on Apocalypticism, Uppsala, August 12-17, 1979*, Tübingen, 1983, 447-59.

5. See, for instance, Barr, 'Jewish Apocalyptic', 14-16; Knibb, 'Prophecy', 160-61.

6. *Apocalypse: The Morphology of a Genre* (Semeia, 14, Missoula, 1979, 9. For a similar definition, cf. Jean Carmignac, 'Qu'est-ce que l'apocalyptique? Son emploi à Qumrân', *RQ* 10 (1979), 3-33.

7. For the most complete collection of apocalypses, see now J.H. Charlesworth, ed., *The Old Testament Pseudepigrapha*, vol. I: *Apocalyptic Literature and Testaments*, Garden City, 1983.

8. *The Dawn of Apocalyptic: The Historical and Sociological Roots of Jewish Apocalyptic Eschatology*, Philadelphia, 1975, 11-12; 'Apocalypticism', 29-30.

9. *The Open Heaven: A Study of Apocalyptic in Judaism and Early Christianity*, London and New York, 1982, 70; cf. 17, 21, etc.

10. *Ibid.*, 75.

11. *Ibid.*, 15, 51-52.

12. *The Method*, 94.

13. *The Relevance of Apocalyptic: A Study of Jewish and Christian Apocalypses from Daniel to the Revelation*, 2nd ed., London 1947, 13. Another contemporary advocate of the prophetic connection is Otto Plöger, *Theocracy and Eschatology*, Oxford, 1968.

14. *The Relevance*, 41.

15. *Ibid.*, 35.

16. For a useful summary of the varied influences from prophecy, see Russell, *The Method*, 73-103, 178-202.

17. *Old Testament Theology*, vol. II: *The Theology of Israel's Prophetic Traditions*, Edinburgh, 1965, 303.

18. *Ibid.*, 306. Von Rad discussed the divine determination of times in wisdom and apocalyptic literature in his *Wisdom in Israel*, London/Nashville/ New York, 1972, 263-83.

19. Cf. Vielhauer, 'Apocalypses', 598; P. von der Osten-Sacken, *Die Apokalyptik in ihrem Verhältnis zu Prophetie und Weisheit* (Theologische Existenz heute, 157), Munich, 1969, 9-10. H.P. Müller summarizes some of the reactions in 'Mantische Weisheit und Apokalyptik', in *Congress Volume, Uppsala, 1971* (SVT, 22), Leiden, 1972, 268-70.

20. *Theologie des Alten Testaments*, vol. II: *Die Theologie der prophetischen Überlieferungen Israels* (Einführung in die evangelische Theologie, 1), 5th ed., Munich, 1968, 331.

21. 'Mantische Weisheit', 268-93 (where he listed another feature, viz. eschatological orientation [280-81]); cf. also his contribution to the article 'חכם', in *TDOT* 4.376-78 (the four features are given on 377-78). Müller's essay 'Magisch-mantische Weisheit und die Gestalt Daniels', *UF* 1 (1969), 79-94, is also relevant in this context.

22. See J.C. VanderKam, *Enoch and the Growth of an Apocalyptic Tradition* (CBQMS, 16), Washington 1984.

23. For the texts, see A.K. Grayson and W. Lambert, 'Akkadian Prophecies',

JCS 18 (1964), 7-30; R.D. Biggs, 'More Babylonian "Prophecies"', *Iraq* 29 (1967), 117-32; R. Borger, 'Gott Marduk und Gott-König Šulgi als Propheten: Zwei prophetische Texte', *BO* 28 (1971), 3-24; H. Hunger and S.A. Kaufman, 'A New Akkadian Prophecy Text', *JAOS* 95 (1975), 371-75; and Grayson, *Babylonian Historical-Literary Texts* (Toronto Semitic Texts and Studies, 3), Toronto, 1975. For discussions of these texts, one can consult Lambert, 'The Background of Jewish Apocalyptic', The Ethel M. Wood Lecture delivered before the University of London on 22 February 1977, London, 1978, 9-17; Helmer Ringgren, 'Akkadian Apocalypses', in D. Hellholm, ed., *Apocalypticism*, 379-86; and VanderKam, *Enoch*, 62-69.

24. 'Akkadian Apocalypses', *IEJ* 16 (1966), 231-42. Ringgren, as the title of his essay indicates (see n. 23 above), still calls them apocalypses.

25. VanderKam, *Enoch*, 62-69.

26. *A History of Prophecy in Israel*, Philadelphia, 1983, 256; cf. 239.

27. *Late Israelite Prophecy: Studies in Deutero-Prophetic Literature and in Chronicles* (SBLMS, 23), Missoula, 1977, 14-15, 21, 25-27, 28, 37-38, 45.

28. See Russell, *The Method*, 195-98.

29. Cf. Susan Niditch, *The Symbolic Vision in Biblical Tradition* (HSM, 30), Chico, 1980, 33-34, 49, 71, 96, 133-34, 174-75, 184-85, 243-48.

30. The Mari 'prophetic' (?) texts are relevant comparisons, and they have often been discussed. See, for example, W.L. Moran, 'New Evidence from Mari on the History of Prophecy', *Biblica* 50 (1969), 15-56; and the brief comments in Klaus Koch, *The Prophets*, vol. I: *The Assyrian Period*, Philadelphia, 1983, 9-12 (who considers the Mari evidence under the rubric 'Inductive and Intuitive Divination in Antiquity and its Connection with Monotheism and Monanthropology in Israel'. For further data on this point, one should consult one of the surveys of Mesopotamian divination, e.g. J. Nougayrol, 'La divination babylonienne', in A. Caquot and M. Leibovici, *La divination*, 2 vols., Paris, 1968, 1.25-81.

31. *Deuteronomy* (ICC), Edinburgh, 102, 221; cf. 227; and Vanderkam, *Enoch*, 71-75.

32. On these passages, see McKane, *Prophets and Wise Men* (SBT, 44), London 1965, 96-97, and also his views on prophecy and apocalyptic thought, 97-101.

33. W. Zimmerli, *Ezekiel*, vol. 1 (Hermeneia), Philadelphia, 1979, 296-97, says about 13.17ff. that the magical and mantic arts noted here constitute a '. . . sphere which can only be put quite improperly under the catchword "prophetic"' (296). But how valid is it for a modern commentator to question whether an ancient writer used a flexible term such as 'prophesy' properly? If one accepts the broader view of prophecy that is here being advocated, then there is nothing improper about Ezekiel's usage.

FOOD FOR THOUGHT:
THE SEPTUAGINT TRANSLATION OF GENESIS 1.11-12

Bryan Paradise

Harrogate

This study is concerned with the attempt of the ancient translator (or translators) to render the Hebrew text of Genesis into Greek. It may be argued that an investigation of such a limited part of the text as verses 11 and 12 of Chapter 1 can have little value in understanding the whole work. These particular verses have, however, been chosen for several reasons. They essentially involve ordinary or common entities like trees, seeds, plants and the like. They include no contentious theological points such as there are at other places in Chapter 1. They also form a neatly self-contained unit in the story of Creation. Further, they come right at the beginning; the translator would almost certainly have had no prior model to guide him and no dictionary, only his own grasp of the two languages. Any solutions to particular problems of translating would naturally be of use when the same problems recurred later. Thus, for example, the choice of particular Greek terms here would be important for the rest of the translation. Presumably, whatever the readership or audience, the intention was to make available the content of the Hebrew original to those who knew only Greek and not Hebrew. The success of the venture must therefore be judged on the accuracy of the translation. The rendering of the straightforward parts is, then, the key to the value of the whole work. Genesis 1.11–12 is such an example of a relatively straightforward part.

We will begin by examining the Hebrew text with the aim of identifying the main areas of likely difficulty for the translator; then the translator's handling of the material will be considered. This study is therefore a contribution to the understanding of the Septuagint as a pioneering work of translation rather than simply a quarry for text-critical notes. In all of what follows it is assumed that the critical editions of the Hebrew and Greek texts bear a sufficiently close resemblance to those handled and produced by the translator.

The Hebrew Text of Genesis 1.11-12[1]

ויאמר אלהים תדשא הארץ דשא עשב מזריע זרע עץ
פרי עשה פרי למינו אשר זרעו־בו על־הארץ ויהי־כן:
ותוצא הארץ דשא עשב מזריע זרע למינהו ועץ עשה פרי אשר
זרעו־בו למינהו וירא אלהים כי־טוב:

The translator was confronted by three distinct problems in the new
material of verses 11 and 12. The first concerned the basic *structure*
of the verses, namely the number of entities or classes of entities that
the earth was called upon to produce. The second was the new
vocabulary for which he had not yet produced a translation. The
third related to the *differences* between the two verses.

Structure

There are three possible ways of looking at the main structural
arrangement of verses 11 and 12: the earth could produce (a) three
classes of things, דשא, עשב and עץ פרי; (b) two classes, דשא עשב and
עץ פרי; (c) one class, דשא, which is then further divided into two
categories עשב and עץ פרי.

A number of considerations favour (c) as the correct reading of the
structure.

1. The punctuation of the Masoretic text (MT) supports this view,
with דשא as the single object of תדשא. דשא is then qualified by the two
nominal clauses which follow.

2. The balance of the structure tells against (a). דשא is completely
unqualified, if this scheme is followed, whilst both עשב and עץ פרי are
carefully qualified according to their means of reproduction.

3. The Hebrew employs a cognate expression תדשא ... דשא to
describe the earth's activity. The verbal form is very rare in the MT,
occurring only here in the *hiphil* and once in the *qal* at Joel 2.22
כי דשאו נאות מדבר. The context here suggests that דשא is the process
whereby the wilderness produces that which it is natural to be
produced when it rains, like trees and vines. The noun דשא (fourteen
times in the MT) refers to that which is grown in fields or in the wild,
essentially vegetation of any kind (see below for a more detailed
treatment). Schmidt[2] and Koehler–Baumgartner[3] suggest that the
verb was derived from the noun דשא. Thus תדשא דשא would be an
example of the common cognate construction. 'There are in the

hiphil a considerable number of denominative verbs which express
the bringing out, the producing of a thing and so they are properly
regarded as causative.'[4] Thus it seems that the structure of the verse
is based on the simple exhortation to the earth that it should
תדשא דשא which is further explained as embracing particularly עשב
and עץ פרי. After the verb דשא it would be strange if the noun דשא
was only one of three different entities to be produced.

4. A further argument against (a) is that the other major categories
of the natural order, the waters, the heavens between the firmament
and the earth, are also productive in a similar way to the earth. המים
are bidden to שְׁרַץ שֶׁרֶץ and עוף are commanded to עוּף. Thus, the
cognate verb and noun are used in all three major areas of the natural
world to express their productive activity.

5. עשב and עץ פרי occur together in several places. In Gen. 1.29
both עשב and עץ פרי are considered as food for men (whilst in Gen.
1.30 עשב ירק is food for animals making דשא appear redundant in the
divine economy). In Ex. 9.25 עשב and עץ are destroyed by hailstones,
i.e. are no longer available for human and animal consumption. In
Ex. 10.15 locusts finish off what is left in both categories. Thus it is
not unknown for both עשב and עץ פרי to occur together to describe all
useful vegetation, without any reference to דשא.

Thus, the simplest way of reading the structure of verses 11 and 12
would be to see דשא as the general category of what is produced,
being explained more fully by עשב and עץ פרי. Such an expression
would be a good Hebrew idiom.[5] However it still remains possible
that דשא עשב are in a construct relationship, i.e. דשא limited or
qualified by עשב, being one category of what the earth is to produce
along with עץ פרי. דשא and עשב nowhere else occur in a construct
relationship in either position. דשא does occur with יֶרֶק at 2 Kgs 19.26
and Ps. 37.2. ירק appears to be a very general term for green thing or
plant. In construct relationship with דשא the general term ירק is
limited by a more specific term דשא denoting a category within the
class of green things (plants) as a whole. This does not of course
prevent דשא being limited by a further more specific term such as
עשב.

Hence interpretation (b) is not completely ruled out, but the
considerations advanced above strongly favour (c). Of modern
commentators only Driver and Dillman favour (a). The majority
prefer (b) or (c), with the majority of those advocating (c).

Vocabulary

The next major problem or series of problems presented to the translator by verses 11-12 is the vocabulary, in particular the lexical items דשא, עשב, עץ, זרע, מין and, in verse 12, יצא.

דשא

דשא springs up after rain (Job 38.27); it provides food for goats (Jer. 14.5) and wild asses (Job 6.5); it is prone to withering under adverse conditions (2 Kgs 19.26; Is. 15.6; Ps. 37.2); it provides a metaphor for prosperity and ease through its luxuriant growth (Is. 66.14; Ps. 23.2, 'in pastures of דשא God makes me lie down'); it forms poetic parallels with עשב (Deut. 32.2: rain falls on both) and חציר (Ps. 37.2: both wither and fade); it grows after חציר has been cut (Prov. 27.25) and there is no other vegetation to hinder growth; it occurs in a construct relationship with יֶרֶק (2 Kgs 19.26) and יֶרֶק (Ps. 37.2); it occurs with חציר and עשב (Prov. 27.25–27, and 2 Kgs 19.26), to describe the inhabitants of a city about to be destroyed, all have the property of fast withering; it needs water to sustain it, like חציר and יֶרֶק (Is. 15.6). In Job 6.5 where it is eaten by wild asses, domestic oxen are on the other hand eating בליל. In Joel 2.22, where the other verbal form of דשא occurs, it is the natural product of the wilderness after abundant rain. Here the context presents a picture of the result of restored rainfall on agriculture. Trees bear fruit, fig trees bear figs and vines produce grapes. Likewise fields or pastures produce their natural crop which will also revive animals. Thus some form of fodder crop results from the action of דשא. Note also the element of wildness, 'wild animals' and 'pastures of the wilderness'. Thus דשא is not a sown crop like wheat but that which springs up naturally as a result of rain.

S. Talmon, in a study of the Gezer Calendar, suggests that there was a definite season of grass cropping or haymaking in Palestine in the early Israelite period as well as in rabbinic times.[6] In 1QS 10.7 this season is referred to as the מועד דשא. It begins after the rainy season in midwinter, and the grass ripens in early spring. Talmon suggests that the crop was essentially unsown, consisting of plants like wild flax which often grew up in grain-sown fields. It was ready to cut before the main harvest. His argument depends in part on a presumed equivalence between דשא and עשב and his claim that in the OT דשא always indicates '(spring) grass'.[7] However, the word serves also to indicate the sprouting grass which occurs after the main hay crop has been removed (cf. Prov. 27.25).

In post-biblical Hebrew דשא is given the value of 'tender grass', 'herbage'. In *b. Rosh Hash.* 11a it is viewed as something which covers the earth.[8] Rashi says in his commentary that 'by דשא is meant that which forms the covering of the earth when it is filled with herbage, meaning all species of herbs growing together collectively'.[9] Modern Hebrew uses דשא for both 'vegetation' and 'grass' as well as that modern horticultural phenomenon 'lawn'.

ירק

יֶרֶק and יָרָק are important to a consideration of the values of דשא and עשב as they relate to the main terms. At 1 Kgs 21.2 Naboth's vineyard will become a גַּן יָרָק for Ahab. In Deut. 11.10 cultivation was required in Egypt where seed was sown and irrigation was necessary in a גן ירק. Prov. 15.17 has that a ארחת ירק is better where love is than a fatted ox and hatred with it. Thus a יָרָק is a plant which grows in a garden as a result of cultivation, or is eaten as a substitute for meat. English 'vegetable' would be a suitable equivalent or perhaps the more colloquial 'greens'. Num. 11.5 gives a list of some of the varieties grown in Egypt.

יֶרֶק occurs infrequently in the MT. In Ex. 10.15 not a יֶרֶק was left after the locusts had covered the land and devoured the עשב and עץ פרי which the hail had left. Not a ירק remained on a tree or on a plant in all Egypt. Here there is an ambiguity. Possibly בעץ and בעשב are the places where no ירק was left, giving the value '(green) leaf' to ירק. Alternatively ירק is in apposition to עץ and עשב and the ב is part of the verbal structure of יתר (cf. the *hiphil*) meaning 'to cause something to be left over' plus ב with the thing so caused. In this case ירק is a more general category of plant life which includes עשב and עץ. In Num. 22.4 the ox licks up the ירק of the field.

In Gen. 1.30 יֶרֶק occurs in close conjunction with עשב. Here it refers to that which animals use for food in distinction to the עשב bearing seed and the עץ פרי which man uses for food. In Gen. 9.3 ירק modifies עשב and refers back to God's giving all the plants to man, including the seed-bearing and fruit-bearing ones. In Ps. 37.2 it occurs with דשא, where ירק דשא will soon fade. Thus its probable value is 'green thing', a more general term than דשא.

BDB gives a meaning of 'herb', 'herbage' ('green, greens') to יָרָק and 'green', 'greenness' to יֶרֶק.[10] K–B describes יֶרֶק as 'greens' or 'vegetables' and יָרָק as 'green (plants)'.[11] Dalman explains יֶרֶק as 'wild, edible vegetables'.[12]

עשב

עשב is produced by the earth (Gen. 1.11, 12; 2.5). It is described as יֶרֶק (Gen. 1.30; 9.3; Ex. 10.15): it can grow in wild locations (Gen. 2.5; 3.18; 2 Kgs 19.26; Ps. 72.16): it is often described as עשב השדה (e.g. Prov. 27.25) and often occurs in agricultural contexts (Deut. 11.15; Ex. 9.22; 10.15; Jer. 12.4; Ps. 104.14); it produces seed (Gen. 1.11, 12, 29); it provides food for animals, especially domestic ones (Gen. 1.30; Deut. 11.15; Jer. 14.6; Ps. 106.20); it provides food for man (Gen. 3.18; 9.3; Ps. 104.14); it is a gift of God to man (Gen. 1.29; 9.3; Zech. 10.1); it withers or dries up quickly, (Is. 42.15; Jer. 12.4; Ps. 102.5, 12); it grows quickly, giving a figure of lush growth (Job 5.25; Ps. 72.16); it occurs in the same context as עץ (Gen. 1.11, 12, 29), שיח (Gen. 2.5) and דשא and חציר (2 Kgs 19.26, Prov. 27.25).

Its occurrence in the same locations as general terms like עץ, שיח and ירק indicates that it too is a general term. It is described by Gen. 1.11, 12, 29 as seed-bearing. It also provides food for both man and animals. Thus it stands as a general term for seed-bearing plants whose food value is in their seed. This would include not only the major cereal crops like wheat, barley and oats but also things like peas, beans and lentils. The reference to עשב being eaten by wild asses recalls the fact that the ancestors of cultivated wheat and barley grew wild in Palestine in ancient times.[13] Dalman gives the meaning 'cereals' to עשב.[14]

חציר

חציר, although not appearing in Gen. 1.11 and 12, commonly occurs with both דשא and עשב. It grows around springs, in valleys and even under adverse conditions (1 Kgs 18.5), on roof tops (2 Kgs 19.26; Ps. 129.6; 147.8) it springs up quickly, especially following rain (Ps. 90.5; Is. 44.4); it withers quickly (Is. 15.6; 40.6–8; Job 8.12); it provides a symbol of man's transitory and feeble condition; it is harvested by reaping; after it is harvested דשא grows up in its place; it provides food for horses and mules (1 Kgs 18.5) and cattle (Ps. 104.14).

In Num. 11.5 it is one of a list of vegetables grown in Egypt. Here it is usually translated as 'leek'. However the normal Hebrew word for 'leek' is כרשה. It is the only word occurring in the singular in the list of Num. 11.5. Young leeks do in fact look remarkably like newly sprouted grass. Apart from this odd reference in Num. 11.5, חציר is nowhere described as eaten by man. It could therefore be defined as grass grown, or allowed to grow, for animal fodder which was cut and left to dry, corresponding to the English word 'hay'.

Other words for general categories of plant life commonly occur in the MT. These include terms like צמח, שיח, ציץ, נטע and מטע. Of these only שיח occurs with one of the terms found in Gen. 1.11 and 12, namely עשב, in Gen. 2.5. Here both עשב and שיח are described as not yet formed upon the earth. At Gen. 21.15 Hagar puts her child under a שיח when the food runs out. At Job 30.4 it is a source of food for the extremely hungry who pick and eat leaves from a שיח. At Job 30.6-7 wild asses in wilderness areas bray among שיח. שיח is thus best understood as a general category of the plant group and not a specific name. 'Bush', 'shrub' or 'scrub' are the best English equivalents. According to biblical usage, עשב is not part of the שיח category and neither is עץ. It may be possible to suggest a classification by size of these general categories, increasing from עשב to שיח to עץ.

The preceding comments may be summed up as follows:

1. In trying to define these terms it is important to remember the picture presented by the ancient Palestinian landscape and climate. It is one which is generally semi-arid with highly seasonal rainfall producing amazingly quick growth from seemingly barren ground. The more temperate areas would be given over to grain crops and fruit trees, particularly vines and the hardier olive.

2. None of the terms discussed represents specific varieties of plants. J. Feliks, who gives a modern scientific classification of the plants of the Bible and the Mishnah, includes none of these terms of this group.[15] All refer to general categories of plant life.

3. חציר is the most straightforward to define. It represents vegetation grown or used for fodder. It is not a specific variety, as there were many types of grass and wild grain plant occurring naturally and available for fodder. It could best be translated by 'hay' in English, especially as it approaches ripeness and harvesting.

4. עשב could at first sight be thought to stand for 'plant' in its most general sense. However its usage in Gen. 1 suggests a more restricted meaning, namely that of 'useful plant' producing a useful (seed) crop including grains, pulses and herbs properly so called.

5. יֶרֶק appears to be the most general term of this group, standing for green plant at any stage of its growth. Often it has only adjectival force as a result of its generality, having then a value roughly

corresponding to English 'green'. A near synonym is צמח which also includes all types of vegetation seen particularly from the point of view of growth from the earth.

6. דשא remains the most difficult term to define and relate to the other terms. Various lexicographers and commentators have attempted definitions.[16]

It seems to do with the earliest stage of plant growth which appears after rainfall when the seed has just sprouted and pushed a new green shoot through the surface of the soil. At this stage the vast majority of plants are very similar in appearance, essentially grasslike. Hence דשא can have a wide range of related referents. First, it may be seen as standing for 'young grass', a similar kind of term to חציר and עשב with which it occurs (i.e. דשא 'young grass', חציר 'fodder grass' or 'hay' and עשב 'grain-bearing plant'). Second, all plants at the very earliest stage have a grass-like appearance, especially in the mass. Then דשא can stand as an *Oberbegriff* for all plants, especially here in Gen. 1.11 and 12 where the very first vegetation is in view. (In this sense it could include such categories of plants as עשב and עץ.) The modern Hebrew usage of דשא for 'lawn' is suggested because lawns are generally kept short and the grass continually remains at the first stage of growth, never becoming חציר. To the English eye דשא could very well stand for the fresh green shoots that spring up a week or two after hay has been taken off a pasture field. No English term exists but the Scots 'brairding' could be appropriate.

Thus, in a hierarchy of increasing specificity the most general terms in Hebrew for 'plants' are ירק or שיח, 'young plants' דשא, general families of plants עץ, שיח, ירק, עשב, חציר and specific varieties בר, כמרן, אלון, רתם, כשרים, דגן, גד.

Perhaps Rashi may be allowed the last word on דשא at Gen. 1.11 and 12. 'דשא means all species of herbs growing together collectively, whilst each root is called an עשב, the species of דשא are all different, each by itself being called this or that עשב . . . by דשא is meant that which forms the covering of the ground when it is filled with herbage.'[17]

עץ פרי

There is really no question that here עץ means 'tree' and that עץ פרי means 'fruit tree' or 'fruit-bearing tree' (cf. ארץ פרי [Ps. 107.34], 'fruitful' or 'fruit-bearing' ground). פרי is a general term for produce of any kind. It refers to fruit of the ground (Gen. 4.3); of the land

(Num. 13.20); of the vineyard (2 Kgs 19.29); of gardens (Amos 9.14); of the womb, meaning offspring (Gen. 30.2). There is also a transferred sense indicating the result or fruit of actions i.e. consequences both good (Is. 3.10) and bad (Hos. 10.13).[18]

However עץ set unusual problems for the translator. In the MT it stands for anything 'woody' both living and dead. Live wood growing as trees is עץ singly, collectively and plurally (Gen. 2.9; Prov. 3.18; Exod. 9.25; Lev. 26.20 Ps. 104.16). It includes anything from shrubs and bushes such as brambles and vines (Judg. 9.8) to the very largest forest trees like the oak and cedar. עץ can be qualified by names of specific varieties such as עץ שמן, an olive tree (Neh. 8.15).

Dead wood in all its forms is also known under the general heading of עץ. This includes items like trees felled for timber for building work (1 Kgs 5.20), small pieces of timber used in building (Hag. 1.8; 2 Kgs 12.13) and articles made from wood (Ezek. 41.25; Hab. 2.11). In Deut. 19.5 the helve of an axe is specifically called העץ. Also covered by this term is the pole on which the bodies of slain criminals were exposed (Gen. 40.19; Josh. 8.29) and later the device for execution itself (Esth. 2.23). Other items included under עץ are firewood (Josh. 9.23; Deut. 19.5) and idols (Deut. 4.28). Presumably ambiguity and confusion could occur, but, like English 'wood' used of both construction material and collections of living trees, the context determined the sense clearly enough.

Other words for 'tree' in the MT are names of species which tended to become generalized e.g. איל, אלון, אלה.[19]

זרע

זרע occurs about 230 times in the MT. Of these 170 have to do with offspring both human and animal, mostly human, standing for 'child', 'son', 'progeny', 'descendants', 'race'. Of the remainder, 50 have to do with plant-produced seed, i.e. about one-fifth of the biblical examples have a natural connection which is not also husbandry. Of these only a few can be unequivocally related to grain, defined as 'seed for food' (e.g. Num. 5.28; Is. 23.3; Job 39.12). זרע in the non-animal and non-human sense is basically that which is scattered upon the ground and from which plants germinate and grow. In other words זרע can be found in sacks, bins or jars earmarked for sowing for next year's crop. Grains found in bins earmarked for food are usually called something else, לחם (Is. 30.23) or דגן, שבר, בר or שבואה. Thus זרע is hardly ever restricted to grain. Its sphere of activity is the reproductive cycle, not the food cycle. It corresponds almost exactly to English 'seed', excluding 'grain'. The verbal form likewise almost always has to do with the scattering of seed upon the ground to produce new plants. Thus עשב in being described as מזריע זרע is not restricted to grain plants like wheat and barley but includes all plants which produce a seed.

למין

This occurs always with some form of third person suffix, and always in the singular, with the possible exception of Gen. 1.21. It is applied to fruit trees (Gen. 1.11, 12); plants (Gen. 1.12); every living sea creature (Gen. 1.21; Ezek. 47.10); birds (Gen. 6.20; 7.14); living creatures of the earth (Gen. 1.24; 6.20); cattle and creeping things (Gen. 7.14).

At Lev. 11.14-29 and Deut. 14.13-18 it is applied to specific examples of birds, e.g. falcon (Lev. 11.14) and ostrich; of insects, e.g. locusts, cricket; of mammals (e.g. mouse); of reptiles and amphibians. All these examples appear in connection with the laws of clean and unclean animals. In this legislation the important thing was identification of the animal. The designation 'clean' or 'unclean' for a particular animal was decided by the features which set it off from other varieties of animal. למין is the term which refers to this collective bundle of features. In modern scientific speech, this would be 'according to its "species"'. All the names in the Leviticus and Deuteronomy lists do in fact refer to individual species rather than general families.

This observation is of value in determining the sense of למינו in Gen. 1. All the animal types mentioned are general categories, orders or families rather than species: birds, fish, sea creatures, creeping things. In these cases למין functions as a way of indicating individual species within a class or family of animals. For example, in Gen. 1.20 the earth is bidden to bring forth 'swarming living things'. It is reported that God made every living swarming creature למינהם, according to their species, namely every kind or species of living swarming creatures.

Thus in Gen. 1.11 and 12 the sense of למין suggests that every kind or species of fruit tree is implied in the command to the earth to bring forth. In the report of the process in verse 12 both עשב and עץ פרי are produced by individual species.[20]

יצא

In v. 12 the command of v. 11, תרשא, is replaced by the reported תוצא. יצא is a very much more common verb than רשא in both *qal* and *hiphil* forms. יצא in the *qal* has the basic meaning of 'to go', or 'to come out' or 'to come forth' with special emphasis on the idea of origin or source.[21] יצא is thus connected with the idea of growth (Job 8.16; 14.2; Is. 11.1 'there shall come forth a shoot from the stump of Jesse . . .'; Job 14.2 'He comes forth like a flower'.) For the *hiphil* the general sense is to 'produce' or 'generate', 'bring into being' (e.g. Is. 61.11, where the earth is described as producing shoots). Schmidt has 'Das Verbum kann der Bedeutung 'Schaffen' nahekommen vgl. Jes. 40.26'.[22]

It would seem to have been more straightforward to use the same verb in the report as in the command. יצא, in being more familiar than רשא, may have been felt to be more appropriate in describing what actually happened. Here the product is not so much in view as the earth in its obedience to the command. The focus is on the activity rather than the end product.

The differences between Gen. 1.11 and 12
The third problem facing the translator was the subtle but significant variations between the two verses. In particular . . . למין occurs with different suffixes and in different places in 1.12 compared with 1.11. This was certainly a problem for early Jewish commentators. 'Although the expression למינהו "according to its kind" was not used when the various kinds of herbage were bidden to come forth, they heard that the trees were so commanded and they applied to themselves the argument *a fortiori*.'[23]

We have already noted above the change in verb from רשא to יצא. There are no stylistic reasons for insisting on the repetition of the same words in both command and reported fulfilment. In fact such repetition does not occur in the rest of the account of creation. In addition, there is an extra copula in v. 12 before עץ and the phrase על הארץ is omitted from v. 12. Such differences, as we shall see, appear to have been of some significance to the translator.

So far we have analysed as far as possible the problems that these verses presented to the translator. We now turn to consider the translator's attempt to render his Hebrew text in Greek.

The Septuagint Translation: The translator's response[24]

καὶ εἶπεν ὁ θεός Βλαστησάτω ἡ γῆ βοτάνην χόρτου, σπεῖρον
σπέρμα κατὰ γένος καὶ καθ' ὁμοιότητα καὶ ξύλον κάρπιμον
ποιοῦν καρπόν, οὗ τὸ σπέρμα αὐτοῦ ἐν αὐτῷ κατὰ γένος ἐπὶ τῆς
γῆς. καὶ ἐγένετο οὕτως. καὶ ἐξήνεγκεν ἡ γῆ βοτάνην χόρτου,
σπεῖρον σπέρμα κατὰ γένος καὶ καθ' ὁμοιώτητα, καὶ ξύλον
κάρπιμον ποιοῦν καρπόν, οὗ τὸ σπέρμα αὐτοῦ ἐν αὐτῷ κατὰ
γένος ἐπὶ τῆς γῆς. καὶ εἶδεν ὁ θεὸς ὅτι καλόν.

The Structure
The translator clearly adopts a *twofold* classification for the things
that are to be produced by the earth, namely βοτάνη χόρτου and
ξύλον κάρπιμον. χόρτου obviously stands in a genitive relationship
with βοτάνη and is not intended to represent a separate entity by
itself. καὶ links the βοτάνην with ξύλον. Both elements are described
in a similar balanced fashion, each having a qualifying adjectival
phrase headed by a participle, σπεῖρον σπέρμα and ποιοῦν καρπόν.
Both parts are clearly categories of things produced by the earth in
the process indicated by βλαστησάτω. Both are apparently equally
specific.

Of the possible ways of understanding the structural relationship
between דשא, עשב and זרע the translator has chosen the least plausible.
He has opposed דשא and זרע rather than עשב and זרע. Instead of seeing
עשב and זרע as explaining the meaning of דשא he has taken עשב as
limiting דשא, regarding דשא עשב as a construct. This is confirmed by
the avoidance of a cognate expression to render תדשא . . . דשא when a
perfectly acceptable solution was available (see below); the translator
does not always avoid such expressions (Gen. 17.13; 40.15).

Thus דשא עשב is treated as one class of entities translated by
βοτάνη χόρτου and on an equal level of specificity with the second
object of βλαστησάτω.

The Vocabulary
βλαστέω *for* דשא
As noted above דשא is a *hapax legomenon* in its *hiphil* form and only
occurs once elsewhere in any other form (Joel 2.22). The translator
was thus guided to its meaning by the context of the verse, including
the agency of the earth and the resulting plants and trees, the much
more common verb in the parallel position in v. 12, the cognate דשא
which occurred more commonly and the wider context of Gen. 1.20,

24. The translator was aware of a difference between תדשא and תוצא,
as is shown by his use of two Greek terms.

The word used here for תרשא is βλαστησάτω from βλαστέω, a
later form of βλαστάνω. (The use of the first aorist is a feature of
koiné and the Septuagint in particular.)[25]

Liddell and Scott define βλαστάνω as firstly 'to bud', 'sprout' or
'grow'.[26] It is thus used properly of plants. It can also have a causal
usage meaning to 'make to grow' or 'propagate'. Hence it is suitable
for translating תרשא. The perspective is that of the earth or the
ground from which the plants are to be produced. The creative
agency of the earth is the important aspect.

In the Septuagint βλαστέω or βλαστάνω occurs thirteen times
with Hebrew originals for ten of these. It translates דשא both times
plus גמל 'ripen' (Num. 17.8: MT 17.23), פרה 'sprout' (Is. 45.8), ציץ
'flower' (Is. 27.6), צמח 'sprout up, grow' (Judg. 16.22) and 'make to
grow' (2 Sam. 23.5). A possible alternative would have been φύειν,
which means 'bring forth', 'produce' even 'beget' and in a passive
form 'grow' 'spring up', used particularly of vegetables (e.g. Plato,
Republic, 621a). φύειν represents four Hebrew originals in the
Septuagint: צמח, פרה, בטע and עלה. However it seems to have been
generally regarded by the translator as intransitive, used in the sense
of 'grow' from the plant's perspective, reflecting general Greek usage.
Thus βλαστέω was a good choice of word for דשא, having a more
vivid active connotation than the prosaic, neutral φύειν.

βοτάνη *for* דֶשֶׁא

If the translator was following the original literally one would have
expected him to have used βλαστός or βλάστημα as the object of
βλαστησάτω. Both were perfectly good, available Greek terms
meaning 'shoots'. Aquila actually uses βλάστηματα in his more
literal translation here.

βοτάνη was used throughout the history of Greek literature. It can
refer to several things, namely 'pasture', 'fodder', 'herbs', 'plants',
'weeds' and 'grass'. It can occur with εὐθέντης meaning 'useful
vegetation', whilst in other places it was used to mean 'weeds'. In
Papyrus Oxyrhynchus 729.22 there is a requirement that vine land
be kept clean from reeds, βοτάνη and all kinds of weeds. This gives,
in this context, a possible meaning of 'long grass'.

In the Septuagint βοτάνη is used to translate דשא, חציר and עשב.
Taking the Septuagintal contexts by themselves, without referring to

the Hebrew word translated, it appears that βοτάνη stands for 'plants' in general, a 'fodder crop' and 'herbs with medicinal properties'. Generally it is used to indicate practically or economically useful plants. In the Pentateuch the more general meaning 'plant' predominates.

On the other hand, in the Septuagint as a whole דשא is variously rendered by βοτάνη (five times), χλόη (four times), χλωροβοτάνη (for דשא ירק), χόρτος and ἄγρωστις, a particular species of grass at Deut. 32.2 (cf. Theophrastus *Historia Plantarum* 1.6.10 and Aristotle, *Historia Animalium* 552.a 15) and πόα.

χλόη is used in Greek to denote the first green shoots of spring, especially young green corn or grass (Herodotus 4.34, Xenophon *Oeconomicus* 17.10). It translates דשא in 2 Sam. 23.4; Ps. 22.2; 36.2 and in Aquila at Gen. 1.29, 30. πόα is used of 'grass' or 'meadow' and refers also to the hay harvest, hence its use in Prov. 27.25. For χόρτος see below.

Thus, several terms are employed in the Septuagint to express the full range of דשא which, as we saw above, meant both a general category of plant growth, i.e. the young green stage, and also 'grass'. Here the translator has adopted a general Greek term, βοτάνη, rather than a more specific term like πόα or even χλόη which was often restricted to 'corn' but could also well express the idea of 'young shoots'.

It is worth noting that φυτόν is the classical word for 'plant' as a general category of nature as opposed to ζῷον, 'animal'. φυτόν can also mean 'garden plant' including 'tree'. The majority of φυτόν compounds have planting or gardening associations. However, in the Septuagint φυτόν often means 'bush' or 'shrub' rather than 'plant'. For example φυτόν renders סנך at Gen. 22.13 and רתם at 1 Kgs 19.5. It is, though, used for 'plant' as a general category at e.g. Job 24.18, Wisdom 7.20. The indication of 'plant' as a general category, however, is more often conveyed by χλωρόν, which function is derived from the Hebrew it is used to translate (ירק) and not its Greek usage.

Thus, φυτόν was probably considered not a suitable translation for דשא. דשא conjures up a particular image of fresh young shoots, whereas φυτόν was too general a term, perhaps even too 'scientific', for the translator's purpose. βοτάνη was a better rendering of the Hebrew imagery. In any case, as noted above, for some reason φυτόν appeared to mean 'bush' for the translators of the Septuagint.

χόρτος *for* עשב

In general Greek usage χόρτος has two basic referents. Firstly, it stands for the place where animals are fed or housed. This can be anything from open pasturage to a closed courtyard. In the plural it can mean, in particular, 'fields'. Secondly, it can stand for that which is fed to animals, 'fodder' or 'provender' and particularly 'hay' (Herodotus 5.16; Xenophon *Anabasis* 1.5.10; 1 Cor. 3.12).[27] Many of the compound derivatives of χόρτος have to do with fodder, e.g. χορτάγω 'to feed' or 'fatten cattle', χορτόβαλον 'hay loft' (*P. Petri* 3. a 139), χορτόκοπη 'hay making' (*P. Tobt.* 337.2) and χορτόκοπος (*P. Cair. Zen* 282 a 123). In the New Testament χόρτος almost always stands for green grass standing in the fields, but the idea of hay or straw is never far away. 1 Cor. 3.12 mentions χόρτος as an inferior building material. Moulton and Milligan have similar evidence from the papyri to show that χόρτος means grass grown for fodder and grazing and hay in all its forms.[28]

In the Septuagint χόρτος is used 46 times with Hebrew originals for 40 of those. It translates דשא at Is. 15.6, as a collective for חציר, חציר and ירק; דשא 11 times; עשב 26 times; קש, meaning 'stubble' or 'chaff', twice. According to the Septuagintal usage χόρτος is a general term designating an economically useful group of plants, not including trees, which can be grown by man to provide grains for food for himself and fodder for his animals. It can designate such plants growing in the wild too. In particular, in Gen. 1.29-30 two classes of χόρτος seem to be distinguished, seed-bearing ones which have been given to humans for food and green ones which have been given to animals for their food.

The Septuagint's choice demonstrates that the meaning of עשב was seen in χόρτος. In general Greek usage however χόρτος is restricted to animal fodder. χόρτος thus appears to be a term whose Septuagintal usage has caused its own semantic borders to become blurred and its range extended.

The use of χόρτος at Gen. 1.11 and 12 seems to indicate that the translator was looking for a term to limit βοτάνη in the direction of a food-crop plant. However, as far as it is possible to judge, the choice of χόρτος has taken the connotation of the phrase βοτάνη χόρτου, for anyone who did not know the Hebrew text, too far in the direction of animal foodstuffs.

It is thus difficult to restrict the value given to χόρτος by the translator to the normal Greek one which is limited to 'grass', 'hay' or 'fodder'. In Genesis χόρτος always stands for עשב whilst βοτάνη always stands for דשא. χόρτος appears to be therefore a standard translation equivalent for עשב. To understand its meaning in the Septuagint translation one must allow that some of the semantic value of עשב has been transferred to χόρτος so that the latter comes to stand for a new category of edible grain and seed-bearing plants. If indeed the normal Greek values for βοτάνη and χόρτος are assigned to them here in Gen. 1.11 and 12, then the phrase βοτάνη χόρτου makes little sense in this situation. It seems that the translator has taken parts of the range of both βοτάνη and χόρτος which were not the most essential or central part of their denotation, i.e. the 'young green shoot' connotation of a word that normally meant 'grass' and the 'edible plant' connotation of a word that normally meant 'hay' or 'fodder'. These have then become the central and significant elements of the translator's usage of the terms in the Septuagint.

This translation technique, whereby a standard though not always appropriate equivalent is adopted and employed throughout, leads our translator into problems with χόρτος at least once more. In Gen. 9.3 ירק עשב is translated by λάχανα χόρτου which in its straightforward sense would give 'vegetables of hay'! Apart from reading ירק as ירֶק this is obviously not what was intended; rather 'edible green plants'—edible by man, that is—are what is meant.

σπεῖρον σπέρμα *for* מזריע זרע

σπέρμα has two related areas of application. When applied to plants, it can mean 'seed' or even 'fruit'; metaphorically it can mean the 'germ' or 'origin' of something. It also has human and animal connections, denoting 'semen' and also the ultimate product of semen, namely 'offspring' or 'descendants' or even 'race', which could be considered as a large collection of offspring. Thus σπέρμα has a similar range to זרע. In general, the usage of σπέρμα reflected the agricultural and horticultural end of its range, whereas זרע was inclined more to the human offspring part of its range. However Gen. 1.11-12 is a very firmly horticultural context. σπέρμα was therefore an appropriate choice for rendering זרע in this context. Of the large number of places where σπέρμα is used in the Septuagint it mostly renders זרע. Of the 210 times זרע occurs in the Hebrew text it is translated by σπέρμα on no less than 190 occasions. It appears that σπέρμα became the standard translation equivalent for זרע.

As noted above in the analysis of זרע, זרע has much more connection with the reproductive cycle than the food cycle, hardly ever indicating grain. The same is also true for σπέρμα. The normal general term for grain is σῖτος. σῖτος and σπέρμα are usually mutually exclusive for a given context. Thus, here in Gen. 1.11-12 σπέρμα was a good choice for זרע.

σπείρειν also has two basic applications. It can mean either sowing (seeds) or begetting (offspring), with many metaphorical extensions. It can be used transitively with seeds as the object, or intransitively as in 'sowing fields'. As with σπέρμα, it has to do with the reproductive cycle rather than with the food production cycle. Essentially it relates to the beginning of the process of reproduction, either putting seeds into soil to produce eventually more seeds, or implanting semen into a womb to produce ultimately more offspring. Hence here in Gen. 1.11-12 the meaning of the phrase is 'edible plants which sow (reproduce themselves by) seeds'.

It would have been possible to render it a little more specifically in order to take account of the Hebrew *hiphil* participle, which tends to bring out the nuance of seed-bearing. Words like σπερμογόνεω (Theophrastus, *H.P.* 1.72.2) and σπερμοφόρεω (Theophrastus, *H.P.* 1.72.2) were available. The later translation ascribed to Aquila employs σπερματίζω, presumably because it was felt that a word which meant simply 'sowing' or 'seeding' was not adequate. σπερματίζω does appear in the Septuagint at Ex. 9.31 to denote that flax was seed-bearing. Here at Gen. 1.11-12 the translator has chosen not to resolve מזריע too sharply in the direction of seed-bearing.

As with σπέρμα, so also σπείρειν became a standard translation equivalent for זרע being used in all but 9 of the 56 cases where זרע occurs.

A further problem of the Greek rendering of this phrase is that the participle σπεῖρον is neuter, either nominative or accusative. Neither βοτάνη nor χόρτος is neuter so that σπεῖρον appears to modify σπέρμα. Possibly however the neuter is used because the masculine and feminine participles σπείρων, σπείρουτα could be applied only to human sowers. If this was the case a more specific term for מזריע would have been even more appropriate.

ξύλον *for* עץ

It was noted earlier that עץ has a wide range of woody applications, covering the whole field from live tree to finished wood product.

There was no similar word available to the Greek translator except possibly ὕλη. Instead, two standard words were generally used in everyday Greek. δένδρον was used to designate 'tree' and ξύλον 'wood' or 'timber'. 'Wood' in the sense of a collection of living trees was denoted by ὕλη. δένδρον appears never to have been used for 'wood' in the ξύλον sense. Although it could cover quite a range of sizes from smaller bushes up to the biggest tree, δένδρον often had a particular connotation of fruit or mast-bearing tree especially in opposition to ὕλη. ὕλη is the term with the closest resemblance to עץ in range, standing for 'forest', 'wood', 'copse'; 'wood cut down' or 'timber' and 'firewood'; the stuff of which a thing was made, originally probably relating to wooden objects but later to more general materials. Later it came to designate the philosophical category of 'matter', especially in Aristotle. In later philosophical writings it was opposed to the formative and intelligent principle νοῦς.[29] Thus, the translator would not have found it particularly useful both because of its philosophical connections and its more general application to forest and wood rather than to tree. Instead, the translator chose ξύλον to represent עץ for almost every example of the latter, so much so that it became a standard translation equivalent no matter what the context.

In Greek usage there appear to be very few examples of the use of ξύλον for tree. The clearest example I have discovered is in Xenophon, *Anabasis* 6.4.5: πολλόις καὶ παντόδαποῖς καὶ μεγάλοις ξύλοις ('plants and large trees of every kind'). Even here the trees may have been seen as potential building material or timber. In a poetic example from Euripedes (*Cyclops* 572) a vine is called a 'clever ξύλον'. Very few other examples have come to light in the literature. By far the greatest usage of ξύλον is to indicate dead wood for building, making things or fuel.[30]

ξύλον occurs 258 times in the Septuagint to translate Hebrew originals of which 255 are עץ. עץ occurs approximately 320 times in the MT, so that the vast majority are translated by ξύλον. Otherwise δένδρον is used on the occasions when the meaning is unambiguously 'large tree' (Gen. 18.4, 8; 23.17; Num. 13.21). For the rest עץ is translated by ξύλον compounds, specific names and ῥάβδος 'stout stick' (Ezek. 37.16). In other words ξύλον for עץ is virtually a technical translation-equivalent. Wherever the translators read עץ they used ξύλον except for the occasions when δένδρον was used, where 'big tree' was definitely meant. However those 16 examples are by no means the majority of cases where 'tree' is the meaning of עץ.

Thus whilst normal Greek usage provided a very common and appropriate term especially for fruit trees, namely δένδρον,[31] the Septuagint preferred ξύλον, which has hardly any contemporary support for the meaning 'tree'. Once again a Greek term has had its range of application extended by association with a Hebrew term whose range overlaps at a certain point. עץ and ξύλον are good equivalents when עץ means 'wood' or 'wooden'. The translator has, however, invested ξύλον with the rest of the range of עץ.

It may be that the restriction of עץ to denote 'timber' and 'wooden' which was noted in post-biblical Hebrew had already begun when the Septuagint was written. Thus in the translator's own usage of Hebrew עץ would possibly have been much closer to ξύλον in its range than the biblical usage. However the context of the biblical usage would clearly have indicated that עץ often means 'tree' and not 'wood' etc.

Alternatively, δένδρον may have been too strongly associated with pagan fertility rites and religious ceremonies. Thus, theological reasons could have meant that a theologically neutral term like ξύλον was preferred. Nevertheless the use of ξύλον to mean 'tree' would have appeared very strange to Greek ears.[32]

κάρπιμον *and* καρπός *for* פרי

καρπός in Greek means 'fruit' in the sense of what grew on trees or vines and the like. It was often used for 'fruit of the earth' or 'produce' in a more general sense including corn, wine, olive oil (Xenophon *Oec.* 5.20). It could also be used of 'seed' (Xenophon *Oec.* 16.12). In a more figurative sense it could be used of 'returns' or 'profit' or the 'fruits' of actions.

Moulton and Milligan give evidence to show that καρπός was common in the papyri in the sense of 'fruit' and 'produce of the land' generally. More particularly it could apply to the product of an olive yard (Pap. Rylands II 130.10), vineyard (P. Fayoum 127.6) and to other fruits like apples.[33]

καρπός occurs frequently in the Septuagint mostly translating פרי. This is true for all but one of the examples in Genesis.

κάρπιμος means 'fruit-bearing' or 'fruitful'. It is related solely to fruitfulness or fruit producing, describing that which produces fruit, e.g. 'ears of corn', 'fields', 'trees', 'summer'. Thus ξύλον κάρπιμον neatly expresses the idea of 'fruit trees' or 'fruit-bearing trees' (given ξύλον for 'tree'). The use of κάρπιμον here, although unique in the Septuagint, is more appropriate than a literal καρπός, which might otherwise have been used. καρποφόρος occurs at Ps. 106.34 to describe the land.

κατὰ γένος καὶ καθ᾽ ὁμοιότητα *for* למינו *and* למינהו

γένος in Greek usage has four main areas of application. Firstly, it can stand for 'race', 'stock', 'kin', denoting a specific relationship within a group of human beings even of a direct descendant. Secondly, it can mean 'offspring' including a single descendant as well as posterity. Thirdly, it can mean more generally 'race' of beings, for example 'animals', 'men', 'gods', or 'family' or 'tribe'. When applied to animals it can mean 'breed'. Fourthly, and more 'scientifically', it can mean 'class' or 'sort' or 'kind', denoting a particular category of the natural world. For example in *Historia Plantarum* 8.1.1 Theophrastus discusses the various classes (γένος) of herbaceous plants. This passage from *Historia Plantarum* also aptly demonstrates the similarities of the agricultural world known to Theophrastus to that of the biblical writers. γένος is also common in the papyri with reference to species or classes of things (P. Fayoum 21.120, 90.11).[34]

In the Septuagint γένος translates מין 17 times in Genesis only. Elsewhere in Genesis γένος stands for משפחה and עם. In the rest of the Septuagint it is used for עם, מור משפחה and זן.

למין is also translated by ὅμοιος particularly at Lev. 11.14-22 and Deut. 14.13-18, the lists of clean and unclean animals. Elsewhere it largely translates כמו. In Leviticus and Deuteronomy much more specific classes of animals are in mind, individual species rather than the general categories of animals, birds, fish of Gen. 1. Thus the translators appear to have distinguished what they saw as two different nuances implied in the Hebrew by using two different translation terms for למין.

ὅμοιος in Greek usage was common at all ages, having three main designations. First, it stands for 'like', 'resembling' or 'same'. Second, it denotes 'of equal rank'. Hence οἱ ὅμοιοι in aristocratic states meant 'peers' or all citizens who had equal rights to hold office (Xenophon *Hist. Graec.* 3.3.5). Third, it was used in geometry to denote similarity or congruence of figures (Euclid 6, Def. 1).

Thus in translating למינו in the context of the laws of clean and unclean animals ὅμοιος means X (= named animal species) and all the same as X. In the context of Gen. 1 למינו intends rather all those of the same class or family, 'every kind of the class of nature called fruit trees'. In that sense γένος is the better term denoting familial relationship but not exact identity, which is the preserve of ὅμοιος.

ὁμοιότης καθ' ὁμοιότητα is added to κατὰ γένος the first time in each verse. This term occurs again in the Septuagint only at Wis. 14.19 and 4 Macc. 15.4. In normal Greek usage it means 'likeness', 'resemblance' or 'corresponding to'. The other Septuagint references have to do with making something in the closest possible resemblance to an original and with family resemblance both physically and characteristically. Thus ὁμοιότης is a useful term in the translation of Gen. 1.11-12, implying a familial relationship but not an exact likeness between the trees or the seed-bearing plants.

καθ' ὁμοιότητα is added to γένος only here at Gen. 1.11-12 and only once in each verse whereas κατα γένος occurs twice in each verse. It may be that it was felt that κατὰ γένος was not precise enough, especially with its wide range of application, and καθ' ὁμοιότητα was added as a kind of parenthesis giving the meaning 'all the kinds of seed-bearing plants, all those which resemble one another'. Having once made the point, the translator felt no further need to repeat the qualification. Alternatively καθ' ὁμοιότητα may have originally been a marginal gloss explaining κατὰ γένος and which was later incorporated into the text. There is a considerable variation in the textual tradition in relation to the number of times and positions in which the phrase occurs in both verses.

ἐκφέρειν *for* יצא

In normal Greek usage ἐκφέρειν has the basic sense of 'carry out of' or 'bring forth'. It is used of physically carrying something away and also of women in childbirth bringing forth a baby, of plants bringing forth or bearing seed, (e.g. Aristotle *G.A.*, 731 a 22) and of the earth bearing fruit (e.g. Herodotus 1.193).

In the Septuagint, ἐκφέρειν occurs approximately 100 times, mostly for יצא in the *hiphil* (e.g. Gen. 14.18; 24.53; Exod. 4.6, 7). This is an exclusive relationship in the Pentateuch. ἐκφέρειν has many objects and is not at all specifically reserved for the plant world. A wide range of applications would be expected from its normal usage.

יצא in the *hiphil* is also translated by ἐξάγειν. ἐξάγειν has a basic sense of 'leading out' or 'away from' which has a different orientation from ἐκφέρειν. An examination of the contexts where ἐκφέρειν and ἐξάγειν are used for יצא in the *hiphil* shows that the distinction is maintained. ἐκφέρειν is used for inanimate objects which have to be carried, and ἐξάγειν is used for animate objects which can be led. Hence ἐκφέρειν is used in Gen. 1.12 of plants which cannot be led forth anywhere, being inanimate, whilst ἐξάγειν is used in Gen. 1.20, 24 of sea creatures and land animals which can be led out (metaphorically) by the waters of the sea and the earth respectively. Cf. Gen. 8.17 where Noah leads out (ἐξάγειν) the animals from the ark and Num. 17.8 [MT 17.23] where Aaron's rod produces (ἐκφέρειν) a bud.

The only confused usage is at Num. 20.8-11, the story of Moses and Aaron producing water from the rock. The translator had difficulty in deciding what exactly happened to the water. The water, being inanimate, cannot be led out of the rock and hence is borne out (ἐκφέρειν) of the rock to the Israelites. On the other hand neither did Moses and Aaron go into the rock to carry out the water, so they figuratively had to lead it out (ἐξάγειν). As a third attempt, deciding that the water could not be borne out nor led out, the translator decided upon ἐκπορεύειν meaning to 'come out' in a more general sense.

The differences between verses 11 and 12

A further problem remained for the translator to solve after he had resolved all the problems of structure and vocabulary. Gen. 1.12 is basically a repetition of 1.11 as the reported fulfilment of the exhortation of 1.11. It is not exactly the same in the Hebrew. There are essentially five basic variations between the verses. These are: the change of verb at the beginning; the various placings and spellings of למינו; verse 12 has ועץ rather than the עץ of verse 11; verse 12 omits the first פרי; verse 12 also omits על הארץ at the end.

The translator's approach is extremely harmonistic. Of the five differences that appear in the traditional text of the Hebrew, only one appears in the text of the Septuagint, namely the different main verbs. κατὰ γένος is inserted twice in verse 11 in the places it appears in verse 12. A copula is inserted in verse 11 before ξύλον and verse 12 has κάρπιμον after both ξύλον and ἐπὶ τῆς γῆς, i.e. it replaces the פרי 'omitted' by the Hebrew original.

It would be difficult to say that all these harmonizations were caused by scribal errors in the transmission of the Greek text. There are many variations in the textual transmission traditions, but it is not possible to reconstruct a sufficiently well-supported text that is closer to the Hebrew.

It seems likely that the translator had a theological motive for harmonizing the two verses. Verse 11 was a command of God to produce various categories of vegetation. Verse 12 was the report of that productive activity. It was not possible that God's will or command should not be fulfilled. Therefore verse 12 had to be as close to 11 as possible.

The biggest problem in this connection is the position of למינו and למינהו. In the Hebrew, verse 11 has למינו after עשה פרי, whilst verse 12 has למינהו after both מזריע זרע and זרעו בו. The Greek text has κατὰ γένος καὶ καθ' ὁμοιότητα after σπεῖρον σπέρμα and κατὰ γένος after σπέρμα αὐτοῦ ἐν αὐτῷ in both verses. Thus the translator has changed verse 11 to agree with verse 12.

למינו is the expected regular form of a word like מין with a third person singular masculine suffix, but למינהו is the common form, occurring 15 times out of 19 instances. The exact significance, for exegetical purposes, of the variation is difficult to estimate. The commentators only note its occurrence. The Greek translator makes no attempt to preserve the variation.

There remains the possibility that למינהו was not in the Hebrew original. However, there is no manuscript evidence for its omission, apart from a cryptic footnote in BHS 'prb. dl. cf. v. 12'. All the Targum texts witness to its presence in the text at the time of their formulation, as do the Vulgate and the Samaritan Pentateuch.[35]

It does seem, however, that למינו is out of place as it stands, breaking the connections of sense and sentence structure between פרי and אשר זרעו בו. As Gunkel remarks, למינו is obviously intended to go with עץ meaning that every kind of tree was to be produced.[36] If so, a better position would have been following זרעו בו as in verse 12. Further, if למינו was original, it is to be wondered why עשב was not also similarly qualified.

In the Septuagint the matter is resolved by adopting the reading of verse 12 in verse 11 as well. Various textual traditions of position, addition and omission of κατὰ γένος and καθ' ὁμοιότητα are recorded in the apparatus of the critical editions of the Greek Genesis. The most significant variant is the Hexaplaric addition of εἰς τὸ γένος αὐτῶν (which is a nearly exact rendering of למינו, or rather למינם) after ποιοῦν κάρπον. This addition suggests both that the Hebrew tradition known to Origen did in fact have למינו in its traditional place and that the Greek text did not have a representation of it after עשה פרי.

In terms of translation technique the translator felt compelled to resolve a difficulty. If למינו was in his Hebrew text then it was in a difficult position for sense and style. Hence it was moved and placed in a more logical position. Then the reading of the sentence structure required its insertion in two places as in verse 12.

Conclusions

The following points can be derived from the Greek translator's attempt to render the Hebrew text of Gen. 1.11-12.

1. The translator understands clearly that there is a twofold classification of plants. However he adopts a less straightforward way of reading the Hebrew by linking דשא and עשב in a construct chain. The solution is unique to him and is not one that has commended itself to any subsequent commentators.

2. The rendering of למינו shows that this word and its position were problems to the translator. If we can rely on the Hexaplaric insertion and the versional support for למינו in the original Hebrew, the translator shows by his treatment of it that he was not averse to moving words around in the text when a difficulty was encountered.

3. The rendering of the vocabulary leads to several further conclusions. The translator was not always slavishly literal. βλαστήσατω... βλάστημα, the most literal possibility, was avoided for the rendering of דשא... תדשא. κάρπιμον is used for פרי where καρπος would have been more literal. Style therefore was not always disregarded.

Nevertheless, even at this early stage in the production of a translation of Genesis, the translator was using stereotyped translation equivalents: χόρτος for עשב, σπεῖρειν for זרע and ξύλον for עץ. This does lead to problems, especially in the phrase βοτάνη χόρτου and later λάχανα χόρτου in Gen. 9.3. σπεῖρειν and particularly ξύλον are examples of problematic renderings caused by this rather inflexible approach, especially as more appropriate terms were available.

However, some good translations were employed, e.g. βλαστήσατω for תדשא, σπέρμα for זרע, κάρπιμος for פרי. κατὰ γένος also communicates well the essential meaning of למין especially when reinforced by καθ' ὁμοιότητα. ἐξήνεγκεν in verse 12 was also according to general usage, with its distinction from ἐξάγειν being preserved.

ξύλον is a classic example of an ordinary Greek word being invested with the whole sense of the Hebrew word which it translates. This is a good illustration of the way in which semantic fields do not always coincide in different languages. In Hebrew עץ is related to the 'plant' field in a way different from that in which ξύλον is related. In fact ξύλον is only very loosely related to that field.

The translation of the other Hebrew terms belonging to the 'plant' group also illustrates the same phenomenon of the lack of coincidence of semantic fields in different languages. The fields are certainly not ὅμοιος even if they might have ὁμοιότης. The Greek translator fails to appreciate the subtle distinctions between דשא, עשב and חציר based on their relationships within the Hebrew 'plant' group. The Greek terms similarly have their own subtle relationships.

The treatment of the vocabulary also illustrates another important feature of words in different languages. A particular word is able to denote a range of related referents. The extent of the range depends on the nature of the referents and their perception by the particular language community. In other words, different languages divide reality in different ways. Individual words in different languages will coincide at one or more points in their range. Their use as translations of each other is thus valid at the point of coincidence. However, the range of those words will almost certainly be different. The employment of the same word in the receptor language for every occurrence of the word in the translated language will be most inappropriate. At the least there will be confusion, if not mistranslation.[37] An example of this is βοτάνη χόρτου, which only makes sense if the range of the Hebrew words translated is added to the normal Greek sense. ξύλον for עץ is again a good example of this phenomenon.

In verses 11-12 there is also an example of the double rendering of one Hebrew term. κατὰ γένος and καθ' ὁμοιότητα are both used to express למין. Either would have been adequate by itself, but both contribute to translating the nuances of the Hebrew.

4. The translator was prone to harmonize variant details. Of the five differences between the verses four have been obliterated. It appears that the concern of the translator to cast no doubt on God's ability to have his commands fulfilled overrode any concern to preserve the detail of the Hebrew text.

If such an 'ordinary' verse in the creation account provides as much food for thought as Gen. 1.11-12 has done, then there are many more meals to be made at the expense of the Greek translators.

NOTES

1. The Hebrew text followed is that of the *Biblia Hebraica Stuttgartensia*, edited by O. Eissfeldt, Stuttgart, 1969.

2. W.H. Schmidt, *Die Schöpfungsgeschichte der Priesterschrift* (WMANT, 17), Neukirchen, 1973, 108.

3. L. Koehler and W. Baumgartner, *Hebräisches und Aramäisches Lexikon zum Alten Testament*, Leiden, 1974, I, 224.

4. E. Kautzsch, *Gesenius Hebrew Grammar*, Oxford, 1910, 145.

5. R.J. Williams, *Hebrew Syntax: An Outline*, Toronto, 1976, 15, n. 65.

6. S. Talmon, 'The Gezer Calendar and the Seasonal Cycle of Ancient Canaan', *JAOS* 83 (1963), 177-87.

7. S. Talmon, *art. cit.*, 184.

8. M. Jastrow, *A Dictionary of the Targumim*, New York, I, 326.

9. Rashi in M. Rosenbaum and A.M. Silbermann, *Pentateuch with Targum Onkelos, Haphtorah and Rashi's Commentary*, New York and Jerusalem, 4, 257f. (n. 4).

10. F. Brown, S.R. Driver and C.A. Briggs, *Hebrew and English Lexicon of the Old Testament*, Oxford, 1907, 438 (= BDB).

11. Koehler and W. Baumgartner, *Lexicon in Veteris Testamenti Libros*, Leiden, 1974, vol. II, 420, (= KB³).

12. G. Dalman, *Arbeit und Sitte in Palästina*, Gütersloh, 1928–42, vol. II, 303.

13. J. Murray, *The First European Agriculture*, Edinburgh, 1970, 5-13.

14. See above, n. 12.

15. J. Feliks, 'Plants', *Encyclopaedia Judaica*, Jerusalem, vol. XIII, 664-627.

16. BDB gives its general meaning as 'grass', specifically standing for a second crop of grass (206). KB¹ gives 'grass, 'season of grass', 'young new grass' (220). KB³ gives 'junges frisches Gras' and an *Oberbegriff* for עשׂב and עץ meaning 'Grünes', 'Vegetation' (I, 224). Gunkel has, 'das junge, frische Grün, wie es damals zuerst und noch jetzt nach dem Winterregen hervorspriesst; aus diesem דשׁא wächst alles Übrige' (H. Gunkel, *Genesis*, Göttingen, 1964, 108). Schmidt has 'Der Oberbegriff דשׁא "junges, frisches Grün" bezeichnet allgemein die Pflanzen im Aussspriessen zur Zeit ihrer Entstehung... Kann man deshalb דשׁא als spätere Einfügung ansehen, die den beiden Pflanzengattungen übergeordnet wurde?' (W.H. Schmidt, *op. cit.*, 107).

Westermann suggests that דשׁא and the verb are used by the writer of Gen. 1 to designate trees and plants in their sprouting out of the earth.

'Tatsächlich sind ja alle Pflanzen im frühesten Wachstumsstadium, d.h. bei ihrem Sprossen, einander ähnlich' (C. Westermann; *Genesis 1–11* [BKAT], Neukirchen, 1974, 173 [ET: SPCK, 1984, 124]).

Von Rad has 'greenness', 'vegetation' (G. von Rad, *Genesis*, London, 1963, 53). Spurrell gives '*grass* or *grass-like plants*, the first verdure that covered the earth young and fresh, appearing after rain . . . or after the old grass had gone' (Spurrell, *Notes on Genesis*, Oxford, 1887, 8). Skinner suggests that דשא means 'fresh, young herbage' and appears here in Gen. 1.11-12 to include all plants in the earliest stages of their growth (J. Skinner, *A Critical and Exegetical Commentary on Genesis*, [ICC], Edinburgh, 1930, 23). Cassuto has 'the noun and verb derived from it refer to vegetation generally' (U. Cassuto, *A Commentary on the Book of Genesis, Part One*, Jerusalem, 1961, 40).

There appears therefore to be a considerable difference of opinion between a value 'grass' or a more general term 'vegetation' or 'young vegetation'.

From its usage דשא shares many of the characteristics of חציר, i.e. springing up out of the ground after rain, being fed to animals or eaten by them, growing and withering quickly. However דשא differs from חציר in being mostly eaten by wild animals, in not being reaped and in being described by ירק. Further and significantly Prov. 27.25 specifically states that דשא springs up after חציר has been harvested. דשא also shares some of the features of עשב including being described by ירק, providing food for animals, although, as with חציר, עשב is eaten more by domestic animals. However דשא differs from עשב in not occurring in agricultural contexts, in not providing food for humans, in not occurring with עץ and שיח and in not providing a metaphor of transitory growth.

17. Rashi; see n. 9 above.

18. BDB, 826; KB¹, 773.

19. The modern Hebrew word for 'tree' is אלון. In the post-biblical period עץ meaning 'tree' was replaced by אילן, and עץ was restricted to 'wood', 'timber'. This suggests the origin of the rabbinic idea that God intended the earth to produce not fruit-bearing trees but fruity-tasting wood shaped like trees, 'that the taste of the tree be exactly the same as that of the fruit'. It did not do this however but 'the earth brought forth a tree yielding fruit' and the tree itself was not a fruit. Therefore when Adam was cursed on account of his sin the earth was also visited and cursed also. H. Friedman and M. Simon (eds.), *Midrash Rabbah*, London, 1951, I, 39. Such an account was possible because the wide range of the biblical term עץ was later limited, leaving part of the original range sounding strange to later commentators.

20. C. Westermann, *op. cit.* (n. 21), on the classifying concerns of P (ET, 18).

21. BDB, 422.

22. W.H. Schmidt, *op. cit.*, 108 (n. 2).

23. Babylonian Talmud, *Hullin* 60a, referred to by Rashi in his commentary.

24. The Greek text followed is that established by J.H. Wevers in *Genesis* (Göttingen Septuagint), vol. I, Göttingen, 1974.

25. H. St. John Thackeray, *A Grammar of the Old Testament in Greek according to the Septuagint*, vol. I, Cambridge, 1909, 233f.

26. H.C. Liddell and R. Scott, *A Greek English Lexicon* (9th ed.), Oxford, 1940, 317 (= Liddell & Scott).

27. W.F. Arndt and F.W. Gingrich, *A Greek English Lexicon of the New Testament*, Chicago and Cambridge, 1970, 892.

28. J.H. Moulton and G. Milligan, *The Vocabulary of the Greek New Testament Illustrated from the Papyri and other Non-literary Sources*, London and New York, 1915-30, 690 (= Moulton & Milligan).

29. Liddell and Scott, 1847f.

30. See below n. 32.

31. In particular note the usage of the Zenon Papyri and the references cited by Moulton and Milligan, 140.

32. J. Barr, 'Aramaic-Greek Notes on the Book of Enoch (I)', *JSS* 23 (1978), 188f. The evidence cited by Moulton and Milligan, 434, for the 'Hellenistic usage of ξύλον to denote a (living) tree' is not altogether convincing. At Luke 23.31 the meaning is clearly 'wood'; green wood as opposed to dry is the basis of a traditional saying. The other evidence is from material that also postdates the Septuagint, if in fact they are unambiguous references to trees as claimed.

33. Moulton and Milligan, 321.

34. Moulton and Milligan, 124.

35. P. Schäfer, *Der Grundtext von Targum Ps. Jonathan*, an unpublished thesis of the Institutum Judaicum der Universität Tübingen 1972, 14.

36. H. Gunkel, *Genesis*, 108.

37. See in particular the works of E.A. Nida especially *Componential Analysis of Meaning*, The Hague, 1975; *Exploring Semantic Structures*, Munich, 1975, esp. 12-28; *Towards a Science of Translating*, Leiden, 1964.

TOWARDS DATING THE TARGUM OF RUTH

D.R.G. Beattie

The Queen's University of Belfast

The problem that attends the dating of the Targum of Ruth may be highlighted by the fact that within the space of two years two very different conclusions on the question were published. In an article entitled 'The Targum of Ruth: A Sectarian Composition',[1] Akiva Schlesinger proposed that its author was a Sadducee, while Ezra-Zion Melamed[2] suggested that it was written at a late date by someone who made use of the Targums of the Pentateuch and Prophets and the Babylonian Talmud, though not always with precision. While it may be hard to imagine a greater divergence than exists between these two conclusions, the two studies share some common ground in that both scholars were attempting to account for the relationship of the Targum of Ruth to rabbinic literature, and both based their conclusions, to some extent, on the same material.

The main thrust of Schlesinger's case comes from *Tg. Ruth* 1.17 where, in the course of a catechism constructed around the several phrases of Ruth's speech in 1.16f., Naomi informs her daughter-in-law that Jewish law prescribes four forms of capital punishment, and Ruth's words באשר תמותי אמות are construed as meaning 'By whatever means you die, I shall die'. What is unique to *Tg. Ruth* is that the fourth death penalty is said there to be crucifixion (literally 'hanging on a tree'), instead of strangling as in *m. Sanh.* 7.1, and elsewhere in rabbinic literature, including the parallel version of the Naomi and Ruth catechism in *Ruth Rabbah* 2.25.

From this fact of its divergence from the unanimous Pharisaic-rabbinic tradition, Schlesinger comes fairly easily to the conclusion that *Tg. Ruth* is a Sadducean[3] document. He was not the first to draw such a conclusion. Schlesinger himself notes[4] that the suggestion had already been made by Moses Sofer (1762-1839) and recorded in the notes *Lishkat Soferim* to the *Shulḥan Arukh, Even ha-Ezer*.

More recently, J. Heinemann[5] has argued forcefully, and independently, that *Tg. Ruth* 1.17 records an ancient pre-tannaitic tradition, noting incidentally that execution by hanging/crucifixion in the Hasmonaean period is attested in *m. Sanh.* 6.4. This conclusion may not be very different from that of Schlesinger inasmuch as the Sadducean author envisaged by the latter would have to be located in the pre-mishnaic period, yet, being altogether more cautious, it is the more deserving of acceptance. Whether it is possible to take the further steps of dating the whole document to such an early period and, with Schlesinger, of assigning it to a non-Pharisaic source is not so clear. Komlosh,[6] for example, while accepting the antiquity of *Tg. Ruth* 1.17 and acknowledging the difficulty in finding a date for the targum with certainty, yet is inclined to see it as post-talmudic.

Schleslinger's own supporting arguments, of which there are two, do not, to my mind, support his conclusion. His second argument is based on Ruth 1.22 where, for MT's 'they came to Bethlehem at the beginning of the barley-harvest', the targum reads 'they came to Bethlehem on the eve of Passover, and on that day the Israelites began to harvest the Omer of the heave-offering which was of barley'. Starting from the fact that we know of a dispute between Pharisees and Sadducees about the presentation of the Omer, Schlesinger reasons that there must also have been a dispute about its cutting and that the Sadducees would have done this before the festival rather than, as the Pharisees, after nightfall on the first festival day. Therefore, since *Tg. Ruth* has a reference to the cutting of the Omer on the day before the Passover festival, he concludes that he has found in it a second specimen of Sadducean halakhah.[7]

This conclusion, however, fails to carry conviction, in my opinion, not only beause Schlesinger's reconstruction of Sadducean halakhah is entirely speculative but because *Tg. Ruth* 1.22 does not say the Omer was cut on the day before Passover: it says 'the Israelites *began* to harvest the Omer' on that day. *m. Menah.* 10.3 describes how agents of the Beth Din would go out on the eve of the festival and tie the barley, while it was still growing, in bundles in order to facilitate its ceremonial reaping after nightfall on the following day. If the statement in *Tg. Ruth* may be construed as referring to these preparations (and it is difficult to imagine why else it should say 'they began . . . '), then *Tg. Ruth* is, in this respect, quite consistent with the Pharisaic halakhah.

Schlesinger's third line of argument does not point directly towards the Sadducees at all, but he offers it as a kind of general support for his contention that *Tg. Ruth* is not, to use his own word, כשר. His starting point is the appearance in *Tg. Ruth* 4.7 of 'glove' in place of MT's 'shoe', and a reference to this in the Ramban's comment on Ex. 28.41, where, according to Schlesinger, he refers to this reading appearing in the Christians' translations (תרגומי הנוצרים).[8]

I have some reservations about Schlesinger's understanding of the Ramban's comment. In particular, the Ramban did not mention 'Christians'; the word he used is שוטים, 'fools'. I do not at present know whether he may have intended thus to indicate 'Christians', but still the general point seems clear. The Ramban was apparently referring to *Tg. Ruth*, for that is the only place (apart from the commentary attributed to D. Kimḥi,[9] which cannot be considered anybody's 'Targum') where the reading 'glove' appears, and describing it as, to borrow Schlesinger's expression, not *kosher*.[10]

The two passages on which Schlesinger based his two main arguments were also discussed in the second article mentioned at the outset of the present paper, where E.Z. Melamed listed them among seven examples of the use by the Targum of midrashim in the Babylonian Talmud, some of which are interpreted incorrectly.[11]

Seeing in *Tg. Ruth* 1.22 a reference to cutting the Omer on the eve of Passover, he says that the Targumist misconstrued *m. Menaḥ*. 10.5 where the description of the preparations is followed directly by an account of the reaping ceremony without any immediate indication that this was to take place a day later. The suggestion has a certain plausibility, but it is unnecessary. Melamed has, like Schlesinger, missed the point that the Targum does not say the Israelites reaped the Omer on Passover-eve, but that they *began* to do so on that day. It is, thus, possible to see *Tg. Ruth* as reflecting the same idea about the reaping of the Omer as is found in the Mishnah. The Targumist may or may not have known the Mishnah as such. It cannot be said with certainty that he did; much less can it be said that he misunderstood it.

In the passage about the four death penalties, listed in *Tg. Ruth* as 'stoning with stones, burning with fire, killing by the sword and crucifixion' (literally 'hanging on a tree'), Melamed finds two matters at variance with the halakhah, for, as he says, 'according to the halakhah burning is not with fire' and 'in Israel there is no death by hanging'.[12] The use of the present tense is significant. Melamed is looking at the matter purely from a rabbinic perspective and, although he refers to the proposal of Moses Sofer that the author of *Tg. Ruth* was a Sadducee, he does not pursue that possibility.

In the former of these two observations there may well be a point which could support Schlesinger's conclusion. *M. Sanh.* 7.2 records two variant opinions on the administration of the death penalty by burning, neither of them involving the direct application of fire. Yet the contradiction (if there is one) between Targum and Mishnah on this point is not so clear-cut as in the case of hanging, for burning 'with fire' is explicitly prescribed in the laws of Lev. 20.14; 21.9, and, presumably, the tannaim saw no conflict between these verses and their preferred methods of carrying out the sentence.

There is, of course, in *m. Sanh.* 7.2, the report of an occasion when a priest's daughter was executed under the law of Lev. 21.9 by having a fire built around her. It is explained there that the court on that occasion was not expert, and in the gemara[13] it is further said that it was a Sadducean court. There might, thus, be here grounds for seeing in *Tg. Ruth* 1.17 a second Sadducean feature, but another interpretation might also be possible (that is, if any explanation of the reference to burning with fire is necessary at all).

The reference to that incident not only shows that the practice of execution by burning in a fire was known; it suggests that there was within the ranks of the tannaim a minority opinion that that was the correct way of administering the penalty of burning. That being so, it is possible that *Tg. Ruth* subscribes to that opinion and that we have here a second feature of the Targum which may be set alongside the reference to crucifixion as a specimen of material which has survived from a period before the halakhah was firmly established. Neither point need be accounted, as Melamed would have them, a misapplication of talmudic statements.

Having treated these two features of *Tg. Ruth* 1.17 together, Melamed finds in the same verse another point, which he treats separately as a specimen of corruption of talmudic material. Ruth's words 'And there I will be buried' are, in the Targum, made in response to Naomi's informing her, 'We have a cemetery', while the parallel accounts of the catechism mention 'two graves' and indeed *m. Sanh.* 6.5 prescribes two graves, 'one for those executed by the sword or strangled and one for those stoned or burnt'. Melamed suggests that the 'two graves' of the halakhah have been turned into the (one) cemetery of the Targum through the error of a scribe who mistook the letter *beth*, representing the numeral 2, for the word *beth* and so wrote בֵּית קְבוּרְתָּא instead of קְבוּרְתָּא (תרתי=) ב'.[14]

The theory is ingenious, and plausible if the matter is approached with the presupposition that the Targum must be in the wrong, but it can be stood on its head. It could be suggested that the halakhah of the two graves started with a mistaken reading of the word בית, or perhaps ב',[15] as the letter ב', meaning '2'. Such an approach would offer not only an explanation for the origin of a very strange halakhah but also an argument for the antiquity of the reading preserved in *Tg. Ruth*.

The statement 'we have a cemetery' need not be so meaningless as Melamed would appear to have thought, for it could be understood as meaning 'We Jews practise burial rather than cremation'. If burial was so distinctively Jewish a practice as Tacitus, *Hist.* 5.5, would appear to imply, it is surely reasonable that Naomi should be made to inform Ruth of it.[16] Then, too, it should be remembered that the kind of expansion encountered in *Tg. Ruth* at this point is almost invited by Ruth's biblical speech. That is to say, the whole thing is providing an answer to the question, 'Why did Ruth say the words recorded in the Bible and not something else?' Given this starting point, what else could Naomi say to elicit the response 'And there I will be buried', apart from 'We have a cemetery'? It would be totally illogical to have Ruth declare her intention to be buried in two places.

Melamed, as I have indicated, also makes several other points, and we shall return to them in due course, but perhaps enough has been said already to show that his conclusion, that *Tg. Ruth* is later than, and made use of, the Babylonian Talmud, is no more securely based than is that of Schlesinger about Sadducean authorship. Thus far we have seen that one detail must be regarded as stemming from a very early period, while perhaps two other details in close proximity to it in the text may arguably also be dated to an early period. However, before I succumb to the temptation to multiply examples of what may arguably be advanced as examples of early material it might be profitable to step back to where it may well be thought I ought to have started and survey *Tg. Ruth* from a broader perspective.

Tg. Ruth contains, as well as an Aramaic translation of the Hebrew text, a considerable quantity of additional material which expands the whole to rather more than twice the length of the Hebrew. The Hebrew text which underlies the Aramaic translation is clearly that which is known to us from MT. The difficult text of 2.7b is already there, as is the second person verb (as in the *qere* text) of 4.5b. In general it may be said that the Aramaic has those readings which are designed *qere* in MT, but in other cases (other, that is, than 4.5) it is difficult to be sure. However, two words, which in MT are marked קרי ולא כתיב, are included in 3.5, 17, while one word, which is כתיב ולא קרי, is omitted from 3.12. Yet there is, I think, at least one clear indication that the translation is pre-masoretic. The opening words of the Targum 'In the days of the judge of judges' (where it is intended to make reference to Boaz, who is identified with the judge Ibzan) are unlikely to have been produced from a vocalized text.

One passage—the second half of 1.7—is omitted from the received Aramaic text, probably through an error in copying at an early stage of the Targum's history.[17] With this one exception, any departure from the wording of MT may be shown to have been precipitated by exegetical considerations of some kind. This general heading includes the Targum's fondness for passive verbs and the avoidance of anthropomorphisms or other 'indelicacies', as well as the drawing out of 'hidden' meanings, and I shall not delay to offer examples at this point.

The additional material in *Tg. Ruth*—that is to say, the material which is not found in the Hebrew text—is often marked in editions of the Aramaic text by use of brackets. This practice goes back to the London polyglot although it has been refined in latter times by the use of different kinds of brackets and other symbols to classify the material into different groups. Thus, for example, Neuhausen[18] used square and round brackets to indicate, respectively, simple explanatory expansions and midrashic additions. Sperber[19] had three classifications: minor additions to MT, marked by daggers; 'additions of Rabbinic interpretation' in square brackets, and 'lengthy midrashic additions' in double square brackets. Levine employed a similar system in his so-called critical translation.[20]

However, the fact that there is little correlation between the classifications assigned to particular passages by different individuals, one man's minor expansion being another man's (major) midrashic addition, suggests to me that there is no great value in this exercise. To be sure, the 'additions' incorporate material of diverse kinds, and I have myself, in my previous work[21] on the Targum in connection with the Jewish exegesis of Ruth, distinguished between the kind of minor addition which is also found in LXX and Peshitta, on the one hand, and the (usually) longer passage of 'midrashic' material, on the other, but the distinction is one which may be made only from a latter-day perspective. To the Targumist, *all* the additional material was exegetical.

I refer deliberately to 'the Targumist' in this connection, because, while suspicion may be entertained that the 'additions' in *Tg. Ruth* may stem from a late period, or indeed that they may have been introduced piecemeal at different times into an earlier, simpler, and literal translation, I do not see any evidence which would warrant such a conclusion. Indeed, the existence in *Tg. Ruth* of even a few passages where literal translation has been abandoned in favour of a paraphrastic rendering which involves the addition of exegetical material, shows that no clear distinction can be made between translation and exegesis.

Given the nature of *Tg. Ruth*, enquiry into its origin must proceed on two fronts. First, a thorough examination of the language of the Targum is called for, in order to determine not only the relationship of *Tg. Ruth* to the other Targums and the rest of Aramaic literature but also whether the 'additions' may be distinguished from the 'translation' on linguistic grounds. But before this can be undertaken a critical edition of the text is needed, for even a casual glance at what textual information is readily available[22] shows that there is some variation in language between different manuscripts.

I do not at present know of any detailed linguistic study of *Tg. Ruth*. Melamed has noted various points of agreement and disagreement between it and Onkelos, Pseudo-Jonathan, and Jonathan on the prophets, and concluded that its author knew and used all these other Targums.[23] Churgin[24] has observed that the resemblance between translations in *Tg. Ruth* and similar things in Onkelos and Jonathan leaves room for the supposition that at some time *Tg. Ruth* held a place among the official targums.

In this connection one point whereby, it might be thought, something might be made to hang is the citation in *Tg. Ruth* 1.1 (in the context of a list of ten famines) of Amos 8.11 in an Aramaic translation which does not conform to that of *Tg. Jonathan*. This suggests to me that the author of *Tg. Ruth* did not use *Tg. Amos*. I doubt whether more can be said, but Churgin saw in the use of למשמע, as opposed to *Tg. Jonathan's* לקבלא, to translate MT לשמוע a sign of *Tg. Ruth*'s late date.[25] Melamed countered that the Targums used two Aramaic verbs to translate the Hebrew שמע, namely שמע when the meaning is 'hear', and קבל when the meaning is 'obey', and that in this instance *Tg. Ruth* had chosen the better word.[26] How this squares with his general conclusion that the writer of *Tg. Ruth* used Jonathan *and* had difficulties with Aramaic,[27] I do not know.

I do not feel able at present to deal in depth with linguistic aspects of *Tg. Ruth*, and it will be understood, therefore, that anything I say hereafter (or indeed herebefore) may be subject to revision in the light of linguistic study, but let us turn now to the second front, which is where most previous studies of *Tg. Ruth* have focussed their attention: the contents of the Targum.

Two questions arise here: (1) Are the 'additions' to be distinguished from the translation as a secondary development?; and (2) Can the 'additions' be dated in relation to parallel material elsewhere? I began above to give my own answer to the first of these questions. Before I resume my theme, I would like to introduce what seems to be the currently received opinion on the subject.

Churgin, speaking of midrashim in *Tg. Ruth*, declared that 'the majority of them are probably late, and imported into the Targum from outside'.[28] The 'flimsy connection' between them and the rest of the text, he said, marks them as something extraneous, and they display the influence of the Babylonian Talmud, yet he allowed the possibility that they might have been included (presumably from the start) by a late translator. Thus far Churgin was speaking of the longer midrashic additions (he mentions eight examples), but later on, speaking of other midrashic comments, which also have parallels in the Talmud and midrash, he envisaged the possibility either that the Targum could have preceded the midrashim or that they could have had a common source.[29] Later still he observed that the majority of the long and short midrashim were probably introduced to the Targum at a later stage.[30]

I shall now attempt to advance from this rather inconsistent position. First, I would question whether any part of *Tg. Ruth* should be hived off and treated as a later accretion. I would suggest that the 'flimsy connection' (which Churgin did not demonstrate) between 'translation' and 'addition' is only apparent to those who recognize the additions as additions on *a priori* grounds. If we did not have a Hebrew text of Ruth, I doubt whether anyone would attempt to distil one out of the Targum. I certainly would not like to undertake such a task myself, although on the basis of Churgin's observation it ought to be straightforward.

To take just one of Churgin's eight examples of midrashic additions with 'flimsy connections', I would refer to *Tg. Ruth* 1.16f.

Ruth said, 'Do not urge me to leave you, to go back from after you for I desire to be a proselyte.'

Naomi said, 'We are commanded to keep Sabbaths and holy days so as not to walk beyond two thousand cubits.'

Ruth said, 'Wherever you go I will go.'

Naomi said, 'We are commanded not to lodge together with gentiles.'

Ruth said, 'Wherever you lodge I will lodge.'

Naomi said, 'We are commanded to keep six hundred and thirteen precepts.'

Ruth said, 'What your people keep I will keep as if they were my people from before this.'

Naomi said, 'We are commanded not to engage in idolatry.'

Ruth said, 'Your God is my god.'

Naomi said, 'We have four death penalties for the guilty, stoning with stones, burning with fire, execution by the sword and crucifixion.'

Ruth said, 'By whatever means you die, I will die.'

Naomi said, 'We have a cemetery.'

Ruth said, 'And there will I be buried. And do not say any more. May the Lord do thus to me and more to me, if even death shall separate me and you.'

The additional material is here so thoroughly integrated with the translation of MT that no-one, surely, would venture to separate them without the sure guide of the Hebrew. Or, again, we may take the passage which, because it patently did not originate specifically as an exegesis of anything in the book of Ruth, is perhaps the most easily suspected of being a later addition in the Targum, that is the aggadah of the ten famines which is 'interpolated' in 1.1.

In the days of the judge of judges there was a severe famine in the land of Israel. Ten severe famines were ordained by Heaven to be in the world, from the day that the world was created until the king Messiah should come, to reprove by them the inhabitants of the earth. The first famine was in the days of Adam, the second famine was in the days of Lamech, the third famine was in the days of Abraham. The fourth famine was in the days of Isaac, the fifth famine was in the days of Jacob, the sixth famine was in the days of Boaz, who is called Ibzan the Righteous, who was from Bethlehem, Judah. The seventh famine was in the days of David, king of Israel, the eighth famine was in the days of Elijah the prophet, the ninth famine was in the days of Elisha in Samaria. The tenth famine is to be in the future, not a famine of eating bread nor a drought of drinking water, but of hearing the word of prophecy from before the Lord. And when that famine was severe in the land of Israel, a great man went out from Bethlehem, Judah, and went to live in the country of Moab, he and his wife and his two sons.

Parallel versions of this list of ten famines are to be found in three places in *Genesis Rabbah*, and in *Ruth Rabbah*,[31] as well as in later midrashim which need not be mentioned here, and it might easily be supposed that the Targum borrowed it from one of those places. However, two observations ought to be made with regard to the version in *Tg. Ruth*. First, the passage is firmly integrated in the text of the Targum, partly by means of additional words at the end—'and, when this famine was severe in the land of Israel, a man went out ...' etc.—and partly by describing the relevant famine (the sixth of the series) as taking place in the time of Boaz, whereas the parallel passages use the opening words of Ruth, 'the time when the judges were judging'. The Targum's distinctive rendering of this phrase at the beginning of the verse provides an anchor for the mention of Boaz/Ibzan in the middle. Second, although the *Genesis Rabbah* passages begin by saying 'there were ten famines' they proceed to list eleven.[32] *Ruth Rabbah* has ten but looks as though it originally had the eleven of *Genesis Rabbah*.[33] *Tg. Ruth* has ten and therefore, I think, a pretty fair case can be made out for saying that its version is the oldest one.

That is, at this precise moment, incidental, although in the long run it may be of some importance. To keep to our present point, I just do not see the 'flimsy connections' or 'inorganic relationship'[34] which have led some to label certain parts of the Targum text as 'imports'. Thus, to return to and elaborate on a point on which I embarked earlier, there are several places where *Tg. Ruth* deviates in its translation and introduces its own material (e.g. 3.9 'Let your name be called over your maidservant by taking me as a wife' for MT 'Spread your wings [or skirt] over your maidservant'). There are also many places where it has minor expansions similar to the sort of thing which is found in LXX and Peshitta (e.g. what the commentators call the 'pregnant usage' of 1.14: 'Orpah kissed her mother-in-law'. The Targum adds 'and went on her way'; LXX 'and she returned to her people'; Peshitta 'and she turned and went away'). No-one would propose to isolate secondary strata in the two latter versions, and no-one should propose to do so with the Targum.

Once some 'additions' are granted to belong to the earliest stratum of the Targum, why should it be suggested that any do not? No distinction may be based on length, for some of the 'long midrashic aditions' are only three or four words long. I propose, therefore, to treat *Tg. Ruth* as a unitary document. The burden of proof lies with those who would suggest otherwise.

But perhaps an exception ought to be made in the case of possible double translations. Churgin suggested that there are a number of these in *Tg. Ruth* and that in the majority of cases an earlier and a later translation are discernible,[35] but I am not at all sure that he has interpreted the phenomenon correctly, because there is rarely, if ever, actual tautology in the Aramaic text. I can think of only one example of this; that is in 3.4, where for MT בשכבו, the Targum reads בעירן משכביה דמכיה, using two verbs for the one in the Hebrew. However, that could simply be the result of a conflation, in the received text, of two variant textual traditions.[36]

But to take up some of the examples offered by Churgin: the rendering of אפרתים (1.2) as אפרתין רבנין might indeed represent a double 'translation' but it might just as easily indicate that the translator chose to retain the Hebrew word in Aramaized form as a technical term alongside a word which explained its meaning as he understood it. Or, again, there is a possibility that we have a conflate reading.[37] The inclusion of 'and she became a proselyte' in 2.6, may well be an interpretation of the Hebrew השבה, which is also translated literally in that verse, but it need not be attributed to a second hand. The translator may have seen a double meaning in the Hebrew and brought it out in his translation. The insertion of 'your god and your people' before 'your father and mother' in 2.11 is not, I think, an example of the double translation of the latter phrase at all, but a bit of narrative expansion similar to the kind of thing we have noted above. 'I am inferior to you and I will be redeemer after you' (4.6) is probably an expansive translation of the Hebrew 'I (am) after you' rather than a translation of that plus a gloss on that translation.

One final example, which Churgin cites not under the head of double translations but in his opening section which deals with longer midrashic additions, has the incidental merit of turning us firmly in the direction of talmudic parallels as well as offering what I think is a clear argument in defence of my policy of not lightly separating 'double' translations and attributing the two parts to different hands. This is in 3.8 where Churgin sees two translations of the Hebrew word וילפת: one is the Aramaic ורתת, 'he was afraid, trembled', the other is midrashic, 'his flesh became as soft as turnip from fear (or, trembling. Aram.: רתיתא)'.[38] The interesting thing here is that it is not possible to achieve the first 'translation' without the second. In other words, there is no way of getting from וילפת to 'fear' or 'trembling' except *via* 'turnip' (boiled, and probably mashed, turnip, at that). Perhaps I should explain more clearly: the Hebrew verb לפת is used rarely (three times in all in the Hebrew Bible). The Targum proposes to explain it from the noun לֶפֶת, 'a turnip'. Now, what could 'he was turnipped' mean? The Targum's answer is that he became like turnip (not 'a turnip'; boiled and mashed turnip is envisaged), and Boaz got like that through fear. Thus, in this case at least, it is clear that the short one-word translation depends on the midrashic explanation which, at first sight, might appear to be an appendage to it.

Now let us turn to the matter of the talmudic parallel, for this very passage is the first one cited by Melamed as an example of the dependence of *Tg. Ruth* on the Babylonian Talmud.[39]

B. Sanh. 19b explains the word וילפת as meaning 'his flesh became like turnip-heads', and this means, according to Rashi, 'his member became hard' ('but nevertheless', he continues, 'he subdued his desire . . . ' etc.). Here, in contrast to the Targum, the turnip is envisaged in its raw state and it is hard to see dependence by *Tg. Ruth* on the talmudic passage. I have considered the possibility that the relationship between Targum and Talmud at this point is one of reaction on the part of one against the other, but I come to the conclusion that there is no actual connection between the two, even though they do have a common root.[40] Both start with 'turnip' but the two conclusions as to the application of 'turnip' to Ruth 3.8 are so diametrically opposed that neither conclusion can have been known to the proponents of the other.

It may seem rather hasty to jump to a conclusion from this single example, but I find myself reflecting that the concept of rabbinic 'parallels' has a peculiar aptness to the study of the relationship of *Tg. Ruth* to rabbinic literature. As I recall from schoolboy geometry, the essence of parallels lies in their never meeting and, certainly, *Tg. Ruth* never seems actually to make contact with any of its many parallels in talmud and midrash.

There are certainly many points of similarity and, even if we leave aside everything which arises from the exegesis of Ruth and which could have been produced independently by different minds working according to similar principles, there are features for which it may appear necessary to postulate borrowing, by one document or another. But even if borrowing were postulated, the question of the direction of this borrowing would remain, and the possibility that all our extant texts derive from a common source could not be discounted.

Two examples may be offered in illustration of the problem: the identification of Boaz with the judge Ibzan,[41] and the attribution of royal ancestry to Ruth.[42] While at first sight there is no discernible reason why either of these two ideas should ever have got started, and therefore some borrowing must be envisaged, to say that the Targum borrowed from the Talmud (or *vice versa*) does not solve the problem of their origin. It occurs to me that the Boaz/Ibzan identification could possibly have its origin in the distinctive Targum rendering of שפט השפטים in Ruth 1.1 as 'the judge of judges'. If Boaz is to be described as 'the judge of judges', then obviously an identification with someone in the book of Judges is called for, and Ibzan, from Bethlehem, is the obvious candidate. The connection could be made without that understanding of Ruth 1.1, but it is easier with it. As for Ruth's being the daughter of Eglon, that could have arisen in connection with Judg. 3.20[43] and thus have been in the public domain, so to speak, for both the Targumist and the authorities of the Talmud, but could it possibly have arisen rather from *Tg. Ruth*, eased by the statement, which is unique to the Targum, that Elimelech's family held high office in Moab?[44] We may here be coming perilously close to special pleading for the priority of the Targum and no doubt other explanations for the origin of these and similar elements could be advanced, but I am struck forcefully by the difficulty in finding anything in *Tg. Ruth* which has to have been derived from some other identifiable source.

There are, of course, also many points of disagreement between *Tg. Ruth* and the Talmud and midrash, which must point towards the conclusion that the Targum is independent of these other traditions, though often sharing the same style of exegesis. A few cases of what might be called head-on confrontation (as opposed to slightly differing presentations of similar exegeses) might allow some speculation as to whether actual opposition may be detected on the part of, say, the Talmud towards the Targum, or *vice versa*. As an example of such material we may take, along with, perhaps, the turnip business already mentioned, the exegesis of 'six barley' in 3.15. The Targum says 'six seahs', but *Ruth Rabbah* 7.2 and *b. Sanh.* 93ab are both adamant that a woman could not carry so much and so the biblical expression must mean 'six grains'; however, the Targum may be accepting the argument in essence because it is careful to record that Ruth received a special gift of strength for the occasion. On the whole such matters are probably best treated as not materially different from other examples of divergence in exegesis.

There are places, too, where the Targum displays complete independence and includes details which are without parallel elsewhere. For example, Elimelech and his sons were 'military tribunes'[45] in Moab; a 'glove' was removed in 4.7, 8, instead of a shoe; in 4.5 the Targum uses the terminology of levirate marriage, whereas Ruth's second marriage was never seen in this light elsewhere in rabbinic literature.

It would seem to follow from all of this that *Tg. Ruth* offers an exegesis of the biblical book which, while at certain points it finds parallels in the Talmud and midrash, is often independent of exegeses found elsewhere in rabbinic literature. I see no reason to question the unity of the Targum, and if asked to assign a date to it I must say I find in it nothing which compels a late dating. The treatment of Ruth's second marriage, at least in 4.5, as a case of levirate marriage might point us in the direction of the Karaites,[46] and therefore towards a late date, but I do not think the Targum is a Karaite document. While certain similarities may be seen between it and the commentary attributed to Salmon ben Yeroham,[47] that commentary is at odds with the Targum on some points distinctive to the latter; for example, in retaining 'shoe' in 4.7, 8 instead of 'glove', and in dating the story to the time of Tola ben Puah, thereby controverting the identification of Boaz with Ibzan.

The Targum has some undoubtedly early features and, as I have suggested, there are grounds for suggesting that other elements may be relatively early too. There is thus a temptation, in the absence of any evidence which points to any other date, to lean on the mention of crucifixion in 1.17 and assign the whole thing to a pre-mishnaic date. However, the caution which guided the formulation of the title of this paper prevents me from yielding to that temptation, especially in view of the fact that no evidence has yet been adduced from linguistic study. It may, nevertheless, not be out of place here to recall the earliest recorded opinion on the origin of the Targum. The Tosafists, commenting on the statement of Rashi that 'there is no Targum on the Writings',[48] observed that 'there is indeed a Targum, but Jonathan did not make it; it was made in the time of the Tannaim'.[49] This statement, at least in so far as it may be applied to the Targum of Ruth, has not yet been proved wrong.

To Willie McKane, to whom may be applied the Targumist's description of Boaz גבר תקיף באורייתא, I have great pleasure in dedicating, on his 65th birthday, this modest supplement to the work I did under his guidance several years ago.

NOTES

1. A. Schlesinger, 'התרגום לספר רות - חיבור כיתתי', כתבי עקיבא שליזנגר: מחקרים במקרא ובלשונו, (Publications of the Israel Society for Biblical Research, 9), Jerusalem, 1962, 12-17.

2. E.Z. Melamed, 'לתרגום מגילת רות', *Bar Ilan, Annual of Bar Ilan University* I (1963), 190-94. He re-stated his conclusion in E.Z. Melamed, המקר אמפרשי, Jerusalem, 1975, ²1978, 341.

3. He explains in a footnote that he uses the term 'Sadducee' as a general term of reference to those non-Pharisaic sects which did not accept the Oral Torah.

4. Schlesinger, 15.

5. J. Heinemann, 'תרגום שמות כב,ר והחלכה הקדומה', *Tarbiz* 38 (1968-69), 294-96.

6. Y. Komlosh, המקרא באור התרגום, Tel Aviv, 1973, 85.

7. Schlesinger, 16.

8. *Ibid.*

9. Hebrew text in Io. Mercerus (Jean Mercier), *Libellus Ruth cum scholiis masorae ad marginem*, Paris: R. Stephanus, 1563. English translation in D.R.G. Beattie, *Jewish Exegesis of the Book of Ruth* (JSOTS, 2), Sheffield, 1977, 149-52.

10. After this paper had been submitted to the editors the reservations expressed above crystallized into a conviction tht the Ramban referred, in the comment cited, neither to Christians nor to *Tg. Ruth*, but to a Karaite document. See D.R.G. Beattie, 'The Targum of Ruth—A Sectarian Composition?', *JJS* 36 (1985), 222-29.

11. Melamed, 191.

12. *Ibid.*

13. *B. Sanh.* 52b.

14. Melamed, 191. Melamed was not the first to make such a suggestion. S.H. Levey, *The Targum to the Book of Ruth: its linguistic and exegetical character*, Hebrew Union College, Cincinnati, 1934 [diss.], translates 'two cemeteries' following the proposal of D. Hartmann, *Das Buch Ruth in der*

Midrasch-Literatur, Leipzig: Bär & Hermann, 1901, 26, n. 4, that the Targum be read בי"ת קבורתא.

15. In the Aramaic text published by Ch. S. Neuhausen, 'התרגום למגילת רות', *Hatsofeh le-Hokhmat Yisrael* 14 (1930), 33-52, the reading בי־קבורתא is offered without comment.

16. According to Hartmann, 26 n.4, W. Bacher interpreted the statement of the Targum as being in opposition to the Persian religion, which knows no burial places.

17. It is present in the Antwerp and Paris polyglots, and some mss., but it may be suspected of being a 'restoration' inasmuch as the verb is a participle, whereas one might have expected a perfect tense to be used to reproduce the Hebrew.

18. See above n. 15.

19. A. Sperber, *The Bible in Aramaic: IV A The Hagiographa*, Leiden: Brill, 1968, 120-24.

20. E. Levine, *The Aramaic Version of Ruth* (Analecta Biblica, 58), Rome, 1973, offers two translations of the Targum, one following his principal ms. (Vat. Cod. Urb. Ebr. 1) and the other based on a comparison of various mss. It is difficult to detect any difference between them.

21. Beattie, *Jewish Exegesis*, 169.

22. Levine records variant readings from seven mss., Walton's polyglot and the edition of Lagarde. C.H.H. Wright, *The Book of Ruth in Hebrew and Chaldee*, London: Williams & Norgate, 1864, collated the London, Antwerp and Paris polyglots and the editions of Bomberg and Buxtorf, as well as one ms. which is no longer extant.

23. Melamed, 192.

24. P. Churgin, תרגום כתובים, New York, 1945, 147f.

25. Churgin, 150.

26. Melamed, 193.

27. Melamed, 194.

28. Churgin, 140. Melamed, 190, has glossed this as meaning 'from the margin'.

29. Churgin, 143.

30. Churgin, 146.

31. *Gen. Rabbah* 25.3; 40.3; 64.2; *Ruth Rabbah* 1.4.

32. The future, spiritual famine, for which Amos 8.11 serves as proof-text, is number eleven. Number ten is a famine 'which rolls around and comes to the world'. Thus all other famines in history, apart from those mentioned specifically in the Bible, are accounted for.

33. Amos 8.11 is, in *Ruth Rabbah*, attached to the tenth famine, which is there the one 'which rolls around and comes to the world'. The illogic of this would suggest that an earlier form of the text, which was in agreement with the version in *Gen. Rabbah*, has been pruned somewhat carelessly in order

to restore the number of famines to ten.

34. Levine, 8.

35. Churgin, 146.

36. In fact most mss. appear to have only one word. Levine, 31, notes one ms. as reading only משכביה with the implication that the other mss. used by him agree with his principal ms. in reading only דמכיה. The Dresden ms. collated by Wright has דמכיה alone.

37. Levine, 19, implies that the reading רבנין (without אפרתין), is commonly found in mss.

38. Churgin, 143.

39. Melamed, 191. Churgin, 143, also saw dependence on the Talmud here.

40. It is hard to resist the temptation to observe that one can hardly ask for a more common root than a turnip.

41. *Tg. Ruth* 1.1, 6; 4.21; *b. Baba Bathra* 91a.

42. *Tg. Ruth* 1.4; *b. Soṭah* 47a; *b. Sanh.* 105b; *b. Nazir* 23b; *b. Hor.* 10b; *Ruth Rabbah* 2.9.

43. According to *Ruth Rabbah* 2.9, Eglon's reward for rising from his throne to receive Ehud (Judg. 3.20) was that a descendant of his should sit on the throne of Israel. In *b. Nazir* 23b; *b. Soṭa* 47a; *b. Sanh.* 105b; *b. Hor.* 10b, where Ruth's ancestry is traced through Eglon to Balak, the reward is said to have been rather for Balak's offering of forty-two sacrifices. The attribution of royal ancestry to Ruth may have preceded both of these midrashim.

44. *Tg. Ruth* 1.2.

45. *Ibid.* The word used—רופילין—is derived from the Latin *rufuli*.

46. The Karaites interpreted the law of levirate marriage in Deut. 25.5f. as applying not to an actual brother-in-law, for whom marriage to the childless widow would have been in their eyes incest, but to more distant relatives.

47. Hebrew text in *Livre d'hommage à la mémoire du Dr Samuel Poznański*, Warsaw, 1927, Hebrew section 78-96. English translation in Beattie, *Jewish Exegesis*, 47-101. Apart from the use of the terminology of levirate marriage, the most striking similarity between this commentary and the Targum—probably the only point which is not also encountered somewhere in rabbinic literature—is in their treatment of the statement ותשאר האשה משני ילדיה ומאישה (1.5), where both offer the same expanded text, 'she was left *bereaved* of her children and *a widow* of her husband'. Salmon adds, 'for it cannot rightly be said that "Reuben was left from Simeon"', showing that he did not understand the privative usage of מן.

48. Rashi, commentary on *b. Meg.* 21b.

49. Tosafot, *ibid.*

A PRELUDE TO THE SAMARITAN PENTATEUCH
TEXTS OF THE PARIS POLYGLOT BIBLE

James G. Fraser

University of Melbourne, Australia

The essential precondition to the publication of an ancient text must be its manuscript evidence, but it would be naive to suggest that this is all that is required. Apart from all the printing and publishing techniques and their support systems, some general data concerning the language, script and the literature within its context are also necessary. In regard to the publication of the Samaritan Pentateuch, perhaps too much emphasis has been given to the collection of the manuscript example acquired by the famous traveller Pietro della Valle. The essential general data for the development of Samaritan studies were probably already in existence at the time of the acquisition of that manuscript, since it would appear that they were assembled and partly assessed in a serious 17th century paper, of which both the author and recipient were at the same time amateur antiquarians and competent political figures involved in affairs of state. Nicolas-Claude Fabri de Peiresc (1580–1637) was no ordinary individual: he has been described by H. Trevor-Roper as 'the dynamo which drove the machine of intellectual discussion throughout the Continent'.[1] In his file on Oriental Languages Pieresc preserved a memoir by the learned Parisian lawyer, Jacques Leschassier (1550–1625), which provides a concise statement of Samaritan studies in Europe as at the midpoint of the second decade of the seventeenth century. From the contents of this memorandum it is possible to ascertain the state of that discipline virtually on the eve of Pietro della Valle's acquisition in 1616 of a Samaritan Pentateuch for Achille de Harlay de Sancy. This latter manuscript is the well-known example which provided the text for the *editio princeps* of the Samaritan Hebrew Pentateuch published in the Paris Polyglot Bible, of which the relevant sixth volume was printed in 1632. As a consequence, knowledge of the Samaritan tradition at that time was not merely a newly erupting phenomenon but rather something that had been anticipated by some of the more brilliant intellects of Europe in the late Renaissance period.

It is the purpose of this present study to examine the text of that memorandum which is printed as an Appendix to this paper, to relate its content to the historical circumstances which appear to have evoked it, and to discuss its contribution towards the rapid growth of interest in the Samaritans during the seventeenth century. The first section of Leschassier's paper consists of a series of quotations drawn from the works of Joseph Juste Scaliger, since certain seminal concepts with which the paper is concerned are derived from him.[2] Then the three sub-sections which form the central section, after making an initial proposition in each case, proceed to substantiate that proposition through carefully ordered evidence. The argument of the whole proceeds as follows:

1. Scaliger's theses or observations
2. Proposition A, with support of five earlier witnesses, reference back to the Scaliger passages, and reference to Duret's statement of the contemporary position
3. Proposition B, with support of three pieces of material evidence
4. Proposition C, differentiated as six specific items
5. Suggestions for effecting the previous Proposition C.

Despite the agreement of the whole with Scaliger's sentiments and objectivity, it cannot be said to be merely a logical extension from his thought. Rather, its development appears to lack the breadth of his view and to be concerned on the one hand with specifics yet on the other with intangibles. Even though the three basic propositions exhibit a graduated divergence from Scaliger's expressed direction of interest, the list of works cited in respect to Proposition C has been modelled on the specific acquisitions of Samaritan works made by Scaliger.

The outward form of the memoir's contents is matched both in superficial simplicity and underlying complexity by its actual writing and layout. It is essential that external features should be considered before any further analysis of the text is made, because there is the possibility that the document as preserved may present the thought of each of these two men who held Scaliger in high esteem. Two distinct styles of writing or possibly two distinct hands may be discerned in the body of the paper, while the customary Peiresc cataloguing data may be seen inscribed at the head of the text and endorsed on the final page. The first is limited to the quotations from Scaliger's works while the second is to be found in the headings to the same Scaliger excerpts, the various propositions, and the details of the various items of supporting evidence. The simplest solution would posit that the first is the hand of Leschassier and the second that of Peiresc, but even if this were the case it would not necessarily signify that the respective written contributions correspond to the actual scholarly contribution made by either. Consequently the major problem afforded by the document as a whole is one of defining the relationship of author and recipient and the role of each in its production.

If the problem were to be limited simply to that of the different styles of writing, then the more likely possibilities would appear to be that either the whole has been copied by the one hand, although at two distinct periods of time or with two distinct value judgments placed on the material, or that there are two distinct stages represented in the transmission of this little tractate, each of which is reflected through its own writing style. The Scaliger excerpts give the appearance of having been copied in a formal documentary script, while the remainder is written in quite an informal hand and was added subsequently after some indefinite interval of time.

The more likely explanations of the observed phenomena include those hypotheses that take Leschassier's contribution seriously, since Peiresc is a witness of excellent repute. On the one hand, Peiresc may have completed an incomplete copy begun either by Leschassier or by some unknown third party as copyist; the memorandum is possibly an epitome of some longer written or orally delivered paper of which Peiresc has had the Scaliger reference copied in full by a secretary while he himself has added to this nucleus the main points drawn from Leschassier's thesis represented by Proposition A, possibly with Proposition B as its corollary, and, although Leschassier appears to have supplied most of the supporting material, Peiresc has supplemented it, so that the overall result features the displaced Scaliger evidence now expanded from mere references to full extracts carefully copied, and Peiresc's personal glosses are seen to serve practical purposes of clarification. On the other hand, Peiresc himself may have deliberately set out to construct a synthesis of Scaliger's, Leschassier's and his own thought, possibly with some secretarial

assistance in delineating Scaliger's position, and with acknowledgment of Leschassier's lucid analysis of the earlier research leading to
its further potential. While the material copied by the second hand
may indeed represent something of the work of Leschassier it is
overlaid by some degree of subjective interpretation the extent of
which is not immediately apparent. Whether any one of these
suggested solutions is the correct explanation is largely immaterial
for present purposes. Obviously their common content is the assumption that Peiresc had access to the concepts of the whole document,
which fact is of far greater relevance in discerning its relationship to
his subsequent actions.

The problem of unravelling the distinctive contributions may be
incapable of a complete and final solution, yet there is sufficient
evidence available to allow some reasonable hypotheses to be postulated. In the event of a selection of data on the part of the recipient,
there is no discernible way in which what has been omitted may be
assessed without recourse to the original author's complete text. Any
relevant hypothesis, in order to be valid, ought so to distinguish the
motivation of the respective parties as to enable an objective presentation of the evidence of the whole memorandum as seen within the
respective contexts of the special interests of each of the two principal
parties. Despite the fact that they shared so many interests, in each
case a relative degree of polarization may be established from their
respective works for certain qualities discernible in the whole as is
presented in the following table:[3]

Quality or Interest	Leschassier	Peiresc
Assembly of manuscript collections	Minimal	Maximal
Classical and patristic tradition	Maximal	Minimal
Numismatics	Minimal	Maximal
Presentation of legal evidence	Maximal	Minimal
Respect for Scaliger	Minimal	Maximal

A simple example may be cited: it is apparent from Peiresc's
correspondence in general that he stood in awe of the great Scaliger.
It follows that if the memoir exhibits any drift away from Scaliger's
thought or interests then any subsequent return may be attributable
to Peiresc's desire to retain his hero's influence. Thus the words from
Item 1 of Proposition B: 'à recouvrir comme requiert tant de fois
Scaliger'; would seem to betray the interests of Peiresc, but obviously

such an instance is too little evidence on which to build a case. Even the cumulative effect of all the interests is only of use as supporting evidence or as an indicator in the absence of concrete facts.

From the outset the notes ascribing the paper to Leschassier are so typical of Peiresc's regular mode of cataloguing that, taken together with the evidence of the handwriting, there is a good *a priori* case for accepting them as derived from Peiresc. Moreover, it is quite apparent from his general correspondence that he was accustomed to make annotations and comments and to endorse a summary of the contents of a letter together with details of the sender, place of origin and date, so that these appeared as well as the sender's inscription of the recipient and his place of residence. Clearly there is much in the structure of the memoir that exhibits the form of a summarized list.[4] If Leschassier had not already supplied the identification of the Scaliger excerpts it is highly probable that Peiresc would have provided this information.

Both the location of the Scaliger excerpts and the use of differing scripts respectively for their substance and their headings suggest something special in regard to his evidence. To elucidate the range of possibilities it is necessary first to ascertain the treatment of both primary and secondary witnesses to the basic propositions and secondly to note any differences in respect to ancient or relatively older sources as compared with sources contemporary with Leschassier and Peiresc. In regard to the primary sources, each item of evidence has been assigned a distinct number in chronological order of publication in association with Proposition A, and in order of discovery in the case of Proposition B. The secondary sources have not been numbered but have been added at the end of the list of items of evidence in association with Proposition A, while in the case of Proposition B they supplement the substance of Item 2. Thus the original structure of the memoir would have assigned Scaliger's evidence a secondary place in regard to Proposition A and a primary place in regard to Proposition B. In many ways the Scaliger evidence is unique since it represents a summary of earlier evidence and produces some entirely new material. If Leschassier had not seen fit to offer it some unique place then assuredly Peiresc would have been prepared to restructure the substance of the tractate to give Scaliger a more prominent place as well as fuller treatment.

It is now appropriate to make an estimate of the possible contributions of either of the two principal parties, although no completely compelling hypothesis is forthcoming. Instead, the relevant indicators may be tabulated in order to demonstrate something of the range of possibilities and probabilities. For this purpose the content of the memoir is classified under four sub-headings which take into account the motivating factors already compared above as significant interests of Leschassier and Peiresc. Such features as additions ought carefully to be consulted in the Appendix, for they provide some fragments of more objective evidence which may indicate development. Thus it is postulated that the respective contributions of the two parties probably lie within the limits indicated on the range of aspects set out below:

		Leschassier	*Peiresc*
I.	*General Structure*	Basic outline	Possible abbreviation of written or oral paper
			Possible advancement of position of the Scaliger references
II.	*Basic Theses*	Proposition A as basis	Possible expansion of Proposition A
			Proposition B as corollary
			Probable addition of Proposition C with its list of desiderata
III.	*Items of Evidence*	Basic lists	Expansion of notes through some minor additions
IV.	*Conclusion*	Possible original expression now incorporated in Proposition C of a general wish to obtain an example of the Samaritan Pentateuch	Details of ways and means of acquiring books and coins in a concluding note

This structural analysis does little more than identify the possible or probable areas where the principal interests of either party could be evident. As a consequence it enables some identification of areas where some significant departure from those interests occurs. The overall substance of the memorandum belongs within very narrow limits and in particular to the years 1613–1616. Thus, on the one hand, its text contains references to Claude Duret, *Thresor de l'histoire des langues de cest univers*, Cologny, 1613, while, on the other, it betrays no knowledge of Pietro della Valle's acquisition in 1616 of the Samaritan Pentateuch. If the position were to be adopted that Leschassier's original draft lacked any reference to the approximately contemporary works of Scaliger and Duret then the lower limit could be put back to a period before 1598 when the first of the relevant Scaliger publications appeared, but this really is an extreme position since the whole does seem to exude the freshness of Scaliger's thought.[5] The other extreme ought most probably to be marked by Leschassier's death in 1625, although in theory if Peiresc had missed marking this it could be extended to 1628, when Peiresc's interest in the Samaritans was re-awakened and he took fresh initiatives in acquiring Samaritan manuscripts. However, it ought to be noted that the longer the *terminus ad quem* is delayed the more likely any alteration to the text of the tractate is limited to the items listed in regard to Proposition C.

Leschassier's contribution must be sought more in fields relative to the memoir's clear palaeographic and implied philological concerns, but it is not unlikely that he learned of some earlier milestones from Scaliger's work. Thus Scaliger had acknowledged the usefulness of Postel's 1538 publication, and it was possibly Leschassier, but more probably Peiresc, who had gone on to consult Duret's work, thereby discovering that Postel had possessed a Samaritan grammar manuscript and that, according to Duret, he too had owned a similar work. In actual fact one manuscript only was involved, and Postel's claim was reported originally in a more correct form by M. Neander.[6] Leschassier had been steeped in the formal education derived ultimately from the classical world, so that, even in regard to his antiquarian interests, he does not report new information so much as classify according to the older categories.

The first two propositions demonstrate a concern with the graphic representation of language, which includes some awareness of the concept of diffusion of the alphabetical script. Leschassier's presentation of these theses introduces no new matter, but, even if it does

appear in an abbreviated form, his basic argument is lucid and
concise. He has called as witnesses to his Proposition A: St. Jerome,
the doyen of western European patristic scholarship on the Bible; the
first-hand report of a respected Jewish traveller, Benjamin of Tudela;
Moses b. Naḥman, an impeccable spokesman for the western Rabbinic
tradition; then Postel and Ambrogio, the earliest Renaissance scholars
in print to bear testimony to the actual form of the script used by the
Samaritans. Furthermore, it would appear likely that he had acknowledged Scaliger as a contemporary witness, although there is some
doubt whether he could have been responsible also for any reference
to Duret. In regard to Proposition B, it should be noted that the
reference to the shekels introduces some difficulties. Here the
evidence is not interpreted accurately, since their palaeo-Hebrew
script is Jewish, while the script of the other items is truly Samaritan.
Postel originally had portrayed something of the differences between
the two, but in his time these subtle differences were attributed to
epigraphical considerations, on the assumption that differing techniques would have been required for recording script on coins or
stone from the simple technique for writing on paper. The essential
point of the proposition holds some validity, because both Samaritan
and the Jewish coin scripts are descendants of the palaeo-Hebrew of
the pre-exilic period of Israel's history.[7] Leschassier may have seen
some of the relevant shekels of the First Jewish Revolt, but it is
highly improbable that he had had access to any of the three or four
Samaritan manuscripts then available in Europe. Consequently, in
these circumstances, it would be difficult to imagine that he could
have omitted to express any desire to see the acquisition of a
Samaritan Pentateuch.

By way of contrast, Peiresc had undergone a less formal education
and had thoroughly imbibed the Renaissance spirit. His personal
contact with Scaliger, his personal interest in coins and his general
spirit of inquiry had combined to await a useful channel in which to
be directed. As a catalyst to scholarship he had longed to be of
maximum assistance to the foremost scholars. When Scaliger had
desired a copy of the Samaritan Pentateuch, he had actually managed
to acquire one in Lebanon, which was consigned into the custody of
Monsr. Mostiere aboard the ship St. Victor, only to have the St.
Victor attacked by pirates with a loss of the unfortunate vice-consul,
Monsr. Mostier, and the manuscript in his charge.[8]

The relationship between Peiresc and Leschassier does not appear to have been very close, despite their common interest. Indeed from the brief summary of their interests and motivations as indicated above it is clear that they applied rather different emphases to those same interests. Yet the internal gleanings from a single memoir, supported by their respective general writings, are meagre evidence, while the factual support for some other theory is not forthcoming. Peiresc's voluminous papers appear to preserve no more than two letters and a few brief undated memoirs from Leschassier.[9] This paucity in quantity of correspondence probably represents a distance in their relationship, so that their respective awareness of a certain overlap in interests was possibly accompanied by some other sense that these interests either diverged or ran in different directions. Accordingly, the common year 1610 in the dates of the two letters may in fact refer to a brief period encompassing the whole of their written communication with one another. In this event Leschassier could have referred to Scaliger's contribution in his Memoir, but any reference to Duret would have to be excluded as something too late for him to include, and thus the Duret references would have to be attributed to Peiresc.

In the cirumstances just indicated, Leschassier's original writing may be seen to be notable for its lucid presentation yet contingent on others' research. Elsewhere Leschassier's logic may be criticized for having been pursued regardless of the accuracy attainable by the philological discipline he has used. However, his logical approach in this tractate must have exercised considerable appeal to Peiresc: its coincidences with Scaliger's thought and its concern with the written aspects of language must have so impressed him that he organized his projected attempt to acquire Samaritan literature on its substance. On certain aspects of what he perceived in its content as having special significance for him, he appears to have added further emphasis. Thus Peiresc would be responsible on this consideration for displacing the Scaliger references from their logical and chronological place to become full excerpts in their present, more prominent position. Consequently, a further contrast between the two men ought to be noticed. Leschassier's work may be characterized as static in essence, whereas there is a distinct dynamic associated with most of Peiresc's scholarly activities. If Leschassier had expressed a wish to see a Samaritan Pentateuch then most assuredly Peiresc would have been concerned with the practical application of translating this into action.

Scope for some immediate reaction by Peiresc would appear to have been provided through two particular aspects of the memoir, though in quite different qualities and proportions between the emotional and academic appeal in either instance. Firstly, Leschassier seems to have taken a simple attitude of acceptance, without any qualification, of Scaliger as a scholar. In the second place, the very subject matter was bound to call to Peiresc's mind that project of Scaliger's in which he himself had already taken part—the quest for historical, literary and linguistic traditions relative to the Samaritan religious heritage.[10] In the light of such effects of the basic contentions of the memoir it is easy to understand how Peiresc's interests and motivations identified above could have introduced some subtle changes into the memoir's form. At the first level that change involved placing a greater degree of emphasis on what was already there with respect to Scaliger, while at the second it would appear that Peiresc perceived in the evidence adduced considerable potential for development along lines which Scaliger had suggested. Thus the references to Duret allowed fuller identification of the sources that Leschassier had found in Scaliger, and that final Scaliger excerpt, whose subject matter is quite distinct from Leschassier's basic propositions, suggested the preparation of a list of desiderata. This list may also represent the expansion either from an actual wish expressed by Leschassier or from a wish that Peiresc believed to be implied in the memoir itself. It is quite conceivable that Peiresc added both the emphasis on Scaliger and the list of desiderata in the belief that he was merely drawing out and expressing what Leschassier already had implied. Whoever it was that provided these aspects, the final paragraph of the memoir, containing its implication of some possible expedition, is so characteristic of Peiresc that it must be attributed to him alone.

Above all, it is the list of desiderata that proves to be of greatest assistance in discerning the particular contribution that Peiresc made not only to the memoir but also to Samaritan studies. In the first place, Peiresc made other related lists, so that it is possible to discern both the course of development of his own interest and the direction in which broader research in the same field was moving. These lists have been set out synoptically in the accompanying table. Peiresc's careful designation of the source lying behind the particular item that he has named enables the making of a precise reference to a particular manuscript. Thus the observant student is able to identify the Scaliger and Postel manuscripts and to determine which coin series is the one from which the exemplar for the desired shekel came. However, when the other lists are taken into consideration, some deeper discernment of Peiresc's motives may be made. The proposed publication of Samaritan texts in the Paris Polyglot Bible seems to have provided a stimulus for Peiresc to bring one of Scaliger's desires to fruition, so that the third list is no longer simply a list of desiderata, but rather it has become specific instructions to acquire examples of all known items. Yet research in the broader field has not stood still since Scaliger's death to await either the opportunity or the necessary funds, so that the third list indicates that Peiresc's plan has been modified by the products of research other than Scaliger's. Thus he appears to have arrived at a more advanced conception for the presentation of Samaritan evidence, which would offer something of that community's particular interpretation of its own Pentateuch and related literature.[11] Such a concept lies in stark contrast to the simple publication of the Samaritan Hebrew and Targum texts of the Pentateuch provided with a single Latin translation to cover both. Rather, Peiresc's vision seems to have been in advance of any publication of Samaritan texts before the critical editions of the twentieth century.[12]

PEIRESC'S LISTS OF SAMARITAN DESIDERATA

Scaliger mss. for printing	Leschassier Memoir	Instructions for Minuti
	Les livres de Moyse en leurs vieils characteres	Les cinq livres de Moyse en langue Hebraique escripts en characteres Samaritains a qui sont touts divers des characteres Hebreus vulgares.
		Les memes cinq livres de Moyse, traduits en langue Samaritaine, escripts en mesme charactere Samaritain.
Chronicum Samaritanum ab excessu Mosis seu ducatu	Le livre qui'ils ont qu'ils appellent Iosue, qui est une chronique de leur	Le livre qui'ils appellent IOSUE qui est une chronique de leur Hist-

Iosuae ad tempora Antoninorum.

histoire depuis la mort de Moyse iusques aus Antonius.
Scaliger en avoit une, . . .

oire depuis le deceds de Moise jusques à cent ans apres Jesus Christ.

Un Alphabet de ceste langue. Postel a escrit qui'il en avait un exemplaire . . .

Une Grammaire en langue Samaritaine, qu'ils appellent leur Alphabet.

Libellus Samaritanus in quo breve chronicon ab Adam ad annum Christi 1584.

Un petit sommaire de leur Chronique depuis Adam qui avoit este continue jusques en l'an de Christ 1584.

Item typus anni samaritani convenienter anno 1584

Leur compost ou embolisme, puis que ils en font tous les ans, semblable a celuy qu'a fait imprimer Scaliger.

Leur Almanach qui'ils renouvellent touts les ans ou computation des jours de leur annee etc.

Les autres livres que l'on pourra trouver escrits en ces characteres.

Leur autres livres que se pourront trouver escripts en caractere desdit Samaritains.

Le sicle en ces mesmes characteres puis qui'il s'en voit fort souvent aus environs de Hierusalem.

The first of the three lists represents an extract taken from a larger catalogue that has been published already and is of far wider concern than Samaritan studies.[13] Within its Latin text, and written in close proximity, appear three Samaritan items of which two provide a nucleus for the list in the Leschassier memoir. The particular section of the catalogue from which the three Samaritan items have been selected in order of their occurrence is a list of Scaliger manuscripts which Peiresc had wished to see printed at the Medici printery in Rome. Consequently, this first list may be dated by reference to the whole from which it is derived so that its *terminus a quo* ought to be set at 1606, when Peiresc visited Scaliger, and its *terminus ad quem* must be set in relation to the death of Giovanni Batista Raimondi, which most probably occurred in 1610. A sub-heading taken from a later point in the catalogue anticipates that Raimondi will exercise oversight in the printing. At the other extreme, for Peiresc to consider publishing a substantial collection of Scaliger manuscripts possibly suggests that the latter had died already, in which case the Peiresc cataloguing notes at the head of the catalogue, referring both to Scaliger and the Medici printery, may have been added no earlier than the year 1609. Although the first of the three Samaritan items is separated from the other two by five intervening non-Samaritan works, the relative order of the Samaritan items remains constant in the later lists, and the actual wording relating to them in the later lists seems to be dependent on the earlier examples despite the change in language. Of the three items named, the first is clearly identifiable with the University of Leiden ms. Or. 249 of the Samaritan Book of Joshua; the second refers to the calendar which was first published by Scaliger in the 1598 edition of his *De emendatione temporum* and the manuscript original of which now seems to be lost; and the third is something of an enigma, since the description is too vague to enable the work to be identified, and the original manuscript copy of this 'brief Chronicle' also is lost.

The Leschassier memoir includes the second of the three lists but it makes no mention of Scaliger's 'brief Chronicle'. Both his other two items from the first list appear despite the fact that the Samaritan Joshua manuscript is predominantly in the Arabic language and script. Perhaps the influence of Peiresc is to be detected in the larger Memoir in regard to Proposition B through the inclusion of both the Samaritan Joshua and the calendar. If this should prove to be the case, then it raises more uncertainty in regard to the 'brief Chronicle', since here Peiresc's silence could signify ignorance or his belief that its language was entirely Arabic. However such speculation is without adequate basis and provides nothing of consequence for the present context. Three further items appear on the Memoir's list, and they too are derived from specific examples. Reference has already been made to Peiresc's abortive attempt on behalf of Scaliger to acquire a copy of the Samaritan Hebrew Pentateuch: the copy lost in transit certainly suffices as a model without searching any further afield.[14] A clear association of the remaining two items with Guillaume Postel, *Linguarum duodecim* (Parisiis, 1538) in its brief chapter on the Samaritans is confirmed through the prominence of both Postel's Samaritan Grammar manuscript and his shekel, but most particularly through Scaliger's approval as indicated in the extracts at the beginning of the Memoir. It would appear that Peiresc had drawn on the expansion of Postel's chapter in Claude Duret's *Thresor*, p. 325, for the Memoir contains its form of the Postel quotation and not the more correct one from which it was derived. The note contained in Proposition A, 4: 'Il y en a en ceste ville', suggests that Peiresc had consulted Postel's works, thus the shekel model is identifiable as one minted during the second year of the First Jewish Revolt, and the exemplar for the grammar, Postel's manuscript, is to be identified with the first four tractates of the University of Leiden ms. Acad. 218. When these matters have been considered, it will be seen that the first group of items on the list from the Memoir is drawn directly from Scaliger's works or through his contact with Peiresc, and the second group which is linked with Postel has been mediated through Scaliger's reference. Therefore it comes as no suprise to find that the non-specific item remaining to be considered which appears as Proposition C, Item 5, in the Memoir, is based on its final Scaliger excerpt.

There is preserved in the Biliothèque Méjanes, Aix-en-Provence, a single leaf that once constituted part of Peiresc's file on Oriental languages. It bears the title: 'Mémoire concernant les livres Samaritains qu'on désire avoir du Levant'.[15] The verso face contains the original text of the third list of desiderata which is completely preserved, although some notes have been lost from the left and lower margins. Its principal supplementary note appears to be directed towards some specific agent as collector on behalf of Peiresc, and the final note, although relevant, is incomplete: '[. . .] entre les MSS apportes par Mr de Sancy, le Pentateuche'. The lacuna at the beginning appears to represent a loss of no more than one or two words, but the text on the recto face has suffered considerably more damage, although it is still intelligible. This reference to the Pentateuch of Achille de Harlay de Sancy and a reference in the list to the Targum, which is none other than that collected by Pietro della Valle, enables the date of the third list to be set within very narrow limits around the year 1628. Early in that year, Jerome Alexander had reported from Rome to Peiresc Morin's plan of publishing the Samaritan Hebrew text for the Polyglot Bible. Subsequently representation was made to Peiresc to persuade della Valle to make his Targum text available for the same purpose. It would appear most probable that the third list was constructed after this, at a time when

Peiresc had conceived a plan of mounting an expedition of his own. In this event, it probably represents either an immediate precursor to, or even a copy of, the list which Peiresc gave to Theophile Minuti before his departure for the Levant in June 1629.

One significant question requiring an answer is the reason why Peiresc sought to acquire copies of texts already collected or deposited in major European libraries. His dependence on his relationship with Scaliger may supply part of the answer, and this relationship is underscored in the third list through the fact that reference to the 'brief Chronicle' is restored. Admittedly it is interlined between the fourth and sixth items of that list, but this only serves to suggest that Peiresc revised the contents in the light of the first list, which, it will be remembered, was extracted from a catalogue of Scaliger manuscripts. Even so, some element that is independent of Scaliger does make an appearance in his proposed acquisitions. If it be conceded that Peiresc took the Paris Polyglot Bible project seriously, then his motives may well have been conditioned by his perception of what was the ideal Samaritan evidence to present. Certainly Scaliger's influence had had much to do with the early formation of Peiresc's motives, but the Polyglot presented a new challenge. In the circumstances, Peiresc's memoir represents a response to that challenge in the form of setting an ideal towards which he had directed careful aim.

Theophile Minuti carried either the original of this memoir or something closely resembling it, together with the remainder of Peiresc's instructions, when he commenced his remarkable combination of pilgrimage to the Holy Land and expedition on behalf of Peiresc.[16] With respect to his Samaritan commission, he reported within a short period that he had had no success at Nablus but had been assured of the likelihood of positive results at Damascus.[17] There it would seem that he met the self-same Maronite priest who had accompanied Pietro della Valle in his quest to meet the Samaritans of Damascus. Fr. Michael was able to supply him with an item which seemed to be even better than the most important Samaritan book on his list. It was a triglot manuscript of the Samaritan Pentateuch, not only in their distinctive Hebrew version with their Aramaic Targum but also provided with an Arabic translation, and all three written in their peculiar script. Under pressure from the Maronite priest, Fr. Michael, Minuti took the decision of allowing him to fill the manuscript's rather extensive lacunae, which Fr.

A Word in Season

Michael proceeded to do after Minuti's departure by substituting some leaves from a Samaritan Hebrew manuscript and by copying out the Syriac text in Syriac characters to fill the remainder. This is how the famous Vatican manuscript, Barberini Or. 1, came to assume its present form. Fr. Michael, either from his own library or at least through his agency, was able to assist in regard to another item on Minuti's list, which was to prove to be a fitting companion to the Triglot Pentateuch. Apparently Minuti had believed that this manuscript was a Samaritan grammar akin to that which he had been commissioned to acquire. When Peiresc received this consignment in November 1629, he discovered that it contained a major remnant of a type of tri-lingual lexicon or glossary, *Hammeliṣ*, interspersed with leaves from some eight distinct liturgical codices.[18] The frustration because of the fragmentary nature of these items was matched and even exceeded by the extreme impatience with which Peiresc awaited the arrival of his Triglot Pentateuch.

Eventually he was to obtain two further Pentateuch manuscripts, but they contained no more than the Hebrew text of the Samaritan tradition, and his wait for the completion of the triglot had proved to be largely in vain. Peiresc appears to have become overwhelmed with a desire to complete each of the three parallel texts. He envisaged that Pietro della Valle's Targum manuscript could supply at least part of the second text tradition, and he expected that della Valle's text would be made available to him on its way to Jean Morin. Unbeknown to him, the manuscript was conveyed directly to Paris, and, as a consequence, Peiresc came to the opinion that Morin, the editor of the Samaritan text for the polyglot, should publish the text of each of the three linguistic witnesses to the Samaritan tradition. To this end he appears to have commissioned Theophile Minuti to return to the Levant to acquire a complete copy of Arabic text of the Samaritan Pentateuch and other items from the original list.

The editors of the great polyglot Bible had already made their decisions in regard to the Samaritan evidence, so that the year 1632 saw printed both the Samaritan Hebrew and Targum texts provided with a single Latin translation to cover both. Despite this, Peiresc continued to hope that Morin would make the fullest use of the manuscripts which he had freely provided for him, and he was particularly anxious that the Samaritan Arabic tradition should be fully investigated. But the great vision of Peiresc of the fullest possible understanding of the Samaritan tradition as a whole was to be cut short. The passage of no more than five years brought about his demise. Energy for research on the text of the Samaritan Pentateuch became dissipated in sectarian debate, which first had been fired by Morin's conclusions too hastily drawn. The Peiresc Samaritan manuscript collection remained intact except for its central item, the famous triglot, which he bequeathed as a legacy to Cardinal Barberini. His private papers, which now reveal so much more of his unfulfilled plans, at that time were not appreciated by those who held custody of what eventually would be described as the national heritage of France. Perhaps his aspirations had been too much coloured by his regard for Scaliger: perhaps they were before their time. One may speculate in regard to the dynamic of the man, that, had he lived, he would have been able to marshal the scholarship to produce at the very least some modest imitation of what his vision implied.

Part of Peiresc's success was his knowledge of human resources for the particular field of research that had aroused his interest. In the very last paragraph of the Leschassier memoir he makes reference to 'un docte Escossois'. When the present writer first read these words he was reminded of a modern parallel, a Scot who was a most effective catalyst to research. Nothing is known of the early Scot's success, but the modern Scot of the writer's thoughts, Professor William McKane, impressed and continues to impress both students and colleagues alike with that very precision in scholarship which Peiresc so desired. How ironic that the great Peiresc, an anagram of whose name is 'precise', could not persuade some scholar to exercise precision in the field that through his relationship with Scaliger had held so great a personal challenge! Today these concepts are more frequently taken for granted, but the conscientious teacher who is both catalyst to research and himself a fine researcher is rare in any generation.

NOTES

1. H. Trevor-Roper, 'The Baroque Century', *The Age of Expansion: Europe and the World 1559-1660*, ed. H. Trevor-Roper, London, 1968, 34f.

2. Certain material from this memorandum which may be traced beyond Scaliger to Postel was noted by the present writer in a paper, 'Guillaume Postel and Samaritan Studies', presented at the conference, *Postel, Venezia e il suo mondo, Convegno internazionale promosso in occasione del quarto*

centenario della morte di Guillaume Postel, 5-9 Sep. 1982: the proceedings are in process of publication.

3. See Peiresc's published correspondence: Nicolas-Claude Fabri de Peiresc, *Lettres de Peiresc, . . . publiées par Philippe Tamizey de Larroque . . .*, 7 vols., Paris: Impr. nationale, 1888–98; and Leschassier's collected works: Jacques Leschassier, *Les Oeuvres de M. Jacques Leschassier . . . contenans plusiers excellens traittez . . . ensemble quelques mémoires servans à l'antiquité de l'Eglise . . . 2e édition augmentée . . .*, Paris: P. Lamy, 1652.

4. Comparison of the respective sections of the memorandum with Peiresc's customary summaries endorsed on inward correspondence as indicators of content, e.g., Bibliothèque Nationale, ms. français 9542, f. 3b, serves to confirm the summary nature of the memorandum's evidence and Peiresc's readiness to modify his summaries in the light of later evidence.

5. Even if due allowance be made for Guillaume Postel's pioneering efforts, some imaginative treatment of the relatively small amount of data from patristic, rabbinic and Samaritan sources available at the end of the seventeenth century was needed to stimulate European interest in Samaritan studies. That need was supplied by *Iosephi Scaligeri Iul. Caesaris f. opus de emendatione temporum: castigatius et multis partibus auctius, ut novum videri possit*, Lugduni Batavorum: F. Raphelengius, 1598.

6. See M. Neander, *Sancta linguae hebraeae erotemata . . . a Michaele Neandro . . . edita*, Basileae: J. Oporinus, 1567, 551.

7. See J.D. Purvis, *The Samaritan Pentateuch and the Origin of the Samaritan Sect* (HSM, 2), Cambridge, Mass., 1968, 36-52; and Joseph Naveh, *Early History of the Alphabet: an Introduction to West Semitic Epigraphy and Palaeography*, Leiden: Brill for The Magnes Press, Jerusalem, 1982, 112-24.

8. See Peiresc's letter dated 26 November, 1628, to Pietro della Valle of which copies are preserved in Bibliothèque Inguimbertine, Carpentras, ms. 1871, ff. 241-3; and Bibliothèque Méjanes, Aix-en-Provence, ms. 1031, pp. 63-5.

9. For the correspondence see Bibliothèque National ms. nouv. acq. français 1147, p. 127, letter no. 443 dated 10 March, 1610, and p. 129, letter no. 444 dated 12 August, 1610; and for the memoirs see Bibliothèque Inguimbertine ms. 1864, ff. 187f., and 252f. Bibliothèque Nationale ms. latin 9340, ff. 317f., is reproduced in an appendix to the present work.

10. See Peiresc's letter to Pietro della Valle identified in n. 8 above.

11. *Ibid.*

12. See Peiresc's letter dated 2 June, 1637, to Jean Morin in *Antiquitates Ecclesiae Orientalis* (ed. R. Simon), London: G. Wells, 1682, 256-9. The texts of the Samaritan Pentateuch, whether Hebrew, Targum or Arabic translation, have all awaited the twentieth century for any substantial improvement over

what was provided in the seventeenth century polyglot editions.

13. See Guillaume Libri, *Histoire des sciences mathématiques en Italie, depuis la renaissance des lettres jusqu'à la fin du dix septième siècle*, 1, Paris: J. Renouard, 1838, 231-47.

14. See Peiresc's letter to Pietro della Valle identified in n. 8 above.

15. This leaf is free and unnumbered and was located in an unbound volume, Bibliothèque Méjanes ms. 1168, when consulted by the present writer, where its approximate position then was shortly after f. 60.

16. For the general instructions see Bibliothèque Inguimbertine ms. 1821, ff. 488f.

17. See the autograph letter dated 20 July, 1629, from Theophile Minuti to Peiresc, Bibliothèque Nationale ms. français 9542, ff. 1, 4.

18. See the covering letter dated 29 August, 1629, from Minuti, Bibliothèque Nationale ms. français, ff. 2-3, and in particular lines 40-1 of the text; Peiresc's reference to his dictionary in three languages in his letter dated 4 March, 1630, to Pierro della Valle, Bibliothèque Méjanes ms. 1031, p. 77; also Peiresc's covering letter, which should be more correctly dated to 8 November, 1632, to Jean Morin, *Antiquitates Ecclesiae Orientalis*, 179-92. The latter, from the end of p. 183 and on part of the following page, gives sufficient details of the loose leaves and quires to enable their identification as Peiresc's liturgical manuscript, Bibliothèque nationale ms. samaritain 8. For a modern edition of *Hammeliṣ* see Ze'ev Ben-Ḥayyim, *The Literary and Oral Tradition of Hebrew and Aramaic among the Samaritans*, 2 (The Academy of the Hebrew Language, Study, 2), Jerusalem: The Bialik Institute and the Academy of the Hebrew Language, 1957, 437-616.

Appendices

In presenting the primary evidence on which this paper is based, the present writer acknowledges first of all the gracious co-operation of the Bibliothèques Nationale, Inguimbertine and Méjanes and then in particular the efficiency, skill and courtesy of the respective members of staff whose aid was invaluable.

The accompanying text of the Leschassier memoir has been subjected to a number of editorial decisions which must necessarily affect its interpretation. As far as is practicable the original orthography, including accents, and the text disposition on the page have been retained, but the following departures should be noted:

1. The underlining of headings to the Scaliger extracts is intended to draw attention to the differences in handwriting in the first part.

2. Consistency in reproducing the manuscript's orthographical usage of u/v and i/j/y has been abandoned in favour of thoroughly

subjective principles whereby u/v render the vowel and consonant respectively while i/j/y are much closer to the manuscript's usage: exceptions are made to enable standardization of proper nouns and final letters.

3. Editorial additions are enclosed within square brackets.

4. Peiresc's additions have been inserted within the text between asterisks, and, where this has affected the length of line, the subsequent point at which the line originally ended has been marked / thus.

5. Minor corrections or alterations are signalled by a preceding dagger (†). In the case of the first hand they mostly signal deliberate omissions, but those referring to the second hand chiefly indicate corrections and stylistic improvements such as are consistent with the process of drafting either a synthesis or a précis.

6. The page reference for the fourth Scaliger extract appears to be an error for 103: it is retained as 107 because it has not been possible to check all editions.

The evidence afforded by the letter dated 26 November, 1628, from Peiresc to della Valle is of particular relevance to the present investigation. Since the original is not available, and the Italian exhibited in the copy is both ornate and formal in style, an English translation, whose style is at the same time simplified and less verbose, seems to be more appropriate for inclusion as the second part of the Appendix. The assistance of the present writer's undergraduate student, Miss Olga Marasco, and also of Dr Stephen Kolsky of the Italian Department of Melbourne Unversity is gratefully acknowledged. However, neither is responsible for the final form as printed, so that any significant errors or misinterpretations must be attributed solely to the present writer.

Appendix I : Bibliothèque Nationale, ms. latin 9340, ff. 317-318

317r.

L'ESCHASSERIUS

Ex libro Opusculorum Scaligeri
Iosephus Scaliger Richardo Thomsoni suo Sal.

pa. 437

Phoenices literàs, quod in extrema Epistola quaeris, diu ante Mosem fuisse noli dubitare, easque esse, quibus olum Hebraei, hodie vero soli Samaritae utuntur. Multa vetustissima numismata eruuntur quotidie in partibus Tyri & Sidonis in quibus Characteres illi sine ulla mutatione extant.

Scaliger in lib. de emendatione
temporum
In computum Samaritarum.

pa. †*620*

In monte Garizim constitutas sedes & sacrarium religionis habent, unde ipsi se vocari volunt †pertinentes ad montem benedictum, neque a temporibus Exodi se inde unquam expulsos fuisse aut aliunde quam ex Aegypto cum Mose huc immigrasse credunt. Reges veteres Samariae defectionem X tribuum, impulsore Ieroboamo, ne fando quidem acceperunt. Nomina Samsonis, Samuelis Davidis & aliorum obiter perstricta habent in Chronico qui liber Iosue ab illis dicitur. In reliqua vetustate omnino peregrini sunt. Erudite de illis Gulielmus Postellus in libello duodecim linguarum disserit; quae quia cognitu digna sunt inde lector hauriat licet, neque operam perdet.

pa. 621

Totidem [enim in] literis ne una quidem minus aut amplius Pentateuchum legunt: et quod caput est, literis non adulterinis, ut Iudaei, sed meris Mosaicis characteribus ut plane a Postello proditum est et res ipsa loquitur./

Scaliger in †*animadversionibus in Cronicon*
Eusebii

pag. 107

Habes exemplum literarum Phoeniciarum una cum figuris diversis Graecarum, ex quarum comparatione per te ipse colligere †potes id quod secundo loco proposuimus, Graecas literas e Phoeniciis natas, quum idem ordo sit eademque forma earum quae Phoeniciarum, quibus omnes olim et Chananaei et Hebraei usi sunt, adhucque Samaritani utuntur; neque aliae in usu fuerunt a temporibus Mosis ad excidium Templi./

317v.

Scaliger de emendatione temporum lib. 7

pag. 627

Qui in Palaestina peregrinantur, possent & alia et Pentateuchum ab illis adipisci. Nam sane Christianae pietatis homines paulo hac in re negligentiores hactenus fueruntur: ex cuius rei cognitione uberrimi fructus in sacram historiam redundarent. Spero non defuturos, qui voto nostro satisfaciant, aut exemplo nostro haec illustraturi sint./

[A]   Que les Samaritains de Sichem et Garizim † n'usent que du Pentateuche de Moyse, qui'ils ont escrit en characteres anciens semblables a ceus du †sicle du santuaire.

1.   Saint Hierosme en la preface du livre des Roys.
2.   Beniamin †Iudaeus Tudelensis in suo Itinerario.† Les parolles en sont dans Iosephus Scaliger de emend. temporum lib. VII. au chapitre Notae in annum Samaritanum pa. 620.
3.   Rabi Moses Gerundesis *Espagnol* qui estoit il y a quatre cens ans et alla en la terre sainte †l'a escrit a la fin du Pentateuque et a veu le sicle du santuaire, monnaye escrite en pareils characteres.
4.   Postel en †son livre des 12. langues, et en son livre de la langue des Phoniciens. Il y en a en ceste ville.
5.   Theseus Ambrosius en son livre, qui est Introductio in linguam Chaldaicam Syriacam et Armeniam, qui est celuy de qui Postel estant sur les lieus en Levant a emprunte ce qui'il en a dit ayant veu son livre depuis a Rome, et transfus dans son livre des 12. langues qui'il fit imprimer en France.
     Scaliger apres eus aus lieus susdits. Le ramas de Duret president de Moulins appellé Histoire de l'origine des langues, a transcrit la plus part de ces passages *au chapitre 37. de la langue Samaritaine* outre que on les peut trouver dans les autheurs / mesmes.

[B]

Il y a convenance de ces characteres anciens, †au livre de

1.   Moyse que ont ces Samaritains ont, a recouvrir comme requiert tant de fois Scaliger,
2.   en la monnaye appelle, le sicle du santuaire dont parle Moyse, laquelle a d'un costé imprimée la figure du vase †plein †de Manne, de l'autre la verge d'Aaron fleurie et a alentour escrit Sekel Israel le sicle d'Israel, et de l'autre costé Ierusalaim Kedossa c'est a dire Ierusalem santa. †
     Rabbi Moses Gerundesis il y a quatre cens ans en avoit veu une. Arias Montanus apres luy en a eu une autre de laquelle il parle et laquelle il explique en son livre †Antiquitatum Iudaicarum au chapitre Thubal Cain sive de mesuris sacris ou il traite au long de sicles.
     Il y a une autre figure dans Beze †en ses notes sur le nouveau testament. Et plusieurs dans le Iesuite Villalpand qui a estendu au long les Antiquites d'Arias Montanus en son Apparatus templi Salomonis.

318r.

3.   †Au compost des Samaritains dont Scaliger a en une coppie recouvree par luy du Caire, et qui estoit envoyee † par les Samaritains de Palaestine a une colonie qu'ils ont au Caire, a laquelle ils envoyent tous les ans l'almanach a observer, ainsi que des longtemps our la conduite de l'an les anciens moins scavantes ont pris instruction †sur le compost de l'annee des plus scavantes et se fait encor aujourdhuy en plusieurs lieus. Ce compost est au 7. livre de Scaliger de emendation avec la representation des mesmes characteres anciens ausquels il loy a esté envoyé et en iceus mesmes il la fait imprimer avec notes au chapitre Computus Samaritanus.

[C]

Les livres a recouvrir de la:

1.   †Les livres de Moyse en leurs vieils characteres
2.   †Le livre qui'ils ont qu'ils appellent Iosue, qui est une cronique de leur histoire depuis la mort de Moyse iusques aus Antonius. Scaliger en avoit une, elle sera dans le thresor de ses livres en Hollande.

3. Un Alphabet de ceste langue. Postel †a escrit qu'il en avoit un exemplaire en ces mots. In grammaticis hebraeis nihil habeo pretiosius uno Samaritanae grammatices hoc est verae hebraicae libro a Sacerdote †Iacobi filio Mugiassin olim scripto; in quo positis exemplis Samaritanis, Arabice, methodo explicatur grammatica hebraea prisca.
   Duret president de Bourbonnois dit page 325. *de son histoire des langues,* dit qui'il en a un / exemplaire

4. Leur compost ou embolisme, puis que ils en font tous les ans, semblable a celuy qu'a fait imprimer Scaliger

5. Les autres livres que l'on pourra trouver escrits en ces characteres

6. Le sicle en ces mesmes characteres puis qu'il s'en voit fort souvent aus environs de Hierusalem.
   †Tout cela par le moyen du Consul des Francois qui est sur les lieus. L'on m'a dit que mons^r de Guise a un docte Escossois en Egypte pour recouvrir des livres qui avec le Consul des Francois sur les lieus pourroit ayder, ou autre homme docte si le Consul en prouve sur les lieus entre les pelerins.

318v.

Memoire de Mr. L'Eschassier.

Appendix II : Translation from the original Italian of the copy of the letter dated 26th November, 1628, from N.-C. Fabri de Peiresc to Pietro della Valle, Bibliothèque Méjanes ms. 1031, pp. 63-5.

To the Illustrious Pietro della Valle,

Rome.

If I were capable of demonstrating my devotion to you, as your genius and distinction demands, I am certain that you would consider me one of your greatest servants. My inability to express my full devotion does in itself however demonstrate my desire to be of service to you. I thank you for your kindness in accepting my letters of praise with regards to your genius.

I shall always be dedicated to you, and I shall always be prepared to follow all your instructions. Due to my feelings of inferiority before you, I shall try to gain your admiration through my obedience and faithful service.

In reference to your letter of 27th of the last month, I was particularly interested in the report thus of the manuscript books in Egyptian as of the Samaritan Pentateuch, of which I believe it would be most valuable to produce a Latin edition. The work of Father Morin may be of service to you here, but I am aware that it would be difficult to convince you that the diligence of this man should be sufficient proof of his expertise even though he has never visited the Levant himself, and thus has never come into contact with the Samaritans still living there, nor has he come into contact with other scholars specialised in the languages of those countries. It would be of great service to the project, if one of the princes were to spend a great deal of money in sponsoring the trip of one of the better educated Samaritan families to Europe, so that they could learn our languages and help us with the translation of these works into Latin. On the other hand it would also be a good idea to send Father Morin to the Levant, or for someone already expert in the oriental languages to translate the works there with the help of the people themselves. Scaliger, who did a great deal of study on the oriental languages, had a great desire to examine the Samaritan tradition and above all to obtain a good grasp of the language in order to understand a particular short but very eloquent chronicle. He made futile attempts to find texts in the language; an exception to this is of course his acquisition of part of the Psalter with which he was able to study the language and form a written grammatical analysis of it which he has shown to me and expressed his desires to see the Pentateuch in that language, hoping to acquire a near perfect understanding of the language. Due to my dedication to him I wrote to the Levant for a copy of the Samaritan Pentateuch. I was not able to acquire this during his lifetime, but years later after his death, one of the merchants who had been assigned to the task of searching for the book went to Damascus and there found a Samaritan willing to sell him a copy of the Pentateuch. He wrote to Marseilles asking if I were willing to buy it, and if so, at a price of forty schudi. I sent the money to Mr. Mostiere, Vice-Consul of Aleppo who bought the book for me and, wanting to deliver it to me, boarded the ship Saint Victor. He was drowned while fighting a group of Corsican bandits, and lost, too, was my copy of the Pentateuch. Actually I thought that that would be the last we would ever see of a Samaritan Pentateuch until I heard the news that you also possessed one. That is why I thought it would be a good idea to translate the work into Latin, so that it can be made available to our scholars of oriental languages who could complete their grammatical analysis of the language and conclude the work begun by Scaliger. I think that it will be necessary to call on Father Morin if you agree to have him work on the project and if I may be of service I shall do my best to produce the edition in Paris. I shall do my best in having the work edited, keeping in mind that the examination and study of the texts will take many years. When I had first considered the work being edited in Paris I thought that it could be made as a contribution from your library, without reducing the value of your collections, since for the edition of the Anecdota of Procopius we are no less grateful to the Vatican Library even though it was printed in Lyon than if it had been put out from the same Vatican Printery. I ask you to allow me to have copied only one or two lines of your Samaritan text as accurately as possible and to compile a complete alphabet with the text of the Pentateuch itself. I also wish to thank you for sending me a verse of one of the Psalms from the Psalter of your Egyptian texts, with the shape of the characters as precise as the original, together with the same verse in Arabic, but above all I would like to thank you for sending me a copy of the entire alphabet of the Egyptian language showing a very different letter formation to that of the Greeks. I would also be very grateful if you could send me a sample of the Egyptian words with Arabic influences in order to attempt to determine their origin, that is if they are influenced by or merely similar to, the other oriental languages or not. I am now working on eighty or more Barbarian-Greek inscriptions dependent on heretical Basilidian Gnostics and others, which prevailed in Egypt, for which some meaningful construction may be made with the help of the Egyptian language with the already existing Greek and Hebrew inscriptions and another unknown, but probably Egyptian.

I shall conclude by saying that we shall be waiting to see the book on Abbas king of Persia, edited in Venice, offering in return all my service.

Your devoted servant,

de Peiresc

From Aix on the 26th November, 1628

BIBLIOGRAPHY OF WILLIAM McKANE

Compiled by R.B. Salters

Books

Al-Ghazali's Book of Fear and Hope, Leiden: E.J. Brill, 1962.
I and II Samuel, London: SCM, 1963.
Tracts for the Times: Ruth, Esther, Lamentations, Ecclesiastes, Song of Songs (Bible Guides, 12), London: Lutterworth, 1965.
Prophets and Wise Men (Studies in Biblical Theology, 44), London: SCM, 1965
Proverbs. A New Approach, London: SCM, 1970.
Studies in the Patriarchal Narratives, Edinburgh: Handsel Press, 1979.
Jeremiah 1–25 (International Critical Commentary), Edinburgh: T. & T. Clark, 1986 [forthcoming].

Articles

'A Manuscript on the Mi'raj in the Bodleian', *JSS* 2 (1957), 366-76.
'The GIBBOR ḤAYIL in the Israelite Community', *TGUOS* 17, (1959), 28-37.
'A Note on 2 Kings 12.10 (EVV 12.9)', *ZAW* 71 (1959), 260-65.
'A Note on Esther IX and I Samuel XV', *JTS* n.s. 12 (1961), 260-61.
'Ruth and Boaz', *TGUOS* 19 (1963), 29-40.
'The Interpretation of Jeremiah XII 1-5', *TGUOS* 20 (1965), 38-48.
'The Earlier History of the Ark', *TGUOS* 21 (1967), 68-76.
'The Interpretation of Isaiah VII 14-25', *VT* 17 (1967), 208-19.
'Modern Trends in Old Testament Theology', *St Mary's College Bulletin* 10 (1968), 7-16.
'Wisdom in Israel', in R.C. Walton (ed.) *A Source Book of the Bible for Teachers*, London: SCM, 1970, 162-73.
'Jeremiah II 23-25: Observations on the Versions and the History of Exegesis', *OTS* 17 (1972), 73-88.
'Martin Buber and the Hasidic Movement', *St Mary's College Bulletin* 15 (1973), 4-15.
'Tradition as a Theological Concept', in *God, Secularisation and History: Essays in Memory of Ronald Gregor Smith*, Columbia: University of South Carolina Press, 1974, 44-59.

'Textual and Philological Notes on the Book of Proverbs with special reference to the New English Bible', *TGUOS* 24 (1974), 76-90.

'Observations on the *TIKKUNE SOPᵉRIM*, in M. Black and W.A. Smalley (eds) *On Language, Culture and Religion: In Honor of E.A. Nida*, The Hague: Mouton 1974, 53-77.

'Jeremiah XVII 5-8: The Resilience of the Man who Trusts in God', *St Mary's College Bulletin* 18 (1976), 4-10.

'Benjamin Kennicott: an Eighteenth-Century Researcher', *JTS* n.s. 28 (1977), 445-64.

'Jeremiah 13.12-14. A Problematic Proverb', in *Israelite Wisdom: Theological and Literary Essays in Honor of Samuel Terrien*, ed. by J.G. Gammie and others, Chico: Scholars Press, 1978, 107-20.

'Functions of Language and Objectives of Discourse according to Proverbs 10–30', in *La Sagesse de l'Ancien Testament*, (Bibliotheca Ephemeridum Theologicarum Lovaniensium, 51) 1979, 166-85.

'Prophecy and the Prophetic Literature', in G.W. Anderson (ed.), *Tradition and Interpretation*, Oxford: Clarendon Press, 1979, 163-88.

'משא in Jeremiah 23.33-40', in *Prophecy, Essays presented to Georg Fohrer* (BZAW, 150), 1980, 35-54.

'Poison, Trial by Ordeal and the Cup of Wrath', *VT* 30 (1980), 474-92.

'ŠPY(Y)M with Special Reference to the Book of Jeremiah' in A. Caquot and M. Delcor (eds), *Mélanges Bibliques et Orientaux: En L'Honneur de H. Cazelles* (Alter Orient und Altes Testament, 212), Kevelaer and Neukirchen 1981, 319-335.

'Relations between Poetry and Prose in the Book of Jeremiah with Special Reference to Jeremiah III 6-11 and XII 14-17', *SVT* 32 (1981), 220-37.

'Prophet and Institution', *ZAW* 94 (1982), 251-66.

'The Construction of Jeremiah chapter XXI', *VT* 32 (1982), 59-73.

'Is the Old Testament a Religious Book?', *St Mary's College Bulletin* 25 (1983), 5-10.

'The Eschatology of Jewish Apocalyptic', in W.C. Van Wyk (ed.) *The Exilic Period: Aspects of Apocalypticism* (OTWSA 25 [1982] and OTWSA 26 [1983] Old Testament Essays), Pretoria, 1984, 79-91.

'Calvin as an Old Testament Commentator', in *Nederduits Gereformeerde Teologiese Tydskrif* 25:3 (1984), 250-59.

'The History of the Text of Jeremiah 10.1-16', in A. Caquot, S. Légasse and M. Tardieu (eds) *Mélanges Bibliques et Orientaux: En l'Honneur de M. Delcor* (Alter Orient und Altes Testament, 215), Kevelaer and Neukirchen, 1985, 297-304.

'Is There a Place for Theology in the Exegesis of the Hebrew Bible?' *SEA* 50 (1985), 7-20.

Editor: *Transactions of Glasgow University Oriental Society* 1965-1972.

Review Articles

W.A. van der Weiden, *Le Livre des Proverbes: notes philologiques* (Biblica et Orientalia, 23), 1960, in *JSS* 16 (1971), 222-36.

D.R. Hillers, *Lamentations* (The Anchor Bible) 1972, in *JSS* 19 (1974), 97-104.

R.N. Whybray, *The Intellectual Tradition in the Old Testament* (BZAW, 135), 1974, in *JSS* 20 (1975), 243-48.

E.W. Heaton, *Solomon's New Men*, in *JTS* n.s. 26 (1975), 439-41.

W. Baumgartner, B. Hartmann, E.Y. Kutscher, *Hebräisches und Aramäisches Lexikon zum Alten Testament von Ludwig Koehler und Walter Baumgartner*, Third edition, in *JTS* n.s. 27 (1976), 148-51.

R. Rendtorff, *Das überlieferungsgeschichtliche Problem des Pentateuch* (BZAW, 147), 1977, in *VT* 28 (1978), 371-82.

H.W.F. Saggs, *The Encounter with the Divine in Mesopotamia and Israel*, 1978, in *BSOAS* 42 (1979), 369-75.

J. Blenkinsopp, *Prophecy and Canon*, 1977, in *JSOT* 12 (1979), 63-69.

Dermot Cox, *The Triumph of Impotence: Job and the Tradition of the Absurd*, in *JTS* n.s. 31 (1980), 139-42.

A. Malamat and I. Eph'al (eds), *The World History of the Jewish People, First Series: Ancient Times. The Age of the Monarchies: I Political History, II Culture and Society*, Jerusalem: Massada Press, 1979, in *JSS* 26 (1981), 281-94.

A.A. MacIntosh, *Isaiah XXI: A Palimpsest*, 1982, in *BSOAS* 45 (1982), 144-47.

T.N.D. Mettinger, *The Dethronement of Sabaoth. Studies in the Shem and Kabod Theologies*, 1982, in *JTS* n.s. 34 (1983), 226-29.

INDEX OF AUTHORS

INDEX OF BIBLICAL REFERENCES

Apocrypha and Pseudepigrapha

Dead Sea Scrolls

Targum

Rabbinic Literature

New Testament

Greek and Roman Authors

Papyri

JOURNAL FOR THE STUDY OF THE OLD TESTAMENT

Supplement Series